Marketing, 37/e

Nisreen N. Bahnan

D1199654

create.mheducation.com

Copyright 2019 by McGraw-Hill Education. All rights reserved.

Printed in the United States of America. Except as permitted under the United States Copyright Act of 1976, no part of this publication may be reproduced or distributed in any form or by any means, or stored in a database or retrieval system, without prior written permission of the publisher.

This McGraw-Hill Create text may include materials submitted to McGraw-Hill for publication by the instructor of this course.The instructor is solely responsible for the editorial content of such materials. Instructors retain copyright of these additional materials.

ISBN-13: 9781308318004

ISBN-10: 1308318006

Contents

Unit 4   157

Preface

The new millennium should continue to be an exciting and challenging time for the American and International business community. Many dynamic changes in the social, economic and technological environments have become an important part of the present marketplace.

Increasing demographic diversity in the U.S. continues to spew new lifestyles and consumer segments, each with a distinct set of needs and interests. Every development in consumer behavior leads to new and exciting marketing opportunities, and strategies that fail to heed this exploding socio-demographic diversity have little chance of success over the long run. Concurrently, the global economy has witnessed enumerable challenges since 2008, challenges that have forced companies to adapt their business practices, be it in regards to product development decisions, pricing and distribution practices, or even promotional tactics. Furthermore, vast and rapid technological changes are enabling new industries to sprout, while making an increasing number of products and services obsolete. The most visible of these developments is perhaps the explosion of social and mobile media, which has fast-tracked the research evolution by making a wealth of online data conveniently available to marketers.

It should be notes that these changes are not unique to the U.S., they have equally altered the consumption rhythms of consumers worldwide, hence requiring a parallel change in companies' definition of marketing concepts and practices. The growth of truly global markets have many small and medium-sized firms looking well beyond their national boundaries. Multinational firms, faced with intense competition, have to acknowledge important economic, political and social changes, which have dramatically altered the landscape of global business.

These changes—accompanied by increasing domestic and foreign competition—are leading a wide array of companies and industries toward the realization that better marketing must become a top priority now to assure future success.

The articles reprinted in this edition of *Annual Editions: Marketing 14/15* have been carefully chosen from numerous public press sources to provide current information on marketing in the world today. Within these pages you will find articles that address marketing theory and application in a wide range of industries. In addition, the selections reveal how several firms interpret and utilize marketing

principles in their daily operations and corporate planning. Collectively, they provide a wide-ranging discussion of how marketing professionals and companies interpret and employ various marketing strategies today.

The volume contains a number of features designed to make it useful for marketing students, educators, researchers, and professionals. These include article abstracts, which summarize each article and highlight key concepts within the *Table of Contents,* and a *Topic Guide* which helps the reader to locate articles on specific marketing subjects. In addition, there are tailored *Learning Outcomes, Critical Thinking Questions* and *Internet References* for each of the 43 articles. Also, the *Correlation Guide* conveniently organizes the articles according to topics and correlates the selections with the Table of Contents of three leading Marketing textbooks.

In this new volume of *Annual Editions: Marketing 14/15,* the articles are organized into four units: *Marketing in the 2000s and Beyond; Research, Markets, and Consumer Behavior; Developing and Implementing Marketing Strategies;* and *Global Marketing.* Selections that focus on similar issues are concentrated into sub*sections within the broader units. Each unit is preceded by a list of unit selections, as well as an overview that provides background for informed reading of the articles and emphasizes critical issues.*

The editor and academic advisory board are pleased to present you with the thirty-seventh edition of *Annual Editions: Marketing.* Since its first edition in the mid-1970s, the efforts of many individuals have contributed toward its success. We believe that this this compilation of reading is a very useful resource for marketing educators and students, and continually strive to make annual improvements.

Editor

Dr. Nisreen Bahnan is Associate Professor of Marketing at Salem State University's Bertolon School of Business. She has earned her PhD in Business Studies from Temple University in Philadelphia. She teaches several marketing courses at the undergraduate and graduate levels, including Principles of Marketing, Consumer Behavior, Services Marketing and Nonprofit Marketing. She has presented her work at various conferences and published several articles in the fields of services marketing and consumer behavior.

Dr. Bahnan resides with her husband and two children in North Reading, Massachusetts.

Academic Advisory Board

Members of the Academic Advisory Board are instrumental in the final selection of articles for Annual Editions books and ExpressBooks. Their review of the articles for content, level, and appropriateness provides critical direction to the editor and staff. We think that you will find their careful consideration reflected here.

Januarius Asongu
Santa Monica University

Connie R. Bateman
University of North Dakota

John Billingsley, Jr.
American Intercontinental University

Howard W. Combs
San Jose State University

Charlie Hardy
Alabama State University

C. Shane Hunt
Arkansas State University

Dale F. Kehr
University of Memphis

Mark Kendrick
Methodist University

Steven J. Lysonski
Marquette University

Mary K. McManamon
Lake Erie College

Keith Neergaard
Pacific Union College

Carol Osborne
University of South Florida—Tampa

Janet Parish
Texas A&M University

Dorothy Pisarski
Drake University

Carlton R. Raines
Lehigh Carbon Community College

David L. Ralph
Pepperdine University

Catherine Rich-Duval
Merrimack College

Catherine Ruggieri
St. John's University

Brad Sago
Wheaton College

Craig Shoemaker
Saint Ambrose University

Joseph R. Stasio
Merrimack College

Paul M. Wellen
Roosevelt University

Kenneth Wong
Boise State University

Correlation Guide

The *Annual Editions* series provides students with convenient, inexpensive access to current, carefully selected articles from the public press. **Annual Editions: Marketing, 37/e** is an easy-to-use reader that presents articles on important topics such as *marketing concepts, social marketing, research, consumer behavior, marketing strategies,* and many more. For more information on *Annual Editions* and other McGraw-Hill Create™ titles and collections, visit www.mcgrawhillcreate.com

This convenient guide matches the articles in **Annual Editions: Marketing, 37/e** with the corresponding chapters in **Essentials of Marketing, 14/e** by Perreault et al.

Essentials of Marketing, 14/e by Perreault et al.	Annual Editions: Marketing, 37/e
Chapter 1: Marketing's Value to Consumers, Firms, and Society	75 Years of Marketing History Made in America? Marketing in 2012: The End of the Middle? Revisiting the Marketing Mix The CMO and the Future of Marketing The Purchasing Power of Entertainment
Chapter 2: Marketing Strategy Planning	Marketing in 2012: The End of the Middle? New World Order for Global Brands Putting Customers First: Nine Surefire Ways to Increase Brand Loyalty *Stop Trying to Delight Your Customers Targeting Demographics in Beverage Marketing The Devolution of Marketing: Is America's Marketing Model Fighting Hard Enough to Keep Up?
Chapter 3: Evaluating Opportunities in the Changing Marketing Environment	Ad Campaigns are Finally Reflecting Diversity of U.S.: But Why Did It Take So Long to Recognize Socially Liberal Shift? Do You Have a Millennial Marketing Strategy? *How Emerging Giants Can Take on the World It's More Than Green to Be Keen Marketing in 2012: The End of the Middle? New World Order for Global Brands Respect Your Elders Selling Green Targeting Demographics in Beverage Marketing The Devolution of Marketing: Is America's Marketing Model Fighting Hard Enough to Keep Up? *The Problem with the "Poverty Premium" Walking the Talk Walmart Wants You to Believe Its Green Makeover Is Changing the World. Just One Hitch: China
Chapter 4: Focusing Marketing Strategy with Segmentation and Positioning	Brand Apathy Calls for New Methods: Turn Customer Preference from "No Brand" to "Some Brand" Made in America? *Make Your Best Customers Even Better Putting Customers First: Nine Surefire Ways to Increase Brand Loyalty Respect Your Elders Six Strategies for Successful Niche Marketing *The Problem with the "Poverty Premium"
Chapter 5: Final Consumers and Their Buying Behavior	Can More Information Be a Bad Thing? Made in America? Our Brands, Ourselves: The Power of Attachment Putting Customers First: Nine Surefire Ways to Increase Brand Loyalty Tapping the Untapped The Purchasing Power of Entertainment
Chapter 6: Business and Organizational Customers and Their Buying Behavior	Walmart Wants You to Believe Its Green Makeover Is Changing the World. Just One Hitch: China

Essentials of Marketing, 14/e by Perreault et al.	Annual Editions: Marketing, 37/e
Chapter 7: Improving Decisions with Marketing Information	Can More Information Be a Bad Thing? Closer to the Truth Do You Have a Millennial Marketing Strategy? Tapping the Untapped
Chapter 8: Elements of Product Planning for Goods and Services	Brand Apathy Calls for New Methods: Turn Customer Preference from "No Brand" to "Some Brand" Branding's Big Guns Fundamental Tenets of Service Excellence How to Make Marketing Brilliance Our Brands, Ourselves: The Power of Attachment Playing Well Together
Chapter 9: Product Management and New-Product Development	Future Tech: The Trends to Watch in 2014 Lessons in App Building
Chapter 10: Place and Development of Channel Systems	*How Emerging Giants Can Take on the World The Devolution of Marketing: Is America's Marketing Model Fighting Hard Enough to Keep Up? *When Marketing Is Strategy
Chapter 11: Distribution Customer Service and Logistics	*When Marketing Is Strategy
Chapter 12: Retailers, Wholesalers, and Their Strategy Planning	Fundamental Tenets of Service Excellence Playing Well Together Social Gathering The Rebirth of Retail
Chapter 13: Promotion—Introduction to Integrated Marketing Communications	Ad Campaigns are Finally Reflecting Diversity of U.S.: But Why Did It Take So Long to Recognize Socially Liberal Shift? Become the Main Attraction How to Make Marketing Brilliance Social Gathering
Chapter 14: Personal Selling and Customer Service	Fundamental Tenets of Service Excellence *Stop Trying to Delight Your Customers
Chapter 15: Advertising, Publicity, and Sales Promotion	Ad Campaigns are Finally Reflecting Diversity of U.S.: But Why Did It Take So Long to Recognize Socially Liberal Shift? Advertising's New Campaign Branding's Big Guns It's More Than Green to Be Keen Marketing Communication in a Digital Era: Marketers Should Focus Efforts on Emerging Social, Mobile and Local Trends Playing Well Together Respect Your Elders Selling Green Walking the Talk
Chapter 16: Pricing Objectives and Policies	*Pricing to Create Shared Value *The Problem with the "Poverty Premium"
Chapter 17: Price Setting in the Business World	*Pricing to Create Shared Value *The Problem with the "Poverty Premium"
Chapter 18: Ethical Marketing in a Consumer-Oriented World: Appraisal and Challenges	Ad Campaigns are Finally Reflecting Diversity of U.S.: But Why Did It Take So Long to Recognize Socially Liberal Shift? Made in America? Walmart Wants You to Believe Its Green Makeover Is Changing the World. Just One Hitch: China

This convenient guide matches the articles in **Annual Editions: Marketing, 37/e** with the corresponding chapters in **Marketing, 12/e** by Kerin et al.

Marketing, 12/e by Kerin et al.	Annual Editions: Marketing, 37/e
Chapter 1: Creating Customer Relationships and Value through Marketing	75 Years of Marketing History Made in America? Marketing in 2012: The End of the Middle? Revisiting the Marketing Mix The CMO and the Future of Marketing The Purchasing Power of Entertainment
Chapter 2: Developing Successful Organizational and Marketing Strategies	Marketing in 2012: The End of the Middle? New World Order for Global Brands Putting Customers First: Nine Surefire Ways to Increase Brand Loyalty *Stop Trying to Delight Your Customers Targeting Demographics in Beverage Marketing The Devolution of Marketing: Is America's Marketing Model Fighting Hard Enough to Keep Up?
Chapter 3: Scanning the Marketing Environment	Ad Campaigns are Finally Reflecting Diversity of U.S.: But Why Did It Take So Long to Recognize Socially Liberal Shift? Do You Have a Millennial Marketing Strategy? Marketing in 2012: The End of the Middle? Respect Your Elders Targeting Demographics in Beverage Marketing The Devolution of Marketing: Is America's Marketing Model Fighting Hard Enough to Keep Up? *The Problem with the "Poverty Premium"
Chapter 4: Ethical and Social Responsibility in Marketing	Ad Campaigns are Finally Reflecting Diversity of U.S.: But Why Did It Take So Long to Recognize Socially Liberal Shift? It's More Than Green to Be Keen Made in America? Selling Green Walking the Talk Walmart Wants You to Believe Its Green Makeover Is Changing the World. Just One Hitch: China
Chapter 5: Understanding Consumer Behavior	Can More Information Be a Bad Thing? Made in America? Our Brands, Ourselves: The Power of Attachment Putting Customers First: Nine Surefire Ways to Increase Brand Loyalty Tapping the Untapped The Purchasing Power of Entertainment
Chapter 6: Understanding Organizations as Customers	Walmart Wants You to Believe Its Green Makeover Is Changing the World. Just One Hitch: China.
Chapter 7: Understanding and Reaching Global Consumers and Markets	*How Emerging Giants Can Take on the World New World Order for Global Brands
Chapter 8: Marketing Research: From Customer Insights to Actions	Can More Information Be a Bad Thing? Closer to the Truth Do You Have a Millennial Marketing Strategy? Tapping the Untapped
Chapter 9: Market Segmentation, Targeting, and Positioning	Brand Apathy Calls for New Methods: Turn Customer Preference from "No Brand" to "Some Brand" Made in America? *Make Your Best Customers Even Better Putting Customers First: Nine Surefire Ways to Increase Brand Loyalty Respect Your Elders Six Strategies for Successful Niche Marketing *The Problem with the "Poverty Premium"
Chapter 10: Developing New Products and Services	Future Tech: The Trends to Watch in 2014 Lessons in App Building

Marketing, 12/e by Kerin et al.	Annual Editions: Marketing, 37/e
Chapter 11: Managing Successful Products, Services, and Brands	Brand Apathy Calls for New Methods: Turn Customer Preference from "No Brand" to "Some Brand" Branding's Big Guns Fundamental Tenets of Service Excellence How to Make Marketing Brilliance Our Brands, Ourselves: the Power of Attachment Playing Well Together
Chapter 12: Services Marketing	Fundamental Tenets of Service Excellence *Stop Trying to Delight Your Customers
Chapter 13: Building the Price Foundation	*Pricing to Create Shared Value *The Problem with the "Poverty Premium"
Chapter 14: Arriving at the Final Price	*Pricing to Create Shared Value *The Problem with the "Poverty Premium"
Chapter 15: Managing Marketing Channels and Supply Chains	*How Emerging Giants Can Take on the World The Devolution of Marketing: Is America's Marketing Model Fighting Hard Enough to Keep Up? *When Marketing Is Strategy
Chapter 16: Retailing and Wholesaling	Fundamental Tenets of Service Excellence Playing Well Together Social Gathering The Rebirth of Retail
Chapter 17: Integrated Marketing Communications and Direct Marketing	Ad Campaigns are Finally Reflecting Diversity of U.S.: But Why Did It Take So Long to Recognize Socially Liberal Shift? Become the Main Attraction How to Make Marketing Brilliance Social Gathering
Chapter 18: Advertising, Sales Promotion, and Public Relations	Ad Campaigns are Finally Reflecting Diversity of U.S.: But Why Did It Take So Long to Recognize Socially Liberal Shift? Advertising's New Campaign Branding's Big Guns It's More Than Green to Be Keen Marketing Communication in a Digital Era: Marketers Should Focus Efforts on Emerging Social, Mobile and Local Trends Playing Well Together Respect Your Elders Selling Green Walking the Talk
Chapter 19: Using Social Media to Connect with Consumers	Advertising's New Campaign Do You Have a Millennial Marketing Strategy? Marketing Communication in a Digital Era: Marketers Should Focus Efforts on Emerging Social, Mobile and Local Trends Respect Your Elders
Chapter 20: Personal Selling and Sales Management	Fundamental Tenets of Service Excellence *Stop Trying to Delight Your Customers
Chapter 21: Implementing Interactive and Multichannel Marketing	
Chapter 22: Pulling It All Together: The Strategic Marketing Process	Putting Customers First: Nine Surefire Ways to Increase Brand Loyalty *Stop Trying to Delight Your Customers The Devolution of Marketing: Is America's Marketing Model Fighting Hard Enough to Keep Up?

This convenient guide matches the articles in **Annual Editions: Marketing, 37/e** with the corresponding chapters in **Marketing, 4/e** by Grewal/Levy.

Marketing, 4/e by Grewal/Levy	Annual Editions: Marketing, 37/e
Chapter 1: Overview of Marketing	75 Years of Marketing History Made in America? Marketing in 2012: The End of the Middle? Revisiting the Marketing Mix The CMO and the Future of Marketing The Purchasing Power of Entertainment
Chapter 2: Developing Marketing Strategies and a Marketing Plan	Marketing in 2012: The End of the Middle? New World Order for Global Brands Putting Customers First: Nine Surefire Ways to Increase Brand Loyalty *Stop Trying to Delight Your Customers Targeting Demographics in Beverage Marketing The Devolution of Marketing: Is America's Marketing Model Fighting Hard Enough to Keep Up?
Chapter 3: Social and Mobile Marketing	Advertising's New Campaign Do You Have a Millennial Marketing Strategy? Marketing Communication in a Digital Era: Marketers Should Focus Efforts on Emerging Social, Mobile and Local Trends Respect Your Elders
Chapter 4: Marketing Ethics	Ad Campaigns are Finally Reflecting Diversity of U.S.: But Why Did It Take So Long to Recognize Socially Liberal Shift? Made in America? Walmart Wants You to Believe Its Green Makeover Is Changing the World. Just One Hitch: China
Chapter 5: Analyzing the Marketing Environment	Ad Campaigns are Finally Reflecting Diversity of U.S.: But Why Did It Take So Long to Recognize Socially Liberal Shift? Do You Have a Millennial Marketing Strategy? It's More Than Green to Be Keen Made in America? Marketing in 2012: The End of the Middle? Respect Your Elders Selling Green Targeting Demographics in Beverage Marketing The Devolution of Marketing: Is America's Marketing Model Fighting Hard Enough to Keep Up? *The Problem with the "Poverty Premium" Walking the Talk Walmart Wants You to Believe Its Green Makeover Is Changing the World. Just One Hitch: China
Chapter 6: Consumer Behavior	Can More Information Be a Bad Thing? Made in America? Our Brands, Ourselves: The Power of Attachment Putting Customers First: Nine Surefire Ways to Increase Brand Loyalty Tapping the Untapped The Purchasing Power of Entertainment
Chapter 7: Business-to-Business Marketing	Walmart Wants You to Believe Its Green Makeover Is Changing the World. Just One Hitch: China
Chapter 8: Global Marketing	*How Emerging Giants Can Take on the World New World Order for Global Brands
Chapter 9: Segmentation, Targeting, and Positioning	Brand Apathy Calls for New Methods: Turn Customer Preference from "No Brand" to "Some Brand" Made in America? *Make Your Best Customers Even Better Putting Customers First: Nine Surefire Ways to Increase Brand Loyalty Respect Your Elders Six Strategies for Successful Niche Marketing *The Problem with the "Poverty Premium"
Chapter 10: Understanding the Marketplace	Can More Information Be a Bad Thing? Closer to the Truth Do You Have a Millennial Marketing Strategy? Tapping the Untapped

Marketing, 4/e by Grewal/Levy	Annual Editions: Marketing, 37/e
Chapter 11: Product, Branding, and Packaging Decisions	Brand Apathy Calls for New Methods: Turn Customer Preference from "No Brand" to "Some Brand" Branding's Big Guns How to Make Marketing Brilliance Our Brands, Ourselves: The Power of Attachment Playing Well Together
Chapter 12: Developing New Products	Future Tech: The Trends to Watch in 2014 Lessons in App Building
Chapter 13: Services: The Intangible Product	Fundamental Tenets of Service Excellence *Stop Trying to Delight Your Customers
Chapter 14: Pricing Concepts for Establishing Value	*Pricing to Create Shared Value *The Problem with the "Poverty Premium"
Chapter 15: Strategic Pricing Methods	*Pricing to Create Shared Value *The Problem with the "Poverty Premium"
Chapter 16: Supply Chain and Channel Management	*How Emerging Giants Can Take on the World The Devolution of Marketing: Is America's Marketing Model Fighting Hard Enough to Keep Up? *When Marketing Is Strategy
Chapter 17: Retailing and Multichannel Marketing	Fundamental Tenets of Service Excellence Playing Well Together Social Gathering The Rebirth of Retail
Chapter 18: Integrated Marketing Communications	Ad Campaigns are Finally Reflecting Diversity of U.S.: But Why Did It Take So Long to Recognize Socially Liberal Shift? Become the Main Attraction How to Make Marketing Brilliance Social Gathering
Chapter 19: Advertising, Public Relations, and Sales Promotions	Ad Campaigns are Finally Reflecting Diversity of U.S.: But Why Did It Take So Long to Recognize Socially Liberal Shift? Advertising's New Campaign Branding's Big Guns It's More Than Green to Be Keen Marketing Communication in a Digital Era: Marketers Should Focus Efforts on Emerging Social, Mobile and Local Trends Playing Well Together Respect Your Elders Selling Green Walking the Talk
Chapter 20: Personal Selling and Sales Management	Fundamental Tenets of Service Excellence *Stop Trying to Delight Your Customers

* These articles are available on McGraw-Hill Create™ at www.mcgrawhillcreate.com as part of the **Expanded** ExpressBook version of Annual Editions: Marketing, 37/e.

Topic Guide

All the articles that relate to each topic are listed below the bold-faced term.

Advertising

Ad Campaigns are Finally Reflecting Diversity of U.S.: But Why Did It Take So Long to Recognize Socially Liberal Shift?
Advertising's New Campaign
Branding's Big Guns
How to Make Marketing Brilliance
Marketing Communication in a Digital Era: Marketers Should Focus Efforts on Emerging Social, Mobile and Local Trends
Playing Well Together
Respect Your Elders
Selling Green
Walking the Talk
Why Traditional Market Research Is a Waste of Time

Branding

Brand Apathy Calls for New Methods: Turn Customer Preference from "No Brand" to "Some Brand"
Branding's Big Guns
How to Make Marketing Brilliance
Our Brands, Ourselves: the Power of Attachment
Playing Well Together

Competition

*How Emerging Giants Can Take on the World
Walmart Wants You to Believe Its Green Makeover Is Changing the World. Just One Hitch: China

Consumer behavior

Can More Information Be a Bad Thing?
Made in America?
Our Brands, Ourselves: The Power of Attachment
Putting Customers First: Nine Surefire Ways to Increase Brand Loyalty
Tapping the Untapped
The Purchasing Power of Entertainment
Understanding the Arab Consumer
Why Traditional Market Research Is a Waste of Time

Consumer demographics

Ad Campaigns are Finally Reflecting Diversity of U.S.: But Why Did It Take So Long to Recognize Socially Liberal Shift?
Do You Have a Millennial Marketing Strategy?
Respect Your Elders
Targeting Demographics in Beverage Marketing
*The Problem with the "Poverty Premium"
Understanding the Arab Consumer
Why Traditional Market Research Is a Waste of Time

Distribution planning

*How Emerging Giants Can Take on the World
The Devolution of Marketing: Is America's Marketing Model Fighting Hard Enough to Keep Up?
The Rebirth of Retail
*When Marketing Is Strategy

Economic environment

*How Emerging Giants Can Take on the World
Marketing in 2012: The End of the Middle?
*The Problem with the "Poverty Premium"

Event marketing

Become the Main Attraction

Franchising

Playing Well Together
Social Gathering

Global marketing

*How Emerging Giants Can Take on the World
New World Order for Global Brands
The Devolution of Marketing: Is America's Marketing Model Fighting Hard Enough to Keep Up?
Walmart Wants You to Believe its Green Makeover Is Changing the World. Just One Hitch: China
Understanding the Arab Consumer
Why Traditional Market Research Is a Waste of Time

Innovation

Future Tech: The Trends to Watch in 2014
The Rebirth of Retail

Internet marketing

Advertising's New Campaign
Closer to the Truth
Marketing Communication in a Digital Era: Marketers Should Focus Efforts on Emerging Social, Mobile and Local Trends
Why Traditional Market Research Is a Waste of Time

Lifestyle marketing

Ad Campaigns are Finally Reflecting Diversity of U.S.: But Why Did It Take So Long to Recognize Socially Liberal Shift?
Advertising's New Campaign
Marketing Communication in a Digital Era: Marketers Should Focus Efforts on Emerging Social, Mobile and Local Trends
Our Brands, Ourselves: the Power of Attachment
Selling Green
Understanding the Arab Consumer
Why Traditional Market Research Is a Waste of Time

Marketing and technology

Closer to the Truth
Lessons in App Building
Why Traditional Market Research Is a Waste of Time

Marketing concept

75 Years of Marketing History
Revisiting the Marketing Mix
The CMO and the Future of Marketing
The Purchasing Power of Entertainment
Why Traditional Market Research Is a Waste of Time

Unit 1

UNIT

Prepared by: Nisreen N. Bahnan, *Salem State University*

Marketing in the 2000s and Beyond

"If we want to know what a business is we must start with its purpose. . . . There is only one valid definition of business purpose: to create a customer. What business thinks it produces is not of first importance—especially not to the future of the business or to its success. What the customer thinks he is buying, what he considers 'value' is decisive—it determines what a business is, what it produces, and whether it will prosper."

— Peter Drucker, *The Practice of Management*

When Peter Drucker penned these words in 1954, American industry was just awakening to the realization that marketing would play an important role in the future success of businesses. The ensuing years have seen an increasing number of firms in highly competitive areas—particularly in the consumer goods industry—adopt a more sophisticated customer orientation and an integrated marketing focus. Over the decades, this marketing epidemic slowly but surely spread to an even broader range of industries—from banking and air travel to communications—as more organizations came to the absolute realization that marketing practices will provide them with sustainable differentiation and the competitive edge necessary for survival and growth.

The last two decades have witnessed dramatic economic and social transformation. Demographic and lifestyle changes have splintered mass, homogeneous markets into distinct segments, each with different needs and interests. Deregulation has made once-protected industries vulnerable to the vagaries of competition. Vast and rapid technological changes are making an increasing number of products and services obsolete. Intense international competition, rapid expansion of the internet-based economy, and the growth of truly global markets have many firms looking well beyond their national boundaries. The selected reading in this unit shed light on these recent developments that have changed the consumption rhythms of consumers worldwide, hence requiring a parallel change in our definition of marketing concepts and practices. The unit's subsections collectively represent different facets of this era of transition, and challenge the reader to question and revisit the status quo.

The first subsection addresses changing *marketing perspectives*. It includes readings that discuss the above-mentioned shift in focus and strategy, even to the extent of challenging the conventional wisdom—and comfortable familiarity—of the traditional marketing mix and its 4Ps. These selections highlight how more organizations are adopting an outward orientation, with attention directed towards creating and catering to niche segments and micro-markets, practices that enable firms to enhance brand loyalty. They also document a growing move among companies to capitalize on innovation to adequately adapt to technology-fueled consumer lifestyles.

The selections that address *the marketing concept* carries the same theme of change and development, and includes a very handy summary to the evolution of marketing thought and practice since the discipline's inception in the 1930s. Some of the other readings tackle the important topic of customer satisfaction, echoing the famous words of author and professor, Michael Leboeuf: "A satisfied customer is the best business strategy of all." These articles illustrate one of many controversies in marketing discipline, this one relating to the issue of cost effectiveness for companies when pursuing obsessive and excessive customer satisfaction efforts. The remaining readings question the robustness of previously established truths in these dynamic and chaotic times.

In the *Services and Social Marketing* subsection, the articles present helpful guidelines for ensuring service excellence, and practical tips encouraging companies to shift away from mass media to more personalized promotional appeals, that speak to individual consumers.

In the final subsection, *Marketing Ethics and Social Responsibility,* a careful look is taken at the strategic process and practice of incorporating ethics and social responsibility into the marketing strategy. Technology makes the world a much smaller place, and consumers are now privy to a wealth of information pertaining to company's outsourcing and manufacturing practices. Educated consumers are more discerning of these practices, and demand high levels of integrity from the brands they patronize. These readings provide a better definition for ethics and social responsibility, resonating with the words of Jeroen De Flander, a seasoned international strategy execution expert and co-founder of The Performance Factory: "Corporate social responsibility should be more than about coloring your annual reports green, and giving a bag of money to your favorite charity in return for some nice pictures." In this subsection, we see an innovative approach to social responsibility, with some companies experimenting with sustainability and conscious consumption.

Article   Prepared by: Nisreen N. Bahnan, *Salem State University*

Marketing in 2012:
The End of the Middle?

A new and more segmented American marketplace has risen from the ashes of the recession, prompting some marketplace watchers to proclaim the demise of the middle class—or, at the very least, to call for a new definition of that expansive consumer group. Once marketers' bread and butter, middle-class consumers are being pushed to the periphery of many marketers' targeting strategies as they focus, instead, on a more cut-and-dry division of the socioeconomic spectrum: into the "haves" and "have-nots." Experts predict that this polarized view of the marketplace could prompt many marketers to shift everything from their product portfolios and pricing to their messaging strategies and marketing mixes this year.

CHRISTINE BIRKNER

Learning Outcomes

After reading this article, you will be able to:

- Identify various socio-economic segments in the U.S. market.

- Understand the significance and purpose of the U.S. Consumer Confidence Index.

- Examine marketing strategies that companies implement to better target a contracting U.S. middle class.

The Economic Outlook

More sophisticated segmentation practices have been parceling out the once-generic middle-class consumer group for years, but now, from a socioeconomic standpoint, the definition of a middle-class consumer—and particularly his wallet size—is anything but generic, and many successful marketers are taking a high-low approach to their targeting and segmentation practices. "There's been a notion in retailing for a long time that you could do better targeting the top end or the bottom end, and you could get lost if you're in the middle. We're seeing more companies focusing on that notion now than ever before," says Jonathan Asher, senior vice president at Perception Research Services International Inc., a consumer research firm based in Fort Lee, N.J.

Given the years of financial unease that many consumers have experienced since the United States economy faltered, it comes as no surprise that "trading down" has become a central consumer behavior. Although not quite as bleak as they were at the beginning of the recession in late 2007, economic statistics and consumer attitudes remain grim. The United States unemployment rate stood at 8.6 percent in November 2011, according to the United States Bureau of Labor Statistics, and while consumer confidence rose in November entering into the holiday shopping season, the United States Consumer Confidence Index, an economic indicator that measures the degree of optimism that consumers feel about the state of the economy, had declined to 39.8 the month before, a level last seen during the 2007–2009 recession. Consumers' overall optimism about the economy slumped to 23 percent in October 2011, down from 35 percent in March 2011 and 41 percent in September 2009, according to a survey on shopper and consumer insights by global management consulting firm McKinsey & Co. Those results don't bode well for marketers targeting beleaguered consumers in 2012, experts say.

"Consumers are still spending money, but they're not feeling good about it. Prices have been increasing and wages are not increasing. The median family income has also fallen three years in a row and a lot of households have lost their net worth. When people don't have any assets, they pursue less. It's very evident that the middle market is being squeezed," says Chris Christopher, senior principal economist at IHS Inc., an

Englewood, Colo.-based global research and consulting company. IHS projects that income inequality will increase in the United States in 2012.

Economic conditions in 2012 will foster a recovery for the upper class in terms of consumer spending, but there will be continued malaise in the middle and lower classes, according to Michael Englund, principal director and chief economist at Boulder, Colo.-based Action Economics, a market analysis firm. "At the low end of income distribution, people dependent on wage income are going to find that labor markets are going to get increasingly dysfunctional. We're not entirely sure the middle class is getting smaller, but what we are finding is people who are depending on wage income can't simply assume ongoing climbs in wage income going forward . . . and they just don't have the income to finance the kind of spending that we've seen in [times of economic] expansion."

Adds Christopher, "We know from economic data that income inequality has increased since the recession hit and that's being reflected in how retailers are approaching things."

Retail and CPG as a Microcosm of the Marketplace

For a barometer of the changing consumer marketplace, look no further than recent moves by Cincinnati-based Procter & Gamble Co. According to *The Wall Street Journal,* P&G expanded its research on low-income households over the past two years and this fall, in response to consumers' needs for lower-cost options, P&G launched bargain-priced Gain dish soap, its first dish soap launch in 38 years. In an attempt to secure the other end of the economic spectrum, P&G introduced higher-priced versions of its Olay and Gillette product lines in 2009 and 2010, respectively. P&G declined to comment for this story.

Shrinking package sizes are another consequence of Americans' shrinking incomes. P&G reduced the size of some Tide laundry detergent packages from 100 oz. to 75 oz., allowing it to sell the smaller package size at under $10 at Wal-Mart compared with $12 for the 100-oz. version, according to *Ad Age.* In October, H.J. Heinz announced plans to produce smaller-sized versions across its product portfolio to target low-income consumers and Coca-Cola introduced 12.5 oz. bottles that sell for less in convenience stores than its 16- and 20-oz. versions.

Consumers still want name-brand products, but they want them for less, says Marshal Cohen, chief industry analyst at Port Washington, New York-based research firm The NPD Group Inc. who specializes in consumer behavior, retail and fashion. "Today, when you ask the consumer, 'What is value?' the No. 1 answer they give is 'brand names for less.' That justifies why companies like Coca-Cola and Procter & Gamble [are

cutting package sizes]. All of those things are a direct reflection of customers saying, 'I want the quality of the trusted brand, the reputation of the product, but I want it at a better value price and I'm willing to pay less to get the experience.'"

The success of discount retailers such as Family Dollar and Dollar General—both of which posted earnings increases in 2011—is evidence of a more permanent shift in purchase behavior than just a reactionary response to the recession's pressures, experts say. "The dollar stores have done a very good job of retaining a customer that gravitated towards them during the recession out of necessity to save money and make their paycheck go further," Cohen says. "The lower-middle and lower-income consumer have engaged with dollar stores and stayed there, and that's why dollar stores continue to grow, because they've offered a more diversified product range, because they've offered new sizes of product at advantageous prices."

On the higher-income end of the spectrum, luxury retailers now are faring well. Tiffany's sales increased 21 percent over the prior year in the third quarter of 2011 and Neiman Marcus Inc. reported total revenues of $1 billion in the first quarter of the 2012 fiscal year compared with $927.2 million in the prior year. "We've been doing a lot of work over the past couple of years on the polarized consumer. Those with incomes of over $100,000 are back in the game. The recession has ended for them. All other income groups are cutting back in terms of spending," says Todd Hale, senior vice president of consumer and shopper insights at the New York-based Nielsen Co.

Granted, experts say that the luxury consumer of 2012 is more cautious than the pre-recession luxury consumer. "The luxury consumer's mindset is one of eagerness and anticipation, but there's also a heavy dose of caution. [Luxury brands] are performing well but not necessarily at pre-recession rates," says Justin Wartell, executive director of brand strategy at Interbrand Design Forum, the shopper sciences and retail arm of Interbrand, a New York-based global branding consultancy.

Pamela Danziger, founder of Unity Marketing, a Stevens, Pa.-based marketing firm that specializes in luxury goods, says that luxury stores have held their own because they've adapted to the changing economy. "Shopping in those stores today is very different than shopping in those stores in 2007. They've opened their doors to lower-priced product lines. Saks is doing more with their own private label, which is more value-oriented, more dollar-friendly. Neiman just started taking MasterCard and Visa, whereas before it was only their own credit cards and American Express. The stores are being rewarded for [their] effective response to the economic climate. They're very smart marketers and as a result, they're showing positive results," Danziger says.

While low-end and high-end retailers have hit their stride in targeting more discerning consumers who've been trained to mind their credit lines by a painful recession, many middle-range retailers haven't been as successful. As *Marketing News* has reported, middle-market retailer Gap Inc. has faltered throughout 2011, with both marketing and earnings troubles. Gap's third quarter 2011 earnings dropped 36 percent and it announced the closure of 21 percent of its United States-based Gap stores in October. Other mid-market retailers struggled in late 2011 as well: J.C. Penney's total company sales in November 2011 decreased 5.9 percent and Sears' domestic comparable sales declined 0.7 percent in the third quarter of 2011.

"We're watching the consumer try to figure out where they belong. Not all of the mass merchants have done as good of a job as the others at reclaiming that lower-end consumer and not all the luxury retailers have recovered from the loss of that aspirational middle-class customer," Cohen says.

"As we see the middle class get stretched further and further into having to buy more diversified product with less income power, luxury is going to get back to pure luxury," he adds. "You're also seeing the low end being able to raise the bar again to at least engage the consumer in figuring out how to put a little bit of luxury there. We're seeing the polarization of luxury very strongly exemplified: the luxury market doing better and the low-end market dipping their toe into affordable luxury, which is eroding the middle even more."

The world of retail is trying to figure out how to reach the two ends of the economic spectrum, Cohen says. And with the disappearance of the aspirational middle-class consumer—or at least with middle-class consumers who are willing and able to spend on aspirational products—some luxury brands are developing products for the middle- or lower-class market, such as fashion retailer Missoni's line of products for Target. "It sold out within two and a half hours in 89 percent of stores they put the product in. That's a phenomenal success story, so successful it crashed Target's website," Cohen says.

And as the marketplace bifurcates based on wallet size, price is, of course, paramount. "If you're going to make price some sort of driver of your message, it has to stand for something, and the middle means nothing. It's either price because it's value, or luxury because it's pricey," says Scott Lucas, executive director of Interbrand Cincinnati. "We're seeing our clients make a clear distinction that if it's going to be a price-based conversation with consumers, it has to be meaningful and that middle tier isn't as rich of a story because price is tied to just being in the middle. . . . It has to be value or premium."

The Broader Implications

Retailers' responses to consumers' new spending behaviors are, of course, emblematic of what's going on throughout the global marketplace, as restaurants, airlines and tourist destinations, service providers, B-to-B organizations, you name it, rethink their targeting and pricing strategies, unbundle or resize their offerings and adjust their thinking to focus on customers who sit right or left of middle on the financial spectrum. In 2012 and beyond, offering a middle-range, average-priced product or service is no longer an enticing marketing proposition for many customers, experts say. Either you beat your competition by offering the most attractive price, or you beat them by convincing customers that the quality and value of your offering is worth the extra cost.

Asher of Perception Research says that for customers across the marketplace, their purchase behavior has become a cost-conscious, either-or proposition: "It's either, 'I'm looking totally for price,' or 'I'm going to spend more for quality because it's going to be worth it in the long run.'"

Critical Thinking

1. What is the United States Consumer Confidence Index?

2. In your opinion, what is the direct and indirect impact of the United States Consumer Confidence Index on consumer consumption patterns and habits?

3. With a small group of peers from your class, brainstorm some alternative strategies that companies could pursue to better target the contracting United States middle class.

Create Central

www.mhhe.com/createcentral

Internet References

Moyers and Company
http://billmoyers.com/2013/09/20/by-the-numbers-the-incredibly-shrinking-american-middle-class/

U.S. Census Bureau
http://www.census.gov/

U.S. Department of Commerce
http://www.commerce.gov/sites/default/files/documents/migrated/Middle%20Class%20Report.pdf

Christine Birkner, "Marketing in 2012: The End of the Middle?" *Marketing News*, January 31, 2012, p. 22–23. Copyright © 2012 by American Marketing Association. All rights reserved. Used with permission.

Article   Prepared by: Nisreen N. Bahnan, *Salem State University*

How to Make Marketing Brilliance

An octogenarian's renaissance, a reinvention of the laptop and a bunch of irate birds—just a few examples of what grips the public's pop-culture consciousness. Some are the result of true innovation, some are examples of grace under pressure—and some things just go viral, because that's what happens now. Here's our look at the best marketing moves of the past year.

JASON DALEY

Learning Outcomes

After reading this article, you will be able to:

- Recognize how marketing strategies and techniques result in competitive advantage and brand success.

- Discuss the elements that qualify as brilliant and that make the brands, discussed in the article, exceptional.

Betty White

It's not like Betty White ever really went away. From radio dramas in the 1940s, TV variety shows in the 1950s and 1960s, a stint on *The Mary Tyler Moore Show* and, of course, her series-stealing turn as Rose Nylund on *The Golden Girls,* White has been a staple of popular entertainment since the cathode ray's beginning. But at the age of 88, White found herself in the middle of one of the strangest entertainment stories of 2010—a popular uprising.

In early 2010, David Mathews of San Antonio, Texas, launched a Facebook page asking for White to host *Saturday Night Live.* A successful Super Bowl Snickers commercial in which White takes a particularly brutal tackle, a surprise *Golden Girls* resurgence and a zany performance in the Sandra Bullock summer rom-com *The Proposal* all had whetted the public's appetite for White. The Facebook petition picked up several hundred thousand signers within a few months, and *SNL* producer Lorne Michaels offered White the Mother's Day

edition of the show. She signed on, and White's digital dominance was complete.

White's performance was edgy and widely praised, and the grandmother with a blue streak finished out 2010 by agreeing to costar in the TV Land sitcom *Hot in Cleveland,* releasing a calendar and popping up in cameo roles on almost every self-respecting comedy in the fall.

The Betty White mania may be winding down, but that doesn't mean she'll ever fade away.

"In earlier days she probably had just as many fans," says Robert Lloyd, TV critic for the Los *Angeles Times.* "But not in the same way we can be a fan now. You can push a button and join a club, and be part of a movement. The thing about Betty White is she belongs to a lot of generations. She's not just a cute old lady. The fact is, she's just funny."

The iPad

In the build-up to the iPad's release last April, Apple, the media and just about everyone else set their expectations pretty high, with claims that the tablet would change everything. It was never possible that the 3G-enabled tablet was going to make the laptop computer obsolete, save the publishing world, upend traditional marketing and buy everyone a Coke like the evangelizers claimed.

But almost a year later, it's hard not to be impressed by the iPad's accomplishments. It became the fastest-selling digital device in history; magazines and newspapers are slowly but

Lady Gaga

Stefani Germanotta who? Hit albums, viral videos, meat dresses and joy rides with Beyonce transformed this unknown NYC girl into the queen of pop.

Shake Weight

You know you've made it big when your awkward infomercials inspire an *SNL* parody.

surely redesigning themselves for a tablet-based world; and marketers have adopted the machine as fast as their industry will allow.

"Tablets are a real market that only Apple could have validated," says Eric Lai, mobile blogger for ZDNet. "A flood of Android tablets and RIM PlayBooks will follow, but it's all due to Apple's trailblazing. The iPad has really lived up to its hype—and more."

Advertisers are impressed, too. According to a survey last November by Nielsen, iPad users are nearly twice as likely to respond to online ads—as long as the ads are new, interesting and use the unique capabilities of the iPad.

The market for the iPad and similar devices and, consequently, their ability to reach consumers, seems set for exponential growth, especially as universities, large businesses and government agencies begin figuring out how to use the tablets in their daily routines.

"Apple just knows how to cater to the technophile early-adopting consumer," Lai says.

"And now that the balance of power has shifted away from the IT department toward the end user, these consumers are forcing enterprises to support and deploy iPads."

JetBlue

Among the many gripes travelers have with airlines, the number one bugaboo is customer service. Weaving our way through labyrinthine phone menus and sending e-mails off into the ether with no guarantee of a reply is the modus operandi for most carriers.

But jetBlue, the low-cost carrier that has been slowly expanding across the country since 1999, decided in 2007 that it would be all about transparency and communication—an idea that led the company to set up a 24/7 Twitter account to answer customer questions and deal with complaints. It's a friendly, wide-ranging back-and-forth banter that covers everything from passengers onboard complaining about delays to people asking which NFL team jetBlue roots for. So far, the @JetBlue Twitter feed has collected 1.6 million followers, along with 150,000 more for its cheap deals feed and more than 440,000 friends on Facebook.

"When we first started, it was just me not sleeping a whole lot," says Morgan Johnston, the only guy fielding the questions at jetBlue when tweeting first began. Now a social media team of 17 supports Johnston, manager of corporate communications. JetBlue initially tried mainly to advertise deals on Twitter, he says, but that strategy fell flat.

"So we asked our customers what they wanted to hear. And we listened. That's how we built our following," he says.

Not only has that following helped engender brand loyalty and trust, it also helped when crisis hit. When flight attendant Steven Slater cursed out passengers on the tarmac at Kennedy International Airport in New York before grabbing a couple of beers and exiting the aircraft via the evacuation slide, jetBlue took a few days before deciding on an appropriate response.

"We understood our reputation for being transparent, and it would have been the wrong action to try and ignore it," Johnston says.

Instead, the company came out with a short, tasteful and funny blog post mentioning the movie *Office Space* and praising its 2,300 other flight crew members who didn't wig out.

The first comment posted sums up the general reaction: "I love you jetBlue."

Angry Birds

Smartphones were pretty revolutionary when they first came out, but experts agree they were missing one key thing—testy little birds willing to fling themselves into concrete walls to destroy smirking green pigs.

Since Finland-based Rovio released the Angry Birds game in December 2009, 36 million gamers have downloaded the cute time-sink. Despite a brief partnership with publisher Chillingo at the app's release, Angry Birds has reached its dominance with a marketing budget close to zero.

"It really is intended for everybody. It's easy to pick up and start playing, even if you've never played any games before," says Ville Heijari, Rovio's vice president of public relations, explaining why the game has become so popular. "Not to forget the unique characters, wacky sound design and the seemingly absurd plotline. It really is the total sum of all its parts that makes it a great game."

Rovio is hoping 2010 was just the first of many years for its birds. This spring, the company plans to roll out Angry Birds versions for Facebook and the web, and it also hopes to launch versions for Xbox 360, Wii, and PS3.

Merchandising of the game's cute birdies and pigs is underway with a plush toy collection, and rumors have been swirling that Angry Birds may get a feature film treatment as well.

In all, Rovio hopes that by the summer, the birds will reach 100 million players, both on and off the phone.

"Consider the Angry Birds like other loved characters, such as Mario," Heijari says. "There's a lot more to the story of Angry Birds than has been seen yet, and infinite possibilities for storytelling."

Conan O'Brien

The only way to describe the departure of late-night host Conan O'Brien from NBC's *The Tonight Show* is this: messy.

After seven months at the helm of the television show made legendary by Steve Allen, Jack Paar and Johnny Carson, O'Brien was given the choice to either move the show to a half hour later to make room for the return of Jay Leno, whose 10 P.M. experiment was a flop, or to hit the road. O'Brien decided that, instead of cheapening the *Tonight Show* brand by moving it later, he'd leave—taking with him $33 million and the status as a beloved underdog.

Though barred from discussing the debacle until last May or returning to television until last fall, O'Brien parlayed his troubles into marketing gold. Within 24 hours of launching his Twitter feed in February, he had more than 300,000 followers. His two-month "The Legally Prohibited From Being Funny on Television" tour launched in April and sold out quickly. Also in April, Conan told the world that he had signed on to begin a new late-night show on TBS starting in November.

Whether his TBS show will capture his old audience remains to be seen, but O'Brien's antics off the small screen were masterful.

"The important thing is he came out of this debacle looking like a folk hero, with a larger stature," says Troy Patterson, television critic for Slate.com and film critic at Spin. "He got to be an underdog that played into his persona as a gawky, aw-shucks type of guy."

The marketing for O'Brien's TBS show was equally inspired: His new logo simply played on the shock of red hair that has been his trademark since his television debut along with the name Team Coco. An orange blimp emblazoned with the word CONAN even traveled the East Coast, checking into Foursquare locations to advertise the show. All that had most of the country repeating the mantra spread by one of Conan's grassroots supporters: "I'm with Coco."

And 10 More...
Old Spice

When actor Isaiah Mustafa appeared as the "Old Spice Man" during last year's Super Bowl, the handsome towel-clad actor inaugurated the most creative advertising campaign of the year. But there was more to the spots spearheaded by ad agency Wieden + Kennedy. In July, Mustafa and a crew of social media experts and production folks began creating and posting YouTube videos of the Old Spice Man answering real questions from the public. Over three days, Mustafa weighed in with 186 videos, advising everyone from Alyssa Milano to George Stephanopoulos. In all, the back and forth generated 34 million YouTube views in a week as well as countless mentions in Facebook, Twitter and the mainstream press.

Domino's Pizza

For years Domino's has been the pizza world's cleanup act. Its low cost and late hours appealed to after-hours partyers and college students. Anyone who cares how their pizza actually tastes abandoned the brand long ago. So when the company began acknowledging its status in the pizza pecking order in ads released early last year, the honesty was a shock.

After reworking its recipe, Domino's head chef brought the new pizzas to the homes of its harshest focus-group critics, where the new pies made their debut. Not only did the ads make customers sit up and listen, they also made them want to try the pizzas for themselves. In the first quarter of 2010, sales jumped 14 percent, and Domino's has recorded 11–12 percent growth each quarter since.

Heineken

Heineken's "Walk-in fridge" ad—in which a group of women goes nuts over their friend's walk-in closet, only to hear their husbands and boyfriends in the next room losing their minds over a walk-in refrigerator stocked with Heineken beer—garnered more than 4 million views on YouTube, not to mention the millions of impressions the ad made on the regular tube.

Glee

In addition to top ratings, singles from the hit musical comedy-drama series demolish the Beatles' record for most hit singles on the Billboard Charts. High school drama kids raise their spirit fingers in solidarity.

But instead of sitting back and waiting for their Clio, the ad company went guerilla. Soon after the ad's launch, groups of young men were spotted throughout Amsterdam trying to push giant cardboard boxes labeled "Walk-in fridge" into apartments and houses.

But Heineken's marketing coup de grâce last year was a video of a 2009 prank pulled on Champions League fans. That October, Heineken had enlisted wives, girlfriends, bosses and professors to sucker 1,136 Italian football fanatics in Milan into skipping the biggest match of the year—AC Milan vs. Real Madrid—to attend a classical music and poetry recital.

It recorded the forlorn men as they filed into the auditorium—then, 15 minutes into the unbearable concert, the game appeared on the screen. We're assuming they all got walk-in fridges as consolation prizes.

Groupon

Groupon, a web company whose name is a mashup of "group" and "coupon," introduced the world to its concept in late 2008. More than two years later, it's one of the marketing world's breakout stars.

The concept is simple: In each of Groupon's 150 North American and 100 international markets, a local deal is offered, say 50 percent off muffins at a bakery. If enough people sign up for the deal, it goes live and is available to everyone. The merchant drives traffic to the store, and Groupon takes a cut.

But last summer, Groupon showed its real muscle when it went national for the first time, with a Gap promotion promising $50 in merchandise for $25. The deal hit critical mass in a few hours, and Gap raked in $11 million in one day.

At press time, it was rumored that Groupon had rebuffed a $5 billion buyout offer from Google. That would have been quite a deal.

World Records

In the past three years, Guinness has seen world-record attempts spike 250 percent, but it's not because of crazy individuals growing out their fingernails or holding their breath. Instead, it's corporations trying to bring attention to their brands.

In 2009, Supercuts set the record for the most haircuts in a day (349). Last year, Sheraton Hotels & Resorts promoted a $120 million upgrade of its fitness facilities with a world-record resistance-band strength-training class (270 people). In November, Nike employees from around the world traveled to Las Vegas to break the record for the largest gathering of Elvis impersonators (645).

Those records may be a far cry from the most lightning strikes survived (7), but they're equally entertaining.

UNICEF

In the middle of Union Square in Manhattan last July, Unicef, the United Nation's Children's Fund, set up a bottled-water vending machine. But instead of spring-fed H20, the machine offered murky bottles labeled dysentery, cholera, dengue, and malaria. The stunt was designed to call attention to the 4,200 children who die each day of water-borne diseases. No one actually drank the water, but the machine did accept donations, and the viral video featuring the stunt reached several hundred thousand people. Not bad for a video without Justin Bieber.

Volkswagen

Volkswagen's Fun Theory claims its mission is to inspire people to do good—and smile at the same time. The carmaker is behind the installation of slides and *Big*-inspired keyboards on subway steps—viral videos from years past. But its mission for 2010 was finding a fun way to make drivers obey the speed limit.

After sifting through hundreds of entries, it chose The Speed Camera Lottery. In cooperation with Swedish authorities, it rigged a camera to photograph all the license plates that went by. Speeding drivers were fined, with the money going into a pot. Drivers who obeyed the speed limit were eligible to win the pot.

The experiment got drivers to drop their speed 22 percent—but, most of all, it gave Volkswagen another viral hit.

Sign Spinning

In an age where marketing seems to revolve around page views, retweets and audience share, a trend as old as, well, signs is making a mark. Sign spinning is a mashup of juggling, performance art and old-fashioned pavement pounding, and it is showing up at grand openings and special events around the country, bringing in foot traffic and attracting crowds.

The driving force and self-proclaimed inventors of sign spinning is AArrow Advertising, a San Diego-based franchise that has locations in 18 states, fielding an army of young spinners nationwide. And they're making waves off the street too. YouTube is full of sign-spinning videos, Ellen DeGeneres has featured sign spinners on her show, and spinners were in FX Network and Ford commercials.

Miracle Whip

In late 2009, Kraft's Miracle Whip began airing a spot showing hip 20-somethings laughing and dancing around a pool on an urban rooftop while smearing their sandwiches with the distinctly unhip dressing. The monotone taglines, "Don't Be So Mayo" and "We Are Miracle Whip, and We Will Not Tone It Down," were youth-pandering at its worst, enough that Stephen Colbert ran a parody of the commercial, throwing his support behind regular mayonnaise on his Comedy Central show. But instead of taking it on the chin, Miracle Whip bought airtime during Colbert's show, running its rooftop ad with new voice-overs calling Colbert "So mayo," making fun of the silent "t" in his name and inviting him to the rooftop to dance. The stunt turned a marketing flop into a publicity juggernaut and icon of customer engagement.

Jersey

If you watched television in 2010, you were smacked in the face by the Garden State's bombardment of pop culture. At its height last October, MTV's "reality" show *Jersey Shore* boasted 6.7 million viewers, but its stars invaded more than the beach. Nicole "Snooki" Polizzi, Mike "The Situation" Sorrentino and DJ Pauly D have parlayed their MTV hit into a minor media empire, creating workout videos, appearing on late-night talk shows, scoring endorsement deals for vodka, bronzer, and pistachios—even writing a novel and getting a gig on *Dancing With the Stars*.

Other Jersey-based shows, including Bravo's *The Real Housewives of New Jersey* and the Style Network's *Jersey-licious,* a reality show about a salon in Green Brook, have kept the state's big hair and spray tans in the spotlight—despite Gov. Chris Christie's lament that *Jersey Shore* doesn't fairly represent his state. But locals don't seem to mind. According to the Seaside Heights Business Improvement District, the "gym, tan, laundry" lifestyle has boosted local revenues 38 percent in just one year.

Critical Thinking

1. Formulate your own definition for 'Marketing Brilliance.'

2. List some additional examples, beyond what's in the article, of marketing brilliance.

Create Central

www.mhhe.com/createcentral

Internet References

Creative Bloq
http://www.creativebloq.com/branding/most-iconic-brands-11121149

Creative Guerilla Marketing
http://www.creativeguerrillamarketing.com/

Marketo Blog
http://blog.marketo.com/2013/05/5-of-the-most-innovative-and-unique-marketing-campaigns-so-far-in-2013.html

---

JASON DALEY is a freelance writer in "Madison, WI."

Jason Daley, "How to Make Marketing Brilliance," *Entrepreneur*, February 2011, p. 48–53. Copyright © 2011 by Entrepreneur Media, Inc. All rights reserved. Used with permission.

Article   Prepared by: Nisreen N. Bahnan, *Salem State University*

Future Tech: The Trends to Watch in 2014

Smartwatches, 3D printing, and connected cars will be in the spotlight

The present is looking quite futuristic. Over the next year, we'll see technologies quickly ramping up toward a tipping point, after which life could change in big ways. Here are several developments that will make headlines very soon.

MARK SULLIVAN

Learning Outcomes

After reading this article, you will be able to:

- Acknowledge the importance of innovation in marketing.
- Recognize the correlation between new product development and changing consumer needs, preferences and lifestyles.

Smartwatches Attract the Masses

A friend of mine said that she bought a watch recently because she was tired of pulling out her phone to see the time. She prefers the familiar motion of swinging her arm up so that she can glance at her wrist.

With the right device, people would probably like to get lots of other information with that same quick gesture. We've already seen Samsung release a smartwatch that largely failed to capture the public imagination (go.pcworld.com/galaxygear). Now it's time for the other heavy hitters—Apple and Google—to swoop in and take the concept mainstream.

Cars Get Connected

Give me a car with screamin'-fast Internet connectivity. Give me enough bandwidth to stream music, stream video at 1080p resolution, connect my mobile devices and wearable tech, make video calls, and enjoy accurate and fast mapping.

GM says it will build 4G LTE connectivity (go.pcworld.com/gm4g) into most of its 2015 cars. Audi's 2015 A3

(go.pcworld.com/audi4g) will have 4G connectivity too. Gartner predicts that in 2014 the majority of car buyers will expect at least basic Web-based information in premium automobiles. And Cisco says that global mobile data traffic will increase 18-fold between 2011 and 2016.

This might be the year that automakers, wireless carriers, and other stakeholders finally manage to figure this concept out.

Your New Password: Your Body

The tech world is beginning to react to the problem of confusing website, service, and mobile-device credentials. Not only are password requirements becoming more stringent (passwords must contain capital letters, numbers, special characters, and so on), but we also have way more usernames and passwords to keep track of than ever before. It's a mess.

Fortunately, interest in biometric alternatives is growing. Instead of typing a complicated password that you have to remember, you'll use your fingerprint, your voice, or maybe the patterns in your eye. Apple got the ball rolling by building the Touch ID fingerprint reader (go.pcworld.com/touchid) into the iPhone 5s, and you can expect other vendors to release their own biometric devices over the next year.

TV Wherever, Whenever

Facing pressure from the TV services of telephone and satellite companies, cable companies will increasingly let subscribers watch their programming on multiple screens. For instance, you might be checking out *Breaking Bad* on the TV in your living room before work, and then grab your tablet and pick up where you left off while you're on the bus.

Cable services such as Comcast's X2 (go.pcworld.com/comcastx2) will finally get the systems (and mindsets) in place to place-shift, time-shift, and device-shift video. It'll be clunky at first, but it will get better.

3D Printing Emerges from the Basement

It took me a while to "get" the utility of 3D printing, but I eventually realized that reasonably priced 3D printers could print out useful household objects—such as the remote-control back cover that disappeared on me last month.

Jupiter Research says 3D printers' popularity (go.pcworld.com/3dprinting) will increase significantly as HP, Microsoft, and Samsung join the party. Soon we'll be printing car parts, batteries, prosthetics, computer chips, jewelry, clothing, and maybe even food, Jupiter muses.

Your Devices Understand You

These days we are surrounded by intelligent devices, wherever we go. We carry them, we wear them, we talk to them, and they talk back to us. But increasingly our devices are getting to know us.

They're learning to understand where we are, what we're doing, how we work and play, what we buy, what we need to remember, and most important, how they can help us with all of those things and more.

Google Now and Apple's Siri are good current examples of such "personal assistant" technology, but similar functionality will take on more AI qualities and will start to appear in more devices, apps, and services this year.

The 'Internet of Things' Goes Mainstream

The digital world is extending into the real world. Objects are growing eyes and ears, connecting to the Internet and becoming searchable. All sorts of objects—smart and dumb, active and passive—are beginning to talk to one another (go.pcworld.com/internetthings). A doorway sensor at a store detects when my smartphone enters and when it leaves. A refrigerator passes data to a grocery-store system. Sensors detect when your car travels over a bridge and when you return.

For the most part, all this new communication will be beneficial and benign. Still, a boatload of data is being generated and logged about every aspect of our lives. As our devices become privy to more and more intimate information about us, the more and more dangerous that data becomes if it were to fall into the wrong hands.

Google Pushes Broadband Forward

When Google Fiber launched in Kansas City (go.pcworld.com/fiberkc), Time Warner Cable promptly announced that it would increase its fastest service to 100 megabits per second in that city. Time Warner Cable also said it would match anything Google rolls out in Austin. AT&T took the bait, too: When Google announced plans for gigabit-fast fiber broadband in Austin, AT&T swiftly outlined plans to offer fiber-based gigabit-per-second broadband service there as well.

Google's fiber march is likely to reach new cities throughout 2014, and the slow and complacent ISPs in those markets will be forced to respond with higher home and business broadband speeds. By the end of the year, gigabit-per-second service could reach half of the large markets in the United States.

Browser Cookies Give Way to Device ID

Advertisers are moving away from using browser cookies to track our identities, interests, and preferences online. Increasingly they'll turn to the unique device IDs (go.pcworld.com/deviceid) associated with our smartphones, tablets, gaming consoles, and wearable computers.

Marketers believe that device IDs might reveal more about all the things people do on their devices. For instance, they might learn how often we make purchases in a certain part of town, or whether we research a product online before we buy it in a brick-and-mortar store. It's just another example of how you'll be giving away more of your privacy over the coming years.

Critical Thinking

1. Formulate a definition for the word "trend." In your opinion, how is a trend different from a fad?

2. Look over the innovations discussed in the article, and give your personal assessment of their potential appeal and success.

Create Central

www.mhhe.com/createcentral

Internet References

Inventables
https://www.inventables.com/
Product Development and Management Association
http://www.pdma.org/p/cm/ld/fid=1

Used with permission of PCWorld Copyright© 2014. All rights reserved.

Article   Prepared by: Nisreen N. Bahnan, *Salem State University*

Six Strategies for Successful Niche Marketing

How to win big by thinking small.

Eric K. Clemons, Paul F. Nunes, and Matt Reilly

Learning Outcomes

After reading this article, you will be able to:

- Define and understand niche marketing in general and resonance marketing in specific.

- Analyze the six marketing principles, discussed in the article, which will allow a company to manage the complexity and reap superior profitability of resonance marketing.

T here's been a lot of buzz about the long-tail phenomenon—the strategy of selling smaller quantities of a wider range of goods that are designed to resonate with consumers' preferences and earn higher margins. And a quick scan of everyday products seems to confirm the long tail's merit: Where once we wore jeans from Levi, Wrangler or Lee, we now have scores of options from design houses. If you're looking for a nutrition bar, there's one exactly right for you, whether you're a triathlete, a dieter or a weight lifter. Hundreds of brewers offer thousands of craft beers suited to every conceivable taste.

It's not surprising that so many companies have embraced this strategy. It allows them to avoid the intense competition found in mass markets. Look at the sales growth that has taken place in low-volume, high-margin products such as super-premium ice cream, noncarbonated beverages, heritage meats and heirloom vegetables.

But the case for the long tail has frequently been overstated. This strategy can be expensive to implement, and it doesn't work for all products or all categories. It's surely better to

Questions to Ask Yourself

1. As part of a strategy of selling a wider range of high-margin goods, are you being careful to distinguish potential future market sweet spots from valueless niches that produce needless complexity?
2. Are you listening carefully to what consumers are saying online about your products, not just to you but also to each other, and are you reacting quickly to make improvements that address any negative comments?
3. Are you standardizing design components as much as possible to limit the costs of producing an extensive product line?
4. Are you aggressively keeping inventory and distribution costs down with strategies that allow you to configure finished products quickly when orders arrive, swap inventory among outlets or share distribution with other producers?
5. Are you continually reviewing your product portfolio to weed out those products that aren't contributing to profits, while being careful not to dump products that aren't big sellers but still contribute to the portfolio's overall profitability?

If you answered no to any of these questions, you're not getting the most out of what we call resonance marketing—selling a variety of precisely targeted goods designed to resonate with consumers. Following the steps in this article will help you manage the complexity of this strategy and reap superior profitability.

For Further Reading

These related articles from MIT Sloan Management Review can be accessed online

From Niches to Riches: Anatomy of the Long Tail

Erik Brynjolfsson, Yu "Jeffrey" Hu and Michael D. Smith (Summer 2006)

The Internet marketplace allows companies to produce and sell a far wider range of products than ever before. This profoundly changes both consumer behavior and business strategy.

Harnessing the Power of the Oh-So-Social Web

Josh Bernoff and Charlene Li (Spring 2008)

People are connecting with one another in increasing numbers, thanks to blogs, social networking sites and countless communities across the Web. Some companies are learning to turn this growing groundswell to their advantage.

Cracking the Code of Mass Customization

Fabrizio Salvador, Pablo Martin de Holan and Frank Piller (Spring 2009)

Most companies can benefit from mass customization, yet few do. The key is to think of it as a process for aligning a business with its customers' needs.

produce a blockbuster film, for instance, than a smattering of low-volume art films.

In other words, simply avoiding the clutter of mass markets isn't enough. Companies need to stake out unique market *sweet spots,* those areas that resonate so strongly with target consumers that they are willing to pay a premium price, which offsets the higher production and distribution costs associated with niche offerings. We call this approach resonance marketing.

The vast amount of information available on the Internet has made this kind of niche marketing more important than ever and easier to do. More important because all that information encourages comparison shopping, putting tremendous downward pressure on prices and profits in highly competitive mass markets. And easier because it eliminates much of consumers' uncertainty about new niche products, since they can easily find reviews, ratings, and comments on everything that hits the market. For decades consumer uncertainty blocked the launch of new offerings that were too focused to be supported by national ad campaigns; today's empowered consumer is truly listening to word-of-mouth.

Finding sweet spots in the market is especially important in these tough economic times, when so many consumers are strapped for cash. Many shoppers will compromise whenever possible by looking for cheaper alternatives to the things they usually buy—but keep buying products that don't have any direct substitutes.

With the right approach, resonance marketing can fulfill its promise. We have found that six marketing principles, taken together, will allow a company to manage the complexity of this strategy and reap superior profitability.

Target Carefully

Sweet-spot offerings aren't better than other products in any absolute sense; they simply have to be different from existing options and better for their target consumers. They have to resonate powerfully with them.

But that's not as easy as it might sound. Finding profitable new niches requires a set of skills different from those needed to build market share or to create variations of an existing product— you're looking for places where no offerings exist, not one where consumers are complaining about existing choices.

Consider the success of Toyota Motor Corp.'s Lexus line of luxury cars. Toyota's research indicated there was an untapped market in the U.S. for Mercedes-quality luxury cars at a lower price, rather than superior quality at a comparable price. The Lexus line was designed to offer quality at a price that indicated the owners could afford whatever they wanted but also were smart enough to get it at a great price. The brand fulfilled an unmet need in the market and enjoyed immediate success.

Simply identifying gaps in the market isn't enough, though. Plenty of unique consumer products have failed to capture the imagination of shoppers. There's no guaranteed way to avoid such failures, but extensive research is essential. Often an ethnologist can help. Many companies use these analysts to explore why consumers buy what they do and what they would buy if it were available.

Listen to Your Customers. Really Listen

Traditional advertising campaigns don't make sense for most niche markets; they're too expensive and too difficult to target precisely enough. Indeed, there are entire product categories, including nutrition bars and craft beers, where most products are never advertised. Their producers have learned how to work with consumer-generated content online—reviews, ratings, or just chatter about a product. They don't just listen when customers talk to them; they listen just as carefully when customers talk about them.

The beauty of consumer-generated content is that companies get immediate and continuous feedback about their products. The key here is to listen closely and react quickly. Marketing executives should watch for the first online comments about their wares with the same excitement and apprehension as Broadway producers waiting for opening-night reviews. Consumers will make it clear right away what they like about the product and what they don't.

Harsh reviews can have devastating consequences. We analyzed two years of data on hotel bookings and found that the length, specificity, and detail of negative online reviews are the best predictors of a hotel's inability to sell itself online.

So what do you do if the product you so carefully crafted to appeal to a particular market segment is trashed by those very consumers? Fix it immediately.

If defects pointed out by consumers are fixed quickly, more-favorable comments will emerge just as quickly. But companies should never assume that they've gotten it right and can stop listening. Continuous monitoring of online comments will alert executives to any new issues that arise, any improvements consumers might like to see as they become more familiar with the product, and even the emergence of any competitors or alternatives that might siphon off buyers.

Some traditional marketing still has its place, and indeed has become more powerful thanks to the way word-of-mouth spreads so quickly over the Internet. Companies can generate positive buzz for niche products with events like the Great American Beer Festival that small, specialty brewers attend every year. The brewers make sure to attract both professional critics and passionate amateur bloggers alike.

Moreover, craft brewers have learned to work together to make these events successful; they understand that at this point in their industry's development, their greatest danger comes not from each other but from consumer acceptance of mass-produced, generic beers.

Control Production Costs

Selling a large number of narrowly targeted products may sound like a production nightmare, but it doesn't have to be. There are several ways to maintain economies of scale over a broad range of product offerings.

Variety and standardization can coexist. For instance, Callaway Golf Co. offers buyers of its drivers multiple options for a club's head, loft angle, and shaft—several hundred different combinations in all. But the company doesn't manufacture every variety separately. Any configuration of the various components can be readily assembled, since the interconnections are standardized.

Manufacturing processes can also be standardized to a large extent. While pumpkin spice ice cream appeals to a very different group of consumers than vanilla does, the manufacturing process is nearly identical for both flavors and any others. Brewing involves cold-fermenting lagers in one set of tanks and warm-fermenting ales in another, but the two varieties share many other processes: mashing grains, adding hops, and bottling.

It also pays for a company to have a high-volume product in its portfolio that will keep its manufacturing equipment and employees from sitting idle for stretches of time. The relatively low volume of sales in narrowly targeted markets means production plants might not need to work to their full capacity to meet demand. A high-volume, if less profitable, product can take up the slack.

Control Distribution Costs

It's not just production costs that will determine the profitability and ultimate success of resonance offerings. Distribution costs are also important. There are ways here, too, to keep costs under control.

It can be difficult to forecast demand for products with limited sales, but that doesn't necessarily mean a company needs to stockpile high levels of inventory to keep from getting caught short. Companies that offer many varieties of a product based on different combinations of components, as Callaway does with its golf clubs, can keep inventory low by postponing final assembly until a particular product is ordered—there's no need to keep a given number of every combination in stock.

Flexible inventory allocation is another way to keep from having to stockpile goods. Auto makers, for instance, often swap needed items. If a customer in New Jersey wants a copper-colored Infiniti FX35 and his dealer has the car in silver, while a customer in Pennsylvania wants the same car in silver and his dealer has the copper, the dealers can arrange an exchange.

Shared distribution is another option worth considering. Small brewers, for instance, cut costs this way.

Selling to customers directly from a company website can reduce costs by eliminating intermediaries. But companies should be aware that shoppers can be less forgiving online than they are offline. A consumer who visits a store to buy a product or orders it from a catalog may be miffed if it is temporarily out of stock. But frustration may rise to the level of anger if the same consumer orders the product online and isn't notified until three days later that the item is out of stock, because of a glitch in the site's inventory software.

Some Apparent Losers Are Worth Keeping

Even with the best research and the most careful marketing, production, and distribution, some products will be unprofitable or only marginally profitable. But before discontinuing a product, a company should consider the product's value in broader terms.

Some products that don't generate significant profit directly still help make a company's other products more profitable. Feeder routes on airlines transport customers to more-profitable routes, such as trans-Atlantic flights. Likewise, niche books that don't account for a significant portion of Amazon.com Inc.'s sales are valuable to the company because they contribute to its reputation as a one-stop source for any book.

Prune Your Portfolio Ruthlessly

Companies must relentlessly drop niche offerings that don't contribute to profitability directly or indirectly. The scores of flavors discontinued over the years by Ben & Jerry's Home-made Inc., remembered fondly in the "flavor graveyard" on the company's website, serve as a reminder to all companies that the flip side of creative expansion of a product line is eliminating those that no longer resonate with consumers. And the success of Ben & Jerry's is a reminder of the power of resonance marketing done right.

Critical Thinking

1. List a possible seventh strategy and explain why you came up with it.

2. What questions would you ask in the pursuit of an additional niche market(s)?

Create Central

www.mhhe.com/createcentral

Internet References

Consumer Psychologist
    http://www.consumerpsychologist.com/cb_Segmentation.html
The U.S. Small Business Association
    http://www.sba.gov/community/blogs/community-blogs/small-business-matters/5-ways-find-right-niche-and-target-market-you

---

DR. CLEMONS is a professor of operations and information management at the Wharton School of the University of Pennsylvania. **MR. NUNES** is executive director of research at the Accenture Institute for High Performance and is based in Boston. **MR. REILLY** is a senior executive in Accenture's management-consulting business, global managing director of the firm's Process and Innovation Performance practice and global co-leader of its Operational Excellence service. They can be reached at reports@wsj.com.

Eric K. Clemons; Paul F. Nunes; Matt Reilly, "Six Strategies for Successful Niche Marketing," *The Wall Street Journal*, May 23, 2010. Copyright © 2010 by Dow Jones & Company, Inc. All rights reserved. Used with permission.

Article   Prepared by: Nisreen N. Bahnan, *Salem State University*

Revisiting the Marketing Mix

The Apple Store experience typifies a new vision for marketing

About seven years ago (January/February, 2005), we published an article in *Marketing Management* titled "In the Mix." In that article, we discussed the traditional concept of the marketing mix, which seemingly originated with Neil Borden of Harvard University in the 1940s, was adopted and adapted as the four Ps (Product, Price, Place, and Promotion) by Jerome McCarthy of Michigan State University in the late 1950s and then popularized by Philip Kotler of Northwestern University over the last several decades. We argued that, while providing a valuable managerial tool for marketing during those times, today's marketing mix fails to truly reflect the marketing situation and planning approach needed by 21st century managers.

DON E. SCHULTZ AND CHEKITAN DEV

Learning Outcomes

After reading this article, you will be able to:

- List and define the elements of the traditional marketing mix (4Ps).

- Analyze SIVA, the customer-based view of the four Ps, and compare it against the traditional marketing mix.

In that initial article, we suggested the four Ps approach, while having a number of virtues, was basically too inward-looking. That is, the concept focused too much on what the marketing organization controlled, the resources it had available and what it hoped to accomplish in the marketplace. And it focused too little on what customers might want, need or desire.

As such, the four Ps are primarily a marketer's view of the world, not a customer's or prospect's view. In an age where consumers and customers are increasingly controlling the marketplace, we questioned whether the concept of a marketing mix, organized and implemented using the four Ps process, as the basic premise of how marketplace exchanges occur might have run its course. Another, more customer- or consumer-focused approach might be needed.

The Siva Approach

In place of the four Ps, we suggested managers employ a market and marketing planning system we called SIVA. The SIVA acronym, which stands for Solution, Information, Value, and Access, simply flips the four Ps methodology around and looks at it from the customer's view. The emphasis is on what customers want, need or require, not what marketers have to sell.

It's as simple as that, but, apparently, based on the responses we got to the original article, was quite a revolutionary concept at the time.

Our premise was very straightforward: Instead of focusing on the product and what it did, how it was made, why it was better than competitors, and so on, we suggested focusing on the customers in terms of the problem they had or might have for which the available product or service might provide a solution.

Likewise, instead of building the marketing effort around price, we proposed value. We viewed value as being of several types. First, of course, is the value the customer will receive from the proposed solution. That value could be monetary, mental, social, time-saving or any other return the customer might seek, enjoy or require. The other side of the value equation, of course, is what value the customer has to give up in order to acquire the marketer's solution. That could be time, money, or some other valuable resource required to obtain and use the solution. We tied that back to the basic concept of reciprocity or shared values or rewards, which we believe is driving the marketplace today and will continue to do so into the future.

Instead of promotion, we suggested focusing on information. This would include supportive details the customer might need to determine how relevant the product was to fill their needs or desires. Not how the marketer wanted to distribute information, but, rather, how the customer wanted to obtain it, whether online, through a retailer, direct, through traditional mass media or newer forms of social media.

Instead of place or distribution, the final element of the SIVA approach is access, or how the customer might acquire the solution. That could come from a wide variety of distribution alternatives such as retail stores, the sales force, online or any other access points where the solution might be available. We also suggested that access include how and where the customer wanted to get information about the solution. Clearly, given today's time-sensitive consumers and customers, ease of access for both the product and the information is critical.

A New Age for Marketing

So, that was how we envisaged SIVA in 2005 . . . a customer-based view of the four Ps. We thought that approach was much more relevant to both marketers and customers in what was becoming an increasingly interactive world and which, given the new social media explosion, is rampant today.

So we wrote the article. *Marketing Management* published it and the rest, as they say, is history. The article created considerable discussion when it was first published and continues to do so. We got numerous comments on the concept and approach. That was and is rewarding, not only intellectually, but practically. Both of us conduct seminars and conferences all over the world. Therefore, we began to embed the SIVA concepts in our various meetings, academic conferences and seminars, generally with great success. People who saw it thought it made eminently good sense.

As we preached the SIVA gospel, numerous acolytes picked up the concept and began to apply it in areas as diverse as business-to-business, consumer package goods, retailing and services, and in locations ranging from Australia, China, India, and the UK to other developed and developing markets.

All that was gratifying, but not nearly as gratifying as the content of an article which appeared in *The Wall Street Journal* on June 15, 2011, under the title, "Secrets from Apple's Genius Bar: Full Loyalty, No Negativity." In that article, Yukari Iwatani Kane and Ian Sherr provided an in-depth analysis of the thought and planning behind the marketplace execution of one of the most successful retail ventures of this or any age . . . the Apple Store.

As we read the article, what literally jumped out at us was the basic framework of SIVA, which we had proposed at about the same time the Apple Stores were being developed. To clarify, however, Apple did not come to us, nor did we go to them to discuss how their retail operations were developed, the concepts behind them and how the Apple Store concept was implemented. But the similarity of our concept of SIVA and what

Apple Stores have done and continue to do seems to have been written from the same script.

Some examples, taken directly from the Apple Store article in *The Wall Street Journal* and the concept of SIVA, as we presented it in 2005, will illustrate the similarity.

In SIVA, we advocated offering or providing customers with solutions, not simply pushing products out toward customers and prospects. Apple Stores do the same. The writers reported: "According to several employees and training manuals, [Apple] sales associates are taught an unusual sales philosophy: not to sell, but rather to help customers solve problems. . . . 'You were never trying to close a sale. It was about finding solutions for a customer and finding their pain points.' . . . 'Your job is to understand all of your customer's needs—some of which they may not even realize they have.' To that end, employees receive no sales commissions and have no sales quotas."

Repositioning products as solutions to customers' problems is the key theme of the SIVA approach. We proposed information as a major element in the SIVA process. Providing information appears to be what Apple Store employees do best. Steve Jobs, former Apple CEO, speaking in a video tour of the first Apple Store, said: "People don't just want to buy personal computers anymore; they want to know what they can do with them." Kane and Sherr also interviewed a former Apple employee: "Keith Bruce, 23, who worked at an Apple store in Virginia for three and one-half years until December, 2009, says he was told the sales floor was a stage where he should focus on things he can do, rather than things he can't."

Value was the third element of the SIVA framework; value not just in the benefits the customer receives from product purchases, but in making the acquisition and use of an Apple product easy and pleasant. For example, Apple Stores look at value in a unique way. According to *The Wall Street Journal* article, "When a new product is launched, such as the second-generation iPad in March, employees cheer customers as they enter and exit the store." And, "Apple's hottest products were placed in the front of the store while a dedicated section for kids was furnished with squishy balls they could sit on while playing with children's software programs loaded onto Macs." And the Apple Stores continue to evolve.

According the story, "Apple now appears to be eyeing business customers at its stores. The company built specially designed 'Briefing Rooms' in some stores and, earlier this year, rolled out a service called 'Joint Venture' to provide a separate program for business customers."

Clearly, Apple Store management believes in providing extra value beyond the product by focusing on the total customer experience. That means value in terms of the solutions provided, but also value in terms of the way and manner in which those products are evaluated, delivered, and used.

In terms of the final SIVA point, access, Apple Stores took a different route to market than most retailers. While traditional retailers were trying to reduce staff, cut services and use technology to provide a less expensive retailing approach, Apple Stores went in exactly the opposite direction . . . building bricks-and-mortar stores in prime locations. The reason for this approach? Simple. Steve Jobs knew that new products would have little impact if consumers couldn't find some people familiar with them. That all comes from employee training.

Why does the Apple Store concept work? Kane and Sherr suggest the following reasons based on their research: "intensive control on how employees interact with customers, scripted training for on-site tech support and considerations of every store detail down to the pre-loaded photos and music on demo devices."

Apple Store management understands access. Not just the retail location, but the customer experience once the person is in the store. And, in terms of access, nothing really beats a well-trained, on-site person who is eager and anxious to help customers find solutions to their wants and needs, not just push products out the door.

Does the Apple Store, SIVA-type approach work? Here are a few numbers provided in *The Wall Street Journal* story to make the case:

- "In 2009, when [total] retail sales declined 2.4%," . . . "Apple's retail sales rose roughly 7%. In 2012, Apple's retail sales, excluding online, jumped 70% to $11.7 billion."
- "More people now visit Apple's 326 stores in a single quarter than the 60 million who visited Walt Disney Co.'s four biggest theme parks last year."

Clearly, the Apple Store concept works. Today's common consumer experience of long lines waiting to get into the Apple stores, while shunning retailers that sell similar products, is marketplace evidence of success. Is the SIVA-type approach that Apple Stores employs = one of the main reasons for that success? We like to think so. Certainly, the methods Apple has employed, as reported in *The Wall Street Journal* article, and our SIVA approach are quite similar.

Will the SIVA approach work for you? In our view, taking a customer's, rather than a marketer's view, of today's interactive marketplace simply makes common sense. It's as simple as that.

Critical Thinking

1. Summarize the article's main premise regarding the need to revisit the traditional four Ps (marketing mix) approach. Do you agree with this argument?
2. List and discuss the elements of the SIVA marketing planning system.

Create Central

www.mhhe.com/createcentral

Internet References

Custom Fit Online
   http://www.customfitonline.com/news/2012/10/19/4-cs-versus-the-4-ps-of-marketing/
Hausman Marketing Letter
   http://www.hausmanmarketingletter.com/marketing-strategy-4ps-marketing/
Help Scout
   https://www.helpscout.net/blog/new-4ps-of-marketing/

Don E. Schultz; Chekitan Dev, "Revisiting the Marketing Mix," Summer 2012. Copyright © 2012 by American Marketing Association. All rights reserved. Used with permission.

Article   Prepared by: Nisreen N. Bahnan, *Salem State University*

75 Years of Marketing History

The world was a vastly different place in 1937. Economies across the globe were still in the throes of the Great Depression. A loaf of bread cost less than a dime. The Golden Gate Bridge was the industrial marvel of the day. Consumers spent their evenings listening to *The Lone Ranger* on their radios or going to the movies to see Spencer Tracy in *Captains Courageous*.

ELISABETH A. SULLIVAN

Learning Outcomes

After reading this article, you will be able to:

- Identify the progressive evolution of marketing thought and concepts.

- Relate external environmental factors to the emergence of marketing practices, trends and theories.

While marketers certainly can't claim to have prompted all of the evolutions and innovations that have powered us through the ensuing three-quarters of a century, over the years the marketing industry has played a significant role in boosting consumer confidence—and spending—to help shore up troubled economies; developing brand images and value propositions to justify higher-priced loaves of bread; creating savvy strategies to promote the innovations of industry titans; and, through promotions, advertising and sponsorships, helping to prompt the proliferation of entertainment channels, from radio and movies, to television, theater, music, sports, and more.

Put simply, marketing has been a dynamic field over the past several decades—and the American Marketing Association has been there to serve practitioners, researchers, academics and students all along the way. To recognize the association's 75th anniversary, *Marketing News* staff writers Christine Birkner and Molly Soat have assembled a compilation of historical highlights from both the evolution of the marketing industry and the growth of the AMA. And in the pages that follow, we feature 22 of the men and women who've dedicated their time and energy to building and directing the association from the helm of the Board of Directors. Their commitment—and that of innumerable volunteers like them—no doubt ensures that the AMA will celebrate many more milestones.

1930s

The concept of **brand management** was introduced in a 1931 memo written by Procter & Gamble executive Neil McElroy in which he proposed that separate teams should be dedicated to managing each of P&G's brands, rather than having all P&G marketers working across the portfolio, and each brand should be handled as a business unto itself, according to *American Business, 1920–2000: How It Worked*, by Thomas K. McCraw.

During the Great Depression, rather than trying to compete on price alone, companies emphasized **value**. For example, the tagline for a 1933 ad for Vicks cold remedies was, "Nobody can afford a cold this year."

In 1934, the **Federal Communications Commission** was created, in part, to help regulate advertisements on the radio, and later, television.

AMA Milestones

1936 PRE-AMA
The *Journal of Marketing* was launched.

1937
On January 1, 1937, the National Association of Teachers in Marketing and Advertising and the American Marketing Society merged to form the American Marketing Association. Frank R. Coutant was the association's first president.

Funfact

In 1938, the U.S. Census Bureau asked the AMA to help unify the marketing definitions used in all government agencies. The AMA has since issued the definition of marketing for the industry, refreshing it periodically by soliciting input and feedback from a broad cross section of the membership.

1940s

Propaganda was used heavily during World War II by the U.S. Office of War Information and the British Political Warfare Executive to promote patriotism, warn of foreign spies and recruit women to the war effort. One important influencer of propaganda in the early 20th century was public relations pioneer Edward Bernays, author of *Propaganda*, who was tapped by President Woodrow Wilson for the Creel Commission, which created anti-German propaganda campaigns during World War I, according to *Selling the Great War: The Making of American Propaganda*.

In the 1930s, Bernays counted Ivory soap, GE and Lucky Strike cigarettes among his PR clients, according to *The New York Times*. Bernays developed campaigns to encourage women to smoke, sponsoring demonstrations for Lucky Strike in which debutantes gathered on street corners to light up, but by the early 1960s, he was a public opponent of smoking and took part in anti-smoking campaigns, according to the *Times*.

In 1949, *Ad Age* published a report called **"Television—Infant Advertising Medium—Where It Stands Today."** Two percent of homes had televisions, according to *Ad Age*, and there were four broadcast networks: ABC, CBS, NBC, and DuMont, which ceased broadcasting in the mid-1950s.

AMA Milestones

1940
AMA had 817 members and 11 chapters.

1945
AMA membership reached 1,557.

1946
Four-page *Monthly News Bulletin*, the predecessor of *Marketing News*, was published.

1947
AMA welcomed Toronto as the 21st chapter; AMA's "first lady," Marguerite (Julian) Kent, was hired as the first staff member; membership was 2,760.

1948
University of Illinois became the first collegiate chapter. Within months, 22 collegiate chapters were established.

Funfact

In 1948, the AMA established its first headquarters at the Hyde Park Bank Building in Chicago. Prior to that, the AMA's "office" was a four-drawer file and a few boxes that moved with the AMA secretary, always a professor, who was provided with space by his college.

AMA Quotes

"You, ladies and gentleman in the market research profession, are actually the home guards of today. . . . You must be on guard to protect the standard of living and to help improve the 'American way of life.' . . . We must never lose sight of the basic fact . . . that 'the consumer is king,' today, tomorrow and always."

—Walter D. Fuller's closing remarks at an AMA conference at Indiana University, June 20, 1941

"The members of two of AMA's most progressive chapters have elected career girls as their presidents."

— AMA *Monthly News Bulletin* in 1948 on the appointment of chapter presidents Bee Angell in St. Louis and Jessie Locke Moffett in Southern California

1950s

The **marketing mix**, a mix of controllable marketing variables used to pursue sales goals in a target market, was proposed by Neil H. Borden in 1950.

Product life cycle, defined by economist Joel Dean in 1950, describes the stages in the sales history of a product. The product life cycle has four premises: (1) that products have a limited life; (2) that product sales pass through distinct stages, each stage having different implications for the seller; (3) that profits from the product vary at different stages in the life cycle; and (4) that products require different strategies at different stages of the life cycle.

The concept of **brand image** was introduced by Sidney J. Levy in 1955. In "The Product and the Brand," published in the *Harvard Business Review*, Levy and Burleigh B. Gardner wrote: "A brand name is more than the label employed to differentiate among the manufacturers of a product. It is a complex symbol that represents a variety of ideas and attributes." The concept of brand image—and of advertising, in general—was given increased visibility by advertising pioneer David Ogilvy in the 1950s.

Market segmentation, the process of subdividing a market into distinct subsets of customers who behave in the same way or have similar needs, was introduced in 1956 by Wendell R. Smith.

AMA Milestones

1950
Membership topped 3,800.

1953
William "Cat" Gorden became the first executive director of the AMA; membership reached 4,700.

1958
AMA division councils were formed.

1959
Membership surpassed 7,000.

AMA Quotes

"The 'weaker sex' has not taken a back seat in the affairs of the American Marketing Association, particularly among the chapters. Six of the lovelies have headed AMA chapters in the past, and the seventh is coming up."
—AMA *Monthly News Bulletin*, 1956

"Tomorrow's office will contain a fleet of machines attended by three or four people with the machines doing all of the paperwork. Stenographers, typists, stock clerks and bookkeepers will slowly and surely disappear."
—AMA *Monthly News Bulletin*, 1956

the process of communications. Trout subsequently co-authored a book with Al Ries on the topic.

Cigarette advertising and marketing was forced to change course when the Surgeon General's Report on Smoking and Health in 1964 stated that smoking may be hazardous to your health. In 1965, Congress passed the Cigarette Labeling and Advertising Act, which required a health warning on all cigarette packs.

AMA Milestones

1964
The *Journal of Marketing Research* debuted.

1966
First AMA Doctoral Consortium was held; membership reached 12,250.

1967
First issue of *Marketing News* was published, replacing the *Monthly News Bulletin*.

AMA Quotes

"I did not think it was such a great idea but it surely has been a great success."
—1967–68 AMA President Robert J. Holloway on the development of *Marketing News*. Holloway also called *MN* the "biggest thing" during his term as AMA president

"It should be clear by now to almost everyone that the revolution of rising expectations in the Negro market has created a new urban economic environment which challenges our realism as well as our profits."
—John H. Johnson, president of Johnson Publishing Co., at a Chicago chapter meeting, as reported by *Marketing News* in 1968

1960s

The **"four Ps"** (product, price, place and promotion) were introduced by E. Jerome McCarthy in 1960. "The four Ps became the basis of a marketing plan. . . . This was an advance over the old definition of a marketing plan as a promotion plan consisting of the budgets for advertising, sales promotion and public relations," says Philip Kotler, S.C. Johnson & Son Distinguished Professor of Marketing at Northwestern University's Kellogg School of Management and an AMA member since 1962.

In 1969, Jack Trout wrote an article in which he introduced **positioning**, a method for differentiating yourself in the mind of your prospect and how the mind works in

> "Basically, marketing moved from a descriptive subject at the time of AMA's founding, with a heavy section on the distribution system and some prescription of what salespeople, wholesalers, retailers and others should be doing, to a managerial and analytical subject in the late 1960s with some scientific aspirations and a focus on optimization in the sense of developing the optimal marketing mix for a given target market."
>
> PHILIP KOTLER Northwestern University's Kellogg School of Management

1970s

In 1971, Kotler and Gerald Zaltman introduced the concept of **social marketing**, by which organizations can market ideas and causes in addition to products and services. The aim of social marketing is to influence behavioral change or maintenance in a direction serving the individual's and society's best interests.

The introduction of **computers** to the general marketplace in the 1970s revolutionized marketing and marketing research. In 1975, Bill Gates and Paul Allen started a company called Micro-Soft, followed one year later by Apple, which was established by Steve Jobs, Steve Wozniak and Ronald Wayne.

Green marketing became more prevalent in the 1970s. The first Earth Day was held in 1970. On Earth Day 1971, Keep America Beautiful's PSA featuring Native American actor Chief Iron Eyes Cody, who became famous as the "Crying Indian," debuted. In 1975, the AMA held a workshop on "ecological marketing."

AMA Milestones

1970
First Agribusiness Marketing Research Conference and first leadership conference were held; AMA had 18,380 members, 63 professional chapters and 190 collegiate chapters.

1972
New AMA "flame of marketing knowledge" logo was adopted.

1974
AMA introduced its Chapter Awards Program to recognize outstanding accomplishments.

1975
First international study tour took 160 AMA members to the Soviet Union. Trips to Russia, Japan, Taiwan, Hong Kong, Czechoslovakia, Hungary, Austria, England, France and China followed.

1977
AMA Office of the President (now Office of the Chairman of the Board) was formed.

1979
First Collegiate Marketing Conference was held; first in-house computer system was installed; membership grew to 21,181.

Funfact

In 1973, the AMA's tagline was "Marketing— it's our middle name."

1980s

Marketing warfare, referring to brands competing for market share, was investigated by Kotler and Ravi Singh in their article "Marketing Warfare in the 1980s," published in the winter 1981 issue of the *Journal of Business Strategy*. The idea was explored further by Al Ries and Jack Trout in their 1986 book *Marketing Warfare*.

In 1983, Theodore Leavitt published an article in the *Harvard Business Review* titled "The Globalization of Markets," introducing marketers to the concept of **global marketing** and emphasizing the value of global operational opportunities to meet larger sales objectives.

That same year, the AMA published the book *Relationship Marketing* by Leonard Berry. Today, the AMA defines **relationship marketing** as "marketing with the conscious aim to develop and manage long-term and trusting relationships with customers, distributors, suppliers or other parties in the marketing environment."

The term **cause-related marketing** was used in 1983 to describe a campaign by American Express in which one cent from each AmEx purchase was donated to fund the restoration of the Statue of Liberty. AmEx raised $1.7 million to restore the statue and Ellis Island, according to the company. Richard Lutz, a longtime AMA member and contributor, and professor at the University of Florida in the department of marketing, says, "[The AmEx campaign] is often talked about as a watershed moment in cause marketing."

AMA Milestones

1980
AMA sponsored the first National Health Care Marketing Symposium and established a council on health services marketing.

1981
AMA launched Alpha Mu Alpha, a student honorary marketing society, and by 1985, more than 2,500 students were initiated; AMA had 82 professional chapters and 368 collegiate chapters.

1987
AMA marked its 50th anniversary with 19,000 student members and 27,000 professional members.

1989
AMA launched its first magazine, *Marketing Research*.

Funfacts

AMA membership nearly doubled within two years, growing from 21,181 in 1979 to 43,000 in 1981.

In 1980, Eli Belil, editorial board member of the AMA New York Chapter's publication *Marketing Review* and director of research for *Playboy* magazine, presented a study titled "The Playboy Report on American Men" to the AMA's Houston chapter. The study surveyed 1,990 men ages 18 to 49 about their values, attitudes and goals. Belil discussed the increasing popularity of "male adornment." "During the past decade, a variety of previously unacceptable forms of male adornment (jewelry, hairpieces, beards) has become part of the changing image of American masculinity," Belil said.

1990s

Online banner ads began to appear in 1994 on HotWired.com, the first digital iteration of *Wired* magazine. AT&T posted the first banner ad, which said: "Have you ever clicked your mouse right HERE? You will."

The concept of **viral marketing** was explored in an article by Harvard Business School faculty member Jeffrey Rayport in the December 31, 1996, issue of *Fast Company* titled "The Virus of Marketing." Viral marketing is defined as a marketing phenomenon that facilitates and encourages people to pass along a marketing message online. Rayport wrote, "When it comes to getting a message out with little time, minimal budgets, and maximum effect, nothing on earth beats a virus."

Integrated marketing communications (IMC) became an accepted practice. Don Schultz presented the concept to Northwestern University students in 1990 and followed up with the 1991 article "Integrated Marketing Communications: The Status of Integrated Marketing Communications Programs in the US Today," published in the *Journal of Promotion Management*. Today, the AMA defines IMC as "a planning process designed to assure that all brand contacts received by a customer or prospect for a product, service or organization are relevant to that person and consistent over time."

AMA Milestones

1990
AMA purchased the *Journal of Public Policy & Marketing*.

1992
AMA Foundation was organized (the AMAF offers resources to nonprofit marketers, scholarships to marketing students and awards to marketing leaders); AMA launched *Marketing Management* magazine.

1994
AMA developed its first online presence with a simple website, known as the Marketing Mix, at AMA.org.

1996
AMA hosted its first global marketing leadership conference, with 19 countries represented.

1997
AMA acquired the *Journal of International Marketing*.

1998
AMA launched a Global Electronic Membership, which allowed members all over the world to access online benefits from the association.

AMA Quote

"Recently toasted for their prowess and good fortune, many of the executives charged with developing on-line, CD-ROM, and other futuristic media options now privately complain they are becoming marginalized. By one industry insider's count, well more than half of those star performers now wish they had stayed with their parent companies' core businesses—publishing and broadcasting—rather than yield to the seductions of cyberspace."

—Bob Donath, a columnist in the July 17, 1995, issue of *Marketing News*.

2000s

Despite the dot-com bubble burst in early 2000, **online marketing** became the norm as marketers raced to augment brands' online presences.

Search engine optimization techniques became an important marketing component and online display advertising gained more popularity.

Social media began to define marketing practices. In 2004, Mark Zuckerberg released the first iteration of Facebook—called "the facebook"—to his fellow Harvard students. Marketers now turn to social channels for everything from market research to branding to customer relations.

"Another manifestation of the Internet is **mass customization**," Lutz says. "You don't have to settle for what someone else has put on the shelf. . . . That has driven segmentation further and further into what they call the long tail: the fact that it's become feasible to serve smaller and smaller and smaller segments, right down to segments of one, using the mass customization approach."

Budgets for **interactive digital campaigns** continue to grow. "The evolution of content from 2003 [to] today is that content can no longer be static.... The content has to be not only searchable, but it also has to provide the user with the opportunity for questions and feedback," says David Bohan, chairman and CEO of Bohan Advertising in Nashville, Tenn., in the December 30, 2010, issue of *Marketing News*.

Beyond the digital evolutions, business strategies underwent socially focused changes as **sustainability** became a buzz word in both operations and marketing. Sustainability now refers to not only ecological concerns and eco-friendly products, but also social sustainability (i.e., responsible supply chain management and cause-related efforts).

AMA Milestones

2000
Special interest groups (SIGs) for practitioners were launched and enhanced; AMAF's assets exceeded $1 million.

2001
MarketingPower.com replaced AMA.org as the association's website to give the AMA presence in the ".com" domain; AMA developed the Professional Certified Marketer (PCM) program.

2002
AMA hosted its first nonprofit conference.

2004
All four AMA journals launched digital access.

2006
AMA's first Mplanet event was held in Orlando, Fla.

2008
AMA hosted its second Mplanet conference.

2010
More than 5,000 marketers from all over the world attended the AMA's first virtual event, Cracking the Code for Business Marketers.

2012
AMA expanded its international reach, creating alliances with the Marketing Association of Spain and the Asia Marketing Federation, among others.

AMA Quotes

"Digital is certainly growing.... That's where the conversation is happening with the consumer. That's where the consumer does his product research, that's where they confide in each other and ask questions and make brand decisions....

This is where you're really going to make or break your relationship with your customer."
—Emily Riley, principal analyst and research director at Forrester Research Inc., in the March 15, 2010, issue of *Marketing News*

"**The definition of marketing, the four Ps, the product lifecycle . . . those concepts haven't changed and they remain at the core of marketing today. The tools and how we're able to assess all of this have changed, but the core concepts haven't changed.**"

DAVID REIBSTEIN Wharton professor and 2012–2013 AMA Chairperson

Insights From Former AMA Leaders

Each AMA chairperson serves just one year in the head post, but his or her involvement in the association extends well beyond that. Past chairs exhibit a noteworthy level of commitment to the association, as evidenced by the robust turnout for the 75th-anniversary chairperson event. Twenty-three former chairs traveled to Chicago for the event and eight took a moment to talk with the *Marketing News* staff about their careers and their involvement in the AMA. What follows are some highlights from *MN's* conversations with chairpersons representing three decades of AMA leadership.

1976

JACK KEANE
AMA Chair 1976–1977; member since 1956

How did you get involved in the AMA?
I'm a different kind of cat. I was in the Air Force, I was the U.S. Census Bureau director, had my own consulting company, worked for J. Walter Thompson advertising and was business school dean at Notre Dame.... I got involved [in the AMA] because I was at U.S. Steel in the commercial department in the corporate headquarters in Pittsburgh and within days of being there, I was marched over to where the Pittsburgh chapter was headquartered and told to join. The company was paying for it.

What momentous events happened at the association during your watch?

One was to decouple the *Journal of Marking* and *Journal of Marketing Research* from the [member] dues. I felt that to be a marketing association and not rely on the free market, what are we doing and saying? We were going to see what the real demand [for the journals] was by seeing what members were willing to pay for them. These journals have great standing and still do.

I was invited to the first meeting of the Brazil Marketing Association in Rio in 1977. [Former AMA Chair] Bill Lazer had high-level connections in Japan. We were having many conferences in London and Germany. . . . There was also a debate on whether advertising was stand-alone or whether it was a part of marketing, which has been pretty well solved.

1981

JOSEPH RABIN

AMA Chair 1981–1982; member since 1954

How did you get involved in the AMA?

I was working for a small research company in Chicago, Gould, Gleiss & Benn, and the president of that company was elected treasurer of the Chicago chapter. He didn't realize that his main job was collecting fees at all of the meetings. When he found that out, he came over and [asked me] how I would like to be a member of the AMA. He said, 'Tomorrow, there's a meeting and you'll go and collect the fees.' That's how I got involved in the AMA, in 1954. It was a very fruitful year because we went to a lot of meetings [and] heard a lot of great speeches.

In your opinion, what has been the most significant development in marketing over the past 75 years?

The computer. It really changed the whole course of marketing. I'm in marketing research, so it totally changed the way we do our data collection and also our data analysis and presentation. It's completely revolutionized everything we do.

Social media is having a huge impact on communication among various constituencies, but it's also changing marketing research. Social media allows companies to listen to what they're customers and non-customers are saying, which is different from doing structured marketing research. . . . Social media is a good additional tool if you can understand what customers are saying. It's easy to collect it, but to understand what it really means is a whole different ballgame. It's a wonderful tool, but it's very dangerous if it's not used properly.

When I started in marketing research in 1951, we were going door to door, talking to people in their homes and bringing it back. Now, nobody sees anything. Our data collection is done on a computer. Its gone a long way from face-to-face interviewing, hand counting of paper questionnaires, then [switching] to IBM counter-sorters, then to computers. It's been a fantastic evolution, it's marvelous what we can do, but it's truly changed the whole ballgame.

1983

ELVIN SCHOFIELD

AMA Chair 1983–1984; member since 1973

What is your professional background?

I'm a practitioner, and I worked for the National Bank of Commerce of San Antonio and the National Bancshares Corporation of Texas as the chief marketing officer. I was a senior vice president.

What impact did being an AMA chair have on your career?

I think it had a very positive impact—namely, the opportunity to meet other professionals, both academic as well as practitioner, and carry that experience over into my job at the bank.

In your opinion, what has been the most significant development in marketing over the past 75 years?

There have been so many individually, but I throw them all together collectively. I think marketing has attained a new level of recognition over the last 75 years in the business world, particularly, and it's because of the intermingling of the academic marketing and the professional marketing.

1984

STEPHEN BROWN

AMA Chair 1984–1985; member since 1969

What momentous events happened at the association during your watch?

In 1984 and 1985, the service economy was really starting to grow, all the way from financial services to healthcare services to travel and tourism. Before 1984 and 1985, some of those industries were quite regulated.

Banking and airlines were regulated and the federal government deregulated a lot of these industries, so suddenly, marketing became important to them. There was tremendous interest in marketing all of a sudden. These industries had all of this competition because you could charge whatever you wanted.

The AMA offered some of the first conferences on the topic of services marketing and encouraged a lot of publications to make the way for legitimizing services [as a category]. At the time, everyone was talking about products. There really is no difference in marketing a service and marketing a product. That was a big debate even among the AMA: Do we need to differentiate the two? Myself and others said yes. . . . Now, in our country and much of the world, services really dominate, approaching 80% of our economy.

1997

SYBIL STERSHIC

AMA Chair 1997–1998; member since 1980

What impact did being an AMA chair have on your career?

The primary reason to get involved was to give back because I love the profession, but it was also to maximize what I could in terms of the AMA for my professional development—to learn from others, to share ideas with other marketers. . . .

When I was contemplating leaving banking and leaving corporate America, I spent a lot of time speaking to my AMA peers and colleagues who were on their own, to ask 'What do I watch out for? Do I do this? Do I not do this?' It was their advice and encouragement that helped me reach that decision. And then when you work on your own and you dont have anybody to bounce ideas off of, I spent a lot of time with my network. . . . Still, if I have a question, I have so many wonderful people that I can call on that I've met through the AMA. I wouldn't do without it.

1995

DAVID GORDON

AMA Chair 1995–1996; member since 1970

What is your professional background?

I started out in marketing research working for a corporation in Connecticut and I decided it would be a good

situation to join the local chapter of the American Marketing Association. . . . My activity with the AMA really got enhanced in 1976. I was transferred to Chicago with a research company and I needed to build up their business. So suddenly, I was in a large city where I knew nobody and I needed to get to know the marketing community as soon as possible. The perfect vehicle for that was the Chicago chapter of the American Marketing Association.

The first event that winter happened to be their Christmas party and during the course of the evening, I probably met three or four hundred people. It sort of launched my career in the business. . . . Little did I know that it would eventually lead to years and years of commitment, and working my way up to Chairman of the Board in 1996.

What impact did being an AMA chair have on your career?

Being involved with the AMA was such a wonderful social networking opportunity and educational opportunity Through the national organizations and through the chapters, there were just so many learning opportunities to stay current on what was going on. . . . It was just a perfect launching pad for my career and an opportunity to stay up to date within marketing.

In your opinion, what has been the most significant development in marketing over the past 75 years?

We've gone from the infancy of marketing into mass marketing, and then the whole movement away from mass marketing to more target marketing, and now I couldn't even begin to touch on all the social media implications on everything that is taking place. . . . It's a different world out there today and technology has had obviously such a major impact, both positive and negative, on marketing efforts. It would be like going into a different business today, to go back into the marketing field. I've been retired for seven years and it's probably changed as much in the last seven years as it did in the preceding 20, 30, maybe 50 years.

1998

CHARLES S. "STAN" MADDEIN

AMA Chair 1998–1999; member since 1967

In your opinion, what has been the most significant development in marketing over the past 75 years?

Marketing is only about 100 years old, so the formation of the American Marketing Association was a big step toward giving marketing stability. It might have come under management, economics, or other disciplines by now had it not had its own defenders, and the AMA has been one of those.

What momentous events happened at the association during your watch?

I hired [current CEO] Dennis [Dunlap] and I'm proud of that.

1999

FRANK HAAS

AMA Chair 1999-00; member since 1981

What impact did being an AMA chair have on your career?

When you live in a place like Hawaii, you naturally feel very isolated. It's a wonderful place to live, but it is very isolated, so networking was very important. To get together in a place like Hawaii with other marketers at the chapter, and then to be plunked into an association that has publications and conferences and things like that, I felt like I was getting a lot of continuing help in my career.

In your opinion, what has been the most significant development in marketing over the past 75 years?

Technology has transformed everything and the change has been increasingly rapid, so the interesting thing, from an association standpoint, is that we've been able to survive and be relevant for 75 years all the way from the sales orientation through the marketing concepts, through the Internet age and through one-on-one customer contact. That's why I'm in marketing. It's a lot of fun because there are these changes and it's refreshing to see an association like the AMA keep up with those.

Critical Thinking

1. Develop your own timeline of marketing history and evolution, including only the most prominent milestone developments.

2. In your opinion, which is the most impactful development within this timeline. Justify your choice.

3. With a group of peers from your class, continue this chronology of marketing evolution to include recent developments since the year 2010 to date. Can you predict some future developments and trends?

Create Central

www.mhhe.com/createcentral

Internet References

Advertising Age
http://adage.com/article/ad-age-graphics/ad-age-a-history-marketing/142967/

Know This
http://www.knowthis.com/what-is-marketing/history-of-marketing

Elisabeth A. Sullivan, "75 Years of Marketing History," *Marketing News*, July 31, 2012. Copyright © 2012 by American Marketing Association. All rights reserved. Used with permission.

Article   Prepared by: Nisreen N. Bahnan, *Salem State University*

Putting Customers First
Nine Surefire Ways to Increase Brand Loyalty

Kyle LaMalfa

Learning Outcomes

After reading this article, you will be able to:

- Comprehend the important role that customer satisfaction and loyalty play in continued business success and growth.
- Discuss techniques that companies can employ to make customer loyalty a powerful competitive advantage.

"Customers first." It's the mantra of businesses everywhere. Yet the average company still loses 10% to 15% of customers each year. Most of them leave due to poor service or a disappointing product experience, yet only 4% of them will tell you about it. And once they've left, it's difficult (not to mention expensive) to get them back.

Fostering true loyalty and engagement with customers starts at a basic level, but here are nine techniques you can employ to make customer loyalty a powerful competitive advantage for your company. They can be broken down into three categories: loyalty basics (one through four), loyalty technologies (five through seven) and loyalty measurement (eight and nine).

1. Give Customers What They Expect

Knowing your customer's expectations and making sure your product or service meets them is Business 101, yet often ignored. At the basic level, business needs to be a balanced transaction where someone pays for something and expects a fair trade in return.

Expectations of product quality come from many sources, including previous quality levels set by your organization, what competitors are saying about you, and the media. Marketing and sales should work together to monitor customer expectations through feedback and surveys.

2. Go Beyond Simple Reward Programs

Points and rewards encourage repeat purchases, but don't actually build loyalty. This is demonstrated by a drop in sales when the rewards are no longer offered. True loyalty comes when customers purchase products without being bribed.

3. Turn Complaints into Opportunities

Managing questions, comments and concerns benefits your business in two important ways. First, research indicates that an upset customer whose problem is addressed with swiftness and certainty can be turned into a highly loyal customer. Second, unstructured feedback, gathered and managed appropriately, can be a rich source of ideas. To that end:

- Establish channels (electronic, phone and written) to build engagement, one customer at a time.
- Encourage customers to voice their thoughts.
- Create metrics to improve response to concerns (i.e., "time to first response," "time to resolution," etc.).
- Create metrics to measure loyalty before and after the problem.
- Use technology to help you centralize the information, create reports and structure drill-downs.

4. Build Opportunities for Repeat Business

Give your customers a chance to be loyal by offering products for repeat business. Monitor what customers request most and offer products or services that compliment other purchases. In addition, exceed expectations by driving product development to offer more value for less cost. Use technology to track, classify and categorize open-ended feedback.

5. Engage Customers in a Two-Way Dialogue

An engaged customer is more than satisfied and more than loyal. They support you during both good and bad times because they believe what you have to offer is superior to others.

Engagement takes your customer beyond passive loyalty to become an active participant and promoter of your product. Engaged customers will give you more feedback so you should be ready to handle it! All this translates into a customer who will spend more money with you over time. Accordingly:

- Listen to customer feedback from comment cards, letters, phone calls and surveys.
- Respond quickly and personally to concerns of high interest to your customers.
- Organize unstructured feedback for tracking and trending over time.
- Trust your customers to tell you what the problem is.
- Use statistical techniques to discover which action items will have the most impact on your business.

6. Survey Customers and Solicit Feedback

Actively soliciting information from a population of customers is a time-tested technique pioneered by Arthur Nielsen (creator of the Nielsen ratings) in the 1920s. Survey research can be used for problem identification or solving. Questions with simple scales such as "agree/disagree" deliver quantitative insight for problem identification. Open-ended follow-up questions can provide rich insight for solving problems. Some tips:

- Make sure your surveys are short, bias-free and well structured.
- Use random sampling to gather feedback continuously without over-surveying.
- Create summary survey indices that can be displayed graphically and tracked over time.

7. Create a Centralized System for Managing Feedback throughout the Enterprise

Technology such as enterprise feedback management (EFM) helps to centralize surveys and customer feedback and track both

qualitative and quantitative information. EFM involves more than just collecting data, though; it adopts a strategic approach to building dialogs with your customers. Follow these steps:

- Empower customers to give feedback through common advertised channels.
- Centralize reporting for proactive surveys and complaint management solutions.
- Structure quantitative feedback into a drill-down or rollup report.
- Make open-ended feedback intuitively searchable.

8. Tie Customer Loyalty and Engagement to Business Outcomes

Orienting your organization to focus on satisfaction, loyalty and engagement is no panacea. But researchers have clearly documented evidence of short-term benefits to customer/employee retention and long-term benefits to profitability. Hence:

- Determine whether to measure your engagement outcome by satisfaction, likelihood to purchase again, likelihood to recommend, or another voice of the customer (VOC) metric.
- If necessary, create hybrid VOC measurements using more than one metric.
- Link your VOC metrics with business outcomes like shareholder returns, annual sales growth, gross margin, market share, cash flows, Tobin's Q or customer churn.
- Be aware that changes in loyalty/engagement scores generally precede changes in business outcomes.

9. Use Analysis to Predict Future Loyalty

Businesses use a variety of statistical techniques to make predictions about the potential for future events. Furthermore, predictive analytics may be used to ascertain the degree to which answers from a survey relate to particular goals (such as loyalty and engagement). Tactical knowledge of how action items impact an outcome discourages the wasting of resources on ineffective programs, and competent statistical modeling reveals which tactical options work. Consequently:

- Analyze data using a statistical technique to reveal the most important areas of focus.
- Ask your analyst about common statistical methods, including correlation and logit models.

- Recognize that the major areas of focus may change in response to changes in your economic, competitive, and demographic environments.

Following these steps may not be the easiest process, but stay focused. Increasing your engagement and loyalty equals increasing profits and a competitive edge.

Critical Thinking

1. Discuss the importance of establishing two-way dialogue with customers and effectively responding to customer feedback.
2. With a small group of peers from your class, develop some ways that companies can achieve effective two-way dialogue with customers.

Create Central

www.mhhe.com/createcentral

Internet References

Customer Loyalty and Retention
  http://www.customerloyalty.org/
Loyalty Research Center
  http://www.loyaltyresearch.com/

KYLE LAMALFA is the best practices manager and loyalty expert for Allegiance, Inc. He can be reached at kyle.lamalfa@allegiance.com. For more information about how to increase your loyalty and engagement, visit www.allegiance.com

Kyle LaMalfa, "Putting Customers First: Nine Surefire Ways to Increase Brand Loyalty," *Sales & Marketing Management,* January/February 2008, p. 12–13. Copyright © 2008 by Lakewood Media Group. All rights reserved. Used with permission.

Article   Prepared by: Nisreen N. Bahnan, *Salem State University*

The Purchasing Power of Entertainment

While it's often said that entertainment spending tends to stay up in a down economy given the escapism element it provides, ironically, no product category's distribution and purchase methods have been altered or affected more radically by recent media and technology advancements.

PATRICK CAULEY

Learning Outcomes

After reading this article, you will be able to:

- Recognize the emotional significance and hedonic value of entertainment to consumers.

- Understand the practice of Direct Response TV promotion in the entertainment industry.

What started with Napster-style shenanigans eventually led to legitimately new, evolving kinds of business models like iTunes, Netflix and Hulu, to name a few. In fact, according to a new report from PricewaterhouseCoopers, online purchases of movies, music and other forms of entertainment will rise to 43 percent of consumer media spending in 2017—from less than a third in 2012.

But while popular perception may pigeonhole direct response products into the fitness, housewares and beauty categories, one segment of the industry that's been showing consistent growth happens to center on all things entertainment.

And, if you can reach the right sweet spot with your target market, the entertainment products featured in direct response television campaigns still provide a unique, nostalgic experience unlike the sometimes cold, less satisfying experience of buying one song online that quickly loses itself among the other flavors of the month you've downloaded. In order to effectively capitalize in this market, it's imperative to understand the way it has changed.

A New Landscape

"The change in the entertainment category is opposite of what you see at the top level," says Jeffrey White, CEO of Philadelphia-based IMS Media Analytics. "Generally, long-form has been declining, while short-form has grown. But, it's been the opposite in the entertainment category. There are certainly more short-forms being shot and broadcast, but if you look at the dollars, there are still a fair amount of dollars going toward long-form."

Some view the category as more stable, rather than growing. "When looking at the past five years, the quantity and quality success of long-form DR entertainment productions, whether it's music or video compilations, tend to be similar," says Clare Kogler, president of Tustin, Calif.-based Jordan Whitney Inc.

However, Kogler has seen a slight decrease in the number of entertainment infomercials that are running with enough frequency to be ranked in the Jordan Whitney report each week. The high was 18 in 2010, 14 in 2012 and 12 so far this year. "Time-Life continues to be the primary producer of music packages, which air the most frequently. Interestingly, five of its entertainment productions in 2012 were among our 'Top 100' for the year."

Kogler claims that typically only one or two entertainment shows air with enough frequency to appear on the rankings, but contends the rise in the entertainment category's success may be partially because of an overall a decline in new infomercials.

While music collection short-form spots reigned supreme in the past, they've certainly declined in recent years. "In the short-form arena, we are seeing far fewer entertainment offers.

This, we believe, is due to the change in the music delivery system with downloading to computers and mobile devices being preferred by a majority of music purchasers," says Kogler.

In fact, music purchases in the U.S., including tickets to live performances, are reversing the multiyear slide caused by illegal downloads and collapsing compact disc revenue. Domestic purchases will rise to $16 billion by 2017 from $15.1 billion this year, driven by digital downloads, streaming services and higher ticket prices, according to a recent *AdAge* article.

However, short-form spots are not to be dismissed entirely in the entertainment category. "On the short-form side, you still see quite a bit on what we call 'the psychics,'" says White. In fact, the top- and fifth-ranked entertainment short-form spots in last month's IMS rankings were for "California Psychics" and "Hollywood Psychics," respectively.

Ticket Holders

If you're looking to break into the entertainment category using DRTV, as usual, the first thing you need to know is who your customer is. "Our overall demographic is from late-40s to well into the 70s. The average age of our customer falls right around 55 years old," says Christopher Hearing, president of Time-Life/Direct Holdings Global. "The overall demographic is a little more female than male, but not dramatically. That is very, very product specific. Some of our military products are 95-percent male. And some of our romance products are skewed in the other direction. The income demographic is right in the heart of America. The quintessential American family is who we're selling to."

Once you understand who your audience is, the next natural question is figuring out what it is they want. "Music is still the top driver in long-form: the compilations, the greatest hits concepts and a lot of country. We are seeing that being a strong sub-category within the music sector," says White.

Kogler concurs. "The target audience for music packages of the sort sold by long-form DR is aging. This is reflected in the offerings that succeed best: nostalgia and country," she says.

Hearing says that what works is something where you can elicit passion. "When we think about selling our nostalgic collections, it's all about making some connection to the consumer's heart, selling romantic songs from the 1960s and 1970s," he contends. "Consumers inevitably say, 'You got me to pick up the phone and call or go on the Web to place an order when I heard the song I had my first kiss to,' or 'our prom theme song,' or whatever it was. It was something that made a very personal connection with consumers. It also applies to video products. We hear our 'Carol Burnett' consumers all the time: 'I remember with my parents or grandparents watching it on Saturday nights.' It's that nostalgic hook that we play on very heavily."

However, the tricky thing about entertainment is that it all boils down to individual's taste. And when considering decades of extensive entertainment choices, who is to say what exactly will catch?

"Fundamentally, when we are looking at the broad array of products that we can bring to the marketplace, we're looking for a product where we can bring something extraordinary. Our producers here have incredibly deep knowledge about both the music and video sides of the business. They know where to go find pockets of material—hard-to-find or never released before. So it's something that's going to resonate with consumers in a way that they might not be able to get anywhere else," says Hearing.

For instance, Time-Life recently released a complete set of products surrounding "China Beach," a TV series from the late 1980s—products never before released on DVD, all re-mastered with extended bonus features attached, including books and signed scripts as part of the package.

"As a very general rule of thumb, we're looking at products that are 20 years old or older. The majority of consumers associate their music choices with their high school and college years. That's when they're thinking nostalgically about music. The intersection of those years with people reaching their direct response buying years is about 20 years post-graduation from high school. So, we're looking to promote to people who are in their late 30s and into their 40s and beyond, because those are the people who are really responsive in the marketplace," says Hearing.

Once you have the collection you've decided to bring to market nailed down, how do you appropriately position it within your creative to make sure that it connects with viewers enough to elicit a response and purchase?

"The trick in being successful with a typical music collection, which has 150 to 180 songs, is finding that 20 or 30 that you're actually going to play in the infomercial. There are a huge number of choices. They're all top songs; most of them were No. 1 hits at some point. How do you wean that down to the 20 percent or the 15 percent that you're actually going to show on TV?" asks Hearing.

He continues, "That's what our producers do. We don't outsource that part of the business, because they have such a deep knowledge about what does connect with consumers, what was important back in that time. That's really the magic in making the programs work."

Targeting the Flops

For every success that surprises studio and label executives across the board, there's always a "Snakes on a Plane": the flop that leaves the once confident marketing team scratching their heads.

"What doesn't work for us is mass appeal. We are not going to compete with the record labels. We're not breaking new artists; we're not putting collections of songs that have been released in the past 10 years because they're still on the radio. And there's nothing nostalgic about it yet," says Hearing.

He referenced a country music program infomercial two years ago titled "Country USA" that people across the board thought would be a surefire win. "We had Larry Gatlin as a host. He was on a bus across America and went to all these great American scenes. He was talking about the music, and it really was just a great collection of country music songs across a whole range of time, and it didn't work," Hearing says.

The company was "dumbfounded" he adds. "When we went out and did research and tried to figure out why it didn't work, it wasn't focused enough! It spoke a little bit to everybody, but it didn't speak deeply to anyone specific. And as the business continues to change and continues to evolve, that's what we're finding. We have to have deep conversations with our consumers. It's not a mass-market product we're selling. It's really a niche product that is focused in an underserved market, targeted to a specific group of people," Hearing says.

Coming Attractions

"The over-50 audience will continue to be a target for nostalgia and country packages—both of music and older TV shows on video," Kogler says. "These seem to work best in long-form. Younger purchasers, and no doubt some older ones as well, will move more and more to downloading, which allows them to buy individual songs rather than albums."

In fact, U.S. consumer spending on media and entertainment will increase 4.8 percent per year through 2017, with digital consumption finally rivaling physical sales, according to Pricewaterhouse-Coopers.

However, DR entertainment products have the potential to be one of digital's few rivals left given the differentiated goods they provide. "We have to constantly be focused on providing services and products that provide more value to our consumer than just downloaded songs," Hearing says.

He adds, "A typical consumer can certainly go out and re-create any of our CD packages. What we have to bring to the market—and what differentiates us from an iTunes—is the editorial standard that we set. If you buy something from us, you're getting the absolute best. You know you're getting the original recording, which is not always easy to find in a download scenario, and also the added value stuff that we bring in. So on a per-song basis, were actually very competitively priced with iTunes, but were selling to our consumers a package of songs plus ancillary materials. If they want to listen to their music digitally, then that's fantastic. But we really provide to our consumers something that they just can't get digitally, which is something that the record labels really struggle with."

Additionally, while a lot of the DR entertainment category may focus on a slightly older demographic now, marketers must also remember that there are bright spots with the younger demographic, as well as the fact that they will eventually be the core DR demographic one day. "We are seeing some new entries and growth in kids' toys and gaming subscriptions," says White.

Moreover, marketers will still be able to reach these consumers through television advertising—it's simply that the screen that they're viewing it on will change. U.S. TV advertising will rise 5.1 percent annually to $81.6 billion in 2017, with more consumers watching on iPads and smartphones, according to PricewaterhouseCoopers.

As the times change, certain products will always come and go with demand, but one thing's for certain: entertainment is something consumers will never be able to live without.

Critical Thinking

1. Explain what is meant by Direct Response TV promotion in the entertainment industry.

2. Develop a profile of the typical customer in the DRTV entertainment category. What are the main competitors within this category?

3. In your opinion, how true is the following statement: "entertainment spending tends to stay up in a down economy given the escapism element it provides"? Justify your response.

Create Central

www.mhhe.com/createcentral

Internet References

Cannella Response Television
http://drtv.com/

InfoWorxDirect
http://www.infoworx.com/drtv_getting_started.shtml

Multichannel Merchant
http://multichannelmerchant.com/crosschannel/how-to-determine-a-drtv-strategy-03042012/

Patrick Cauley, "The Purchasing Power of Entertainment," *Response Magazine*, July 2013. Copyright © 2013 by Response Magazine. All rights reserved. Used with permission.

Article   Prepared by: Nisreen N. Bahnan, *Salem State University*

Become the Main Attraction

People go to summer events for music, food and fun—not for marketing materials.
Here's how you get them to pay attention to you.

Piet Levy

Learning Outcomes

After reading this article, you will be able to:

- Define *event marketing* and its role within the promotional mix.

- Identify the many advantages that companies gain from using event marketing to promote their product(s).

There are hundreds, maybe thousands of people here. Many of them are just the types of customers you are looking for. But odds are that none of them are here to see you. Instead, the masses have gathered at this event to hear music, watch sports, eat food or, in the case of conferences, network and listen to keynote presentations.

The consumers are there for their reasons and you're there for yours: to market your brand and increase awareness and sales. In a sea of noise, surrounded by hordes of talking people, distracting attractions and numerous marketing booths and street teams competing for consumers' attention, you have to stand out. But in addition to turning heads, you have to open minds. Beyond handing out coupons or samples or tchotchkes, you must showcase the value of your product or service in an interactive and engaging way, which also means training the right people to serve as brand messengers. If you make sure you're memorable, when the event ends and the consumers go about their daily lives, they'll remember you, tell others about you and pay to experience your product or service.

Step Right Up

Event marketing is important because it "places your product or service face to face with your target audience," argues Brad Horowitz, vice president of marketing for Elite Marketing Group, an experiential agency with headquarters in New Hyde Park, N.Y. "Brands can have a conversation with consumers rather than delivering a monologue. Conversations allow for customized learning, which fosters purchasing behavior. Additionally, it allows for valuable feedback from consumers about the product or service and the perception out there in the real world."

To be the most effective event marketer, you have to go beyond just being at a popular event and set up shop in a premium position. "Juxtaposing your footprint to a high-traffic location at an event such as the entry or the food court will allow for the greatest reach and greatest amount of impressions," Horowitz says.

That's also where a lot of other marketing booths or street teams will be hanging out. But don't worry about them; worry about yourself, and calm those concerns by establishing a physical presence that pops.

Overland Park, Kan.-based Sprint Nextel Corp., which sponsors the National Association for Stock Car Auto Racing's (NASCAR) Sprint Cup Series, incorporates a jumbotron, trophy replica and NASCAR driver appearances at its display at races, says Tim Considine, general manager of the sponsorship. To attract mechanics to its travelling display last year, the U.S. Air Force showcased customized vehicles that incorporated Air Force technology, says Kristin Krajecki, director of experiential marketing at the Air Force's experiential agency, GSD&M Idea City in Austin, Texas. For its presence at the

National Religious Broadcasters Convention and Exposition earlier this year, TV Magic Inc., a San Diego-based broadcast solutions provider, presented a cross designed out of televisions at its booth, the sort of visual element that conference-attending pastors may want at their churches, says Stephen Rosen, president and CEO of the company. "You've got to make an impressive impression and let [consumers] feel that spending a few minutes with you of their very precious time is worth it," Sprint's Considine says.

You may not have the budget to bring your own jumbotron, super car, or elaborate TV display to an event, but you can find creative ways to cut costs. TV Magic actually reduced its trade show budget by 50% this year and was still able to replace its "worse than blah" booth from last year with one featuring the TV display, Rosen says. Savings came from two areas: TV Magic reduced the number of company representatives at the booth from seven to three, and the company partnered with electronic suppliers such as Sony and Panasonic to provide equipment at no cost, says Jeff Symon, President and CEO of San Diego-based Aim Agency, TV Magic's agency. In some cases, you may even be able to find a company partner to participate with you at the event and subsidize expenses, he also suggests.

Whatever you put together, make sure the element is relevant to the audience and reflective of your brand. The cars at the Air Force display appealed to gear heads, but given the Air Force-inspired modifications, including an ejection seat, vertical doors, and aircraft style controls, the brand was even more reinforced. In addition to the church-friendly TV display at its convention booth, TV Magic put together a system where pastors could be filmed and the video edited and broadcast to a TV, online, and mobile device on the spot as a way to demonstrate the type of service the company provides, Symon says.

It's also a good idea to make your display interactive to increase the odds and length of time that consumers will stick around. Incentives are another way to draw people in. Sprint stages racing video games on its jumbotron that people can participate in and offers free gifts to customers, Considine says.

You should also try to design the space to allow for easier traffic flow. Symon suggests removing any table separating consumers from brand messengers to allow greater interactivity and openness. Considine says the Sprint layout features no walls or interiors to better increase impressions and interaction, and the jumbotron is in place to increase the possibility of engaging people from the periphery.

Razzle-Dazzle Them

The wow factor and selling points are crucial event marketing criteria, but Considine argues that "the hand you shake, the kindness that you show to someone in an [event] marketing environment, may be more powerful than the information you present."

By the Numbers

The Norwalk, Conn.-based Event Marketing Institute and Auburn Hills, Mich.-based experiential agency George P. Johnson Co. interviewed 108 sales and marketing management leaders for its EventView report, an annual study assessing the relevance of event marketing. Some key findings:

62% of respondents say their marketing budget for events has either remained constant or increased in 2010.

32% consider event marketing a "vital component" of their marketing plan.

64% cited event marketing as one of the top three elements for accelerating and deepening relationships, followed by social marketing (55%) and online marketing (54%).

Want a Ticket to Ride?

Follow These 10 Instructions for Successful Event Marketing:

1. Set up your booth or street team in highly trafficked areas.
2. Have a visual element that turns heads but connects back to your brand.
3. Find participating partners to subsidize costs.
4. Present an interactive element, like a game, so consumers stick around for a while.
5. Make your space as open as possible to maximize traffic and engagement.
6. Entice visitors with incentives like coupons or samples.
7. Find upbeat, extroverted, professional, articulate people to act as brand representatives.
8. Cast people who can relate with the target demographic, like employing NASCAR fans for booths at NASCAR events.
9. Train representatives with quizzes and run-throughs, but don't overwhelm them with details.
10. Dress your staff so they stand out, but make sure they look approachable.

In addition to head-turning displays, you have to rely on your brand representatives to present the brand properly, yet oftentimes marketers may have to outsource for those services, as Sprint does for its NASCAR display.

To find the right people for the job, Aim Agency first profiles what the brand stands for and the type of people who would best represent it. Then comes an online evaluation process that serves as a screener to see if candidates match brand objectives, Symon says.

If you don't have the budget to recruit an agency to help you with staffing, use the interview process to determine which candidates are extroverted, upbeat, articulate, and professional, Considine and Symon say. Jessica Fisher, Senior Manager of events for athletic apparel company Reebok International Ltd. in Canton, Mass., says that before an interview begins it's important to have a casual conversation about the candidate's perspective of the brand to gauge his enthusiasm and understanding. It also helps to recruit people who can relate to the target audience. For its M&M's supporting street team at NASCAR races, Mars Chocolate North America utilizes two employees from the company's PR agency, Weber Shandwick, who are actual fans of NASCAR so their interaction with fans will be authentic, says Suzanne Beaudoin, Vice President of sponsorship and sports marketing for the Hackettstown, N.J.-based company.

Once your team is in place, make sure staff members dress the part to not only physically represent the brand but also attract consumers. The M&M's street team stands out with NASCAR-style jumpsuits, Beaudoin argues, to help communicate the brand's Most Colorful Fan website and Facebook page, which encourage NASCAR fans to submit photos displaying their love of the sport for a cash prize. Similarly, the Air Force tries to place its brand representatives in the most appropriate attire based on the event, says Captain Homero Martinez, the former chief of event marketing for the Air Force Recruiting Service. For a recent Memorial Day race, Martinez says, formal dress was appropriate given the holiday weekend's correlation with the Air Force. For more casual events like music festivals, staff wear more relaxed uniforms to reduce any consumer concern that they will be pressured to sign up.

The U.S. Air Force paraded customized cars equipped with jet-inspired technology at events last year in an effort to attract mechanics for the Air Force on the spot, he says.

Beyond looking the part, training must be done so that brand representatives can act the part. Training should include quizzing participants about the brand and business objectives in addition to on-site run-throughs, Symon says, and participants should be encouraged to ask questions for clarification's sake. Fisher recommends giving representatives the product when applicable, so that when they are on site, "they are not just giving out words, but talking from their own experiences." It's ideal to have people who work for the company on hand to help address consumer questions, but for those assigned with attracting people with their presence and interaction, it's important not to overwhelm them with instructions during the training process. Considine says his advice boils down to one simple philosophy: Treat passing consumers like guests at your home. If they feel welcome, there's a greater chance they'll welcome your product or service into their lives.

Critical Thinking

1. What makes event marketing an attractive promotion option for businesses?
2. With a small group of peers from your class, design an event marketing plan for any business of your choice.

Create Central

www.mhhe.com/createcentral

Internet References

Event Marketer
 http://www.eventmarketer.com/
Corporate Event Marketing Association
 http://cemaonline.com/

Piet Levy, "Become the Main Attraction," *Marketing News,* July 30, 2010, p. 16–17, 20. Copyright © 2010 by American Marketing Association. All rights reserved. Used with permission.

Article   Prepared by: Nisreen N. Bahnan, *Salem State University*

Fundamental Tenets of Service Excellence

A look at your company's strengths and weaknesses in five key areas can greatly improve how you serve your customers.

LANCE A. BETTENCOURT

Learning Outcomes

After reading this article, you will be able to:

- Recognize the important role of customer service in business success.

- Identify the elements of excellent service.

Service is a critical factor to business success now more than ever. Research shows that improved service drives customer loyalty and willingness to pay, which then drive improved sales and profitability. On the flip side, poor service leads to customer defections and loss of market share. Despite its importance though, some companies seem to perpetually struggle with providing exceptional service.

So what is it that sets the likes of Southwest Airlines, United Services Automobile Association and, more recently, Zappos apart for their exceptional service? Certainly, there are some exceptional tools out there to help improve service, such as service guarantees, transaction surveys, and database management. However, companies that excel at service recognize that excellence is not achieved by a particular tool or technique. Rather, it requires a disciplined focus on the fundamentals of service excellence. Some organizations, such as the U.S. Postal Service, may talk about service excellence, but don't approach it with the discipline required. Competing priorities cause others, such as The Home Depot, to lose their focus. Still others, such as J.C. Penney, are finding their way back with renewed focus.

Service excellence demands that a company knows what its customers need, is oriented toward the customer, is aligned for service excellence, manages its people to deliver what matters and coordinates resources to stay ahead. These tenets draw on both practical experience and research, and are as applicable in a B-to-B setting as B-to-C. In fact, recent research finds that manufacturers who are seeking to add services to their portfolio struggle more with issues of culture, organizational structure, delivery capabilities, and partner collaboration than coming up with valuable service ideas. As one executive shared with researchers, "The soft stuff really is the hard stuff" ("Growing Service Solutions—Implementing the Service Infusion Continuum," ASU W.P. Carey School of Business, webinar, 2012).

A company wanting to excel at service must have a disciplined approach to each of the five areas. This article will focus on understanding the key principles at work, and illustrate how some companies have put the five tenets into practice.

Tenet 1: Know What Your Customer Needs

Companies that excel at service know where to focus their resources: They know where they need to be better, where they need to maintain performance and even what facets of service they can choose to do worse. Great service businesses accept that they cannot and should not try to be all things to all customers. They must focus on what matters to their priority customers and accept lower performance on what does not. Though one might think that such focus would lower overall customer satisfaction, the above average ratings of Amazon, Costco, and Southwest Airlines indicate that this is not the case. But such focus does beg the following questions:

- How do your customers measure service excellence? What are their needs?
- Which needs are the drivers of critical customer outcomes? Which are not?

Though there is no shortage of approaches to measuring customer needs for service, there is a shortage of approaches to doing this well. To be an effective guide to service improvement, a company must understand how its customers judge value based on what they are trying to get done, independent of how service is delivered today. This is a common failure point. For example, it is not uncommon for measures of customers' service needs to include such service attributes as long hours of operation, Web access and price guarantees.

The problem is that a focus on the attributes of a current service constrains thinking for how to improve service, because it fails to understand why these features are valuable to customers in terms of their functional and emotional needs. Features are not needs, and a failure to properly distinguish them causes confusion. Further, whereas companies tend to think in terms of Web vs. telephone service or billing vs. logistics, the ideal service from the customer perspective may have to cut across these company boundaries.

In addition, a company's understanding of customer needs must be detailed enough to guide specific decisions among service improvements. Overall customer satisfaction or net promoter scores (NPS) are useful as objectives, but too many companies fail to get insight into specific customer needs that drive customer satisfaction or NPS. This inhibits the ability to dig beneath the surface of rising, falling or even stagnant scores to know what is happening and what needs to change.

In contrast, a focus on measuring specific customer needs that are functional (e.g., quickly getting a question answered) and emotional (e.g., feeling respected) across the steps the customer must take to obtain a product or service (e.g., access, select, order, receive, resolve and so on) provides the actionable insight a company requires.

What you measure matters. Office Depot learned an important lesson about this after Kevin Peters became the company's president in 2010, according to an article he wrote for the November 2011 *Harvard Business Review*. Peters was perplexed at why the company's retail sales were declining faster than its competitors, when its customer service scores from mystery shoppers were going through the roof. A look at what was being measured answered the riddle. The customer service scores were based on things like restroom cleanliness and full shelves, but what drove sales were customer needs like getting around

the store quickly, finding products they are seeking and choosing the best products for their needs. In line with what was being measured, store employees were spending their time cleaning and stocking shelves, rather than engaging customers to satisfy their shopping needs. With a new appreciation for what matters to its customers, Office Depot is changing store sizes and employee responsibilities to align with customer needs.

Tenet 2: Orient Your Company Toward the Customer

Great service companies appreciate the value of people to their business—not only customers, but also employees. As such, they make it a priority to understand what factors drive customer and employee satisfaction and loyalty, and they ensure that these insights pervade their values, success metrics and decision making. Starting with the executive suite, they create a culture that makes people and service priorities.

Of course, what really matters for service excellence has little to do with what a company says it values. Rather, what really matters is whether there is shared belief throughout die organization that exceptional service is expected and valued. Companies with that shared belief have employees who are more likely to provide service that is above and beyond the call of duty, which then leads to higher customer satisfaction and better market performance (Schneider, Benjamin, Mark G. Ehrhart, David M. Mayer, Jessica L. Saltz and Kathryn Niles-Jolly "Understanding Organization-Customer Links in Service Settings," December 2005 *Academy of Management Journal*, 48, 1017–1032).

To achieve a shared belief that exceptional service is expected, a company must communicate the value of customer satisfaction and loyalty to all employees; ensure that they understand what the ideal experience looks like from a customer perspective; and make decisions concerning systems, standards, policies and management practices that exemplify the value of serving customers and employees. As Glenn Forbes, the CEO of Mayo Clinic in Rochester, Minn., explains: "If you've just communicated a value but you haven't driven it into the operations, into the policy, into the decision making, into the allocation of resources, and ultimately into the culture of the organization, then it's just words," according to *Management Lessons from Mayo Clinic: Inside One of the World's Most Admired Service Organizations* by Leonard L. Berry and Kent B. Seltman (New York: McGraw-Hill, 2008).

Consider how Zappos, the online retailer, has ensured that there is a shared belief around the importance of its No. 1 core value, "Deliver WOW Through Service," by making some unconventional choices that reinforce the importance of this value, according to CEO Tony Hsieh's *Delivering Happiness: A Path to Profits, Passion, and Purpose* (New York: Business

Plus, 2010). For one thing, Zappos provides its customer service number at the top of every Zappos Web page, rather than burying it on some obscure page. The company is willing to take on the extra cost of telephone service for the goodwill it creates. In a similar way, Zappos runs its warehouse 24/7, a decision that Hsieh says, "actually isn't the most efficient way to run a warehouse." That may be true, but the decision speaks volumes of the priority that Zappos places on customer service over efficiency.

Tenet 3: Align Your Organization for Service Excellence

To excel at serving customers, a company must also align its organizational structure, offerings, systems, and service processes to deliver the experience that customers are seeking.

To begin, organizational structures must be designed with the total experience of customers in mind. When organizations are structured around products rather than customers, for example, there is little to no accountability for improving the customer experience. This leads to customers who experience cross-functional problems, suboptimal solutions and inefficient interactions. When customers are diverse and derive value from integrated and customized offerings, it requires an organization that is aligned with satisfying customer jobs, segments or key accounts—rather than selling products.

Though there are different approaches to making this happen, a common structure that has been implemented successfully in firms such as IBM, Fidelity Investments and Cisco Systems is called a front/back hybrid design (according to George S. Day in "Aligning the Organization with the Market," 2006). In this design, a front-end, customer-facing group is aligned with customer jobs, segments or key accounts, and the rest of the organization is structured around products. The front-end groups are responsible for understanding customer needs, creating customized solutions and serving customers. The back-end groups are responsible for developing and managing products and processes that can be combined into bundles and experiences. Cross-functional service delivery teams, such as care teams within a hospital, provide similar benefits.

Organizational systems, processes and offerings must also be designed with specific customer and company needs in mind. This is critical, because design choices—such as customization vs. standardization, team vs. individual service and company vs. customer production—inevitably involve choosing not only what the company will do well, but also what the company will not do well, relative to the competition. Different design choices are sure to appeal to distinct customer segments or distinct occasions. This is why WebMD, Just Answer, Minute Clinic, the family physician and the hospital emergency room can all successfully co-exist.

Of course, there are also a thousand tactical decisions to reinforce an overall service vision that can benefit from a systematic service design process. Service blueprinting, for example, enables the company to create a simple visual depiction of customer actions and how they interface with onstage and backstage company tasks to complete several essential design tasks. These include defining employee, customer and technology roles; identifying equipment and material requirements; discovering potential failure points; determining what clues to offer at distinct points to reinforce the service vision; and designing specific processes to deliver against customer needs in a seamless manner.

Tenet 4: Manage Your People to Deliver What Matters

A company's service orientation is implemented on the frontline of the business in each and every customer interaction. To the customer, the employee is part resource, part marketer, and part solution. This is why management practices are so critical to success. To ensure that your employees are prepared to deliver against your company's service standards, your company must answer three critical employee questions:

- What is expected of me?
- What is in it for me?
- Do I have what it takes to succeed?

First, employees must understand what their role is and what their priorities are in delivering exceptional service. Whether through values, training, job design, service standards, management coaching, reward systems or (preferably) all of the above, it is important to align employee role expectations with customer needs. All employees should understand the impact of their roles on customer satisfaction and loyalty. At Zappos, for example, every new employee—lawyers, accountants and other staff included—goes through the exact same 4-week training program on the importance of service and the vision and philosophy of the company.

Second, employees must also be motivated to deliver exceptional service. One of the most powerful motivators is recognition for excellent service, and great service organizations make sure this happens on a regular basis. This might be as small as a "thank you" from one's manager or a more substantial bonus tied to customer satisfaction. Perhaps an even more critical motivational factor, however, is hiring service-oriented people. Recognizing that it is inherently difficult to train someone to be a people person, great service companies such as Southwest Airlines spend well above the average amount of time and money to find the right people to serve their customers.

Briefly

- When it comes to exceptional service, there are no quick fixes or magical tools.
- Research shows that improved service drives customer loyalty and willingness to pay, which then drive improved sales and profitability.
- A company must focus first and foremost on five fundamental tenets of service excellence: knowing what customers need, orienting the company toward the customer, aligning the organization for service excellence, managing people to deliver what matters, and coordinating resources to stay ahead.

Third, employees must have the knowledge and skills to succeed in their service roles. Certainly, employees must have the necessary technical capabilities. However, great service organizations pay as much or more attention to ensuring that their employees have the interpersonal skills required to succeed, such as listening effectively, asking valuable questions, and building trust. As Pal Barger, chairman of Baldrige Award winner Pal's Sudden Service, once shared, "When we open a new store, we give every hourly employee 120 hours of training. Someone said, 'What if you spend all that money and time and they leave?' And I said, 'What if you don't and they stay?'"

Of course, it is not enough to give employees the knowledge and skills to provide service and conclude that the company is ready for success. What at first appears to be a provider problem may in fact be evidence of a deficiency in systems, tools, and support to enable employees to do their jobs. Your company's best source of insight into such deficiencies still comes from those on the frontline of your organization. Your employees have a job to do—to provide service—and their success depends on how well your organization satisfies their needs at every step of the process. In other words, frontline employees should be viewed as internal customers who depend on internal services from the company to get their job done.

In a parallel manner to employee management, companies that excel at service give equal consideration to helping their customers to be ready, willing and able to perform their roles. In a professional B-to-B setting, for example, leading service companies screen potential clients to ensure that goals and resources are aligned for project success, orient clients in a series of kickoff meetings concerning the roles and behaviors that are necessary for project success, and conduct post-project reviews to identify client performance problems.

Tenet 5: Coordinate Your Resources to Stay Ahead

There are several characteristics of service that demand effective resource coordination. As processes, many services require multiple individuals to do their part at the right point in time. In addition, service is often provided across geographically far-flung operations. Finally, service excellence demands consistency with thousands of customers, and consistency from just as many employees. When it comes to addressing these coordination challenges, information management is critical.

First, service excellence hinges on systematic information capture from customers, employees and operations to monitor, control and improve service delivery. The use of multiple listening approaches is necessary to identify where service is doing well and where it is poor, uncover root causes and best practices, monitor the impact of investments and provide feedback (Berry, Leonard L. and A. Parasuraman, "Listening to the Customer—The Concept of a Service-Quality Information System," *MIT Sloan Management Review,* 38, Spring, 1997, 65–76). A typical day at a Charles Schwab branch, for example, begins with the branch manager pulling up a customer feedback report based on surveys sent to clients the prior day. The verbatim responses are used to identify patterns in customer frustrations, follow up with specific customers, engage employees in suggesting service improvements, celebrate successes, and counsel employees on individual struggles. Schwab credits its customer feedback approach with helping it stay connected to customers' service needs, which has led to significant improvement in both its customer ratings and sales.

Second, service excellence often demands that frontline service employees have ready access to relevant customer information to support coordination of service activities and relationship building. At Mayo Clinic, for example, fully interconnected systems improve patient care that requires coordination among multiple departments and specialists. When a physician enters an order for a patient to receive a particular medication at particular time intervals, the system automatically notifies physicians, pharmacists, and other medical staff when a particular treatment should be given. The system also highlights new test results in the patient file so that other nurses and doctors do not overlook critical patient information.

Third, because services are processes that are often delivered in geographically dispersed locations, a company must coordinate use of its physical resources so they are available when and where they are needed. Consider a Zipcar experience. Zipcar provides an alternative to using a traditional rental car, public transportation or borrowing a car from a friend when a person needs a car for short trips around town. The cars are located in designated Zipcar locations in a particular city. Members reserve a car via the company website or from their mobile phone. Once at the car, the renter waves a membership card over a windshield sensor, which initiates a wireless inquiry to the company to confirm that the member is approved to use the car. If everything checks out, the car's doors are unlocked remotely. Upon return of the car to a Zipcar location, the car's status and the member's account are automatically updated ("The Four Technologies You Need to Be Working With," by Adam Richardson, *Harvard Business Review*, 2011).

Achieve Service Excellence Success

Service excellence is not easy to achieve, but the success of the companies in this article demonstrates that it is both possible and worthwhile. However, it will not be achieved by simply adopting a particular tool or technology; nor will it be achieved simply by reading examples of service excellence. To excel at service, a company must understand the fundamental principles that underlie the value of particular tools or the success of individual companies.

Careful attention to the five fundamental tenets reviewed in this article won't provide a quick fix, but companies that do so will manage to create lasting value for their customers and themselves.

Whether the goal is to improve or sustain service excellence, a company should begin by assessing strengths and weaknesses in each tenet area. Improvement efforts should focus first on weaknesses that are most critical to a strategic position. Though new resource commitments may be required, a lot can be achieved with the same resources and an improved focus. This is certainly true as it pertains to how decisions are made, what policies allow and restrict, what is communicated to the organization, how jobs are designed, what behaviors are rewarded, what information is made available to employees, and so on.

Finally, where new resources are required, the market performance of service leaders should be kept in mind. Failure to spend what is needed to achieve and sustain service excellence may be the most costly decision of all!

Critical Thinking

1. Explain the concept of 'Service Excellence' as defined by the authors.

2. List and summarize the five tenets of service excellence discussed in the article.

3. Discuss the following statement from the article: "Service is a critical factor to business success now more than ever." Do you agree?

Create Central

www.mhhe.com/createcentral

Internet References

Help Scout
https://www.helpscout.net/blog/
International Customer Service Association
http://icsatoday.org/
National Customer Service Association
www.nationalcsa.com/

Lance A. Bettencourt, "Fundamental Tenets of Service Excellence," *Marketing Power*, Fall 2012. Copyright © 2012 by American Marketing Association. All rights reserved. Used with permission.

Article   Prepared by: Nisreen N. Bahnan, *Salem State University*

Walking the Talk

Eco-minded retailer, Patagonia caused a stir with its recent "conscious-consumption" holiday campaign that told consumers *not* to buy the featured product. Marketing VP Rob BonDurant discusses the strategy and shares some early results.

KATHERINE LING

Learning Outcomes

After reading this article, you will be able to:

- Understand the concept of "conscious consumerism," and the ethical implications of production and consumption of products.

- Analyze the effect of alternative promotional strategies, such as Patagonia's "Common Thread Initiative" on consumers' perceptions and behaviors.

Last fall on Cyber Monday, the busiest online shopping day of the year, Patagonia customers opened their e-mail inboxes to see these words in the outdoor apparel retailer's promotional message: "Don't Buy This Jacket."

The ensuing message read, in part: "Cyber Monday was created by the National Retail Federation in 2005 to focus media and public attention on online shopping. But Cyber Monday, and the culture of consumption it reflects, puts the economy of natural systems that support all life firmly in the red. . . .

"We ask you to buy less and to reflect before you spend a dime on this jacket or anything else. . . .

"The environmental cost of everything we make is astonishing. Consider the R2 Jacket shown, one of our best sellers. To make it required 135 liters of water, enough to meet the daily needs (three glasses a day) of 45 people. Its journey from its origin as 60 percent recycled polyester to our Reno warehouse generated nearly 20 pounds of carbon dioxide, 24 times the weight of the finished product. This jacket left behind, on its way to Reno, two-thirds its weight in waste.

"And this is a 60 percent recycled polyester jacket, knit and sewn to a high standard; it is exceptionally durable, so you won't have to replace it as often. . . . But, as is true of all the things we can make and you can buy, this jacket comes with an environmental cost higher than its price.

"There is much to be done and plenty for us all to do. Don't buy what you don't need. Think twice before you buy anything. Go to patagonia.com/CommonThreads, take the Common Threads Initiative pledge and join us in the fifth 'R,' to reimagine a world where we take only what nature can replace."

The e-mail message—and a related full-page ad that Patagonia ran in *The New York Times* for Black Friday—came on the heels of an ad campaign that told consumers to "Reduce what you buy," and prompted a whirlwind of media attention and online chatter about whether the message would hurt Patagonia's sales or help secure customer loyalty, or would simply be perceived as a marketing gimmick.

Rob BonDurant, vice president of marketing and communications at Ventura, Calif.-based Patagonia Inc., recently told *Marketing News* that the campaign has more than paid for itself with the amount of interest that it has generated for the brand and its Common Threads Initiative, a sustainability effort intended to prompt consumers to think twice about the environmental impact of buying any product and to encourage companies to be transparent about how their products are made.

If the "Don't Buy This Jacket" message boosts sales, that'd be an ancillary benefit, BonDurant says. The campaign's goal is to get consumers who aren't yet familiar with Patagonia and its sustainability-minded practices to take note of the company's culture and eco-minded business strategy, and to prompt more consumers to shop and live sustainably.

What follow are excerpts from *Marketing News'* interview with BonDurant. To see more of his insights, check out the March 1 issue of *Marketing News Exclusives* at Marketing Power.com/newsletters.

Q: What was the strategy behind this direct marketing effort?

A: It was really a comment on consumption for the sake of consumption. As a company, we have always been absolutely fascinated and committed to this idea of quality in place of consumption. We build our ethos around that because of where we came from. . . .

In 1972, before [Yvon Chouinard] founded the company, roughly, [mountain climbers] would pound nails into rocks that would leave marks and it would lead, ultimately, to degradation to the environment and against the very reason to go to these wild places. So he built these tools that you could pull out and remove and left no marks whatsoever. . . . He caused a disruption that changed the way we look at the rock climbing industry forever. . . .

Because we don't even consider ourselves a marketing company—we consider ourselves a company that makes products that solve problems—we are able to do things other companies can't. . . . When we began discussing this Black Friday/Cyber Monday thing . . . for Black Friday we are told to go out and consume a resource that is not renewable and we just couldn't really live with that. We decided to be exactly who we are and say: "Hey, look: Only purchase what you need. We want you to be aware of what goes into the products that we make so you can make an educated choice about when you buy those products" . . .

That, in and of itself, was our counter to the myriad of discounts, offers, sweepstakes and tchotchkes, and traditional marketing tactics that are meant to pull us into retail stores and aren't necessarily going to improve the quality of our lives. They are temporary. . . . The message, "Don't buy this jacket," is obviously super counterintuitive to what a for-profit company would say, especially on a day like Black Friday, but honesty is what we really were after.

As a measurement tool, I needed to see that we created a dialogue. I mean, we only ran one ad in *The New York Times* and that one ad has actually generated so much PR that, literally, the interview process that we have been going through, that I have been going through since that very day, has gained steam. So it has more than paid for itself in value and it has gotten a dialogue going.

Q: Who were you targeting in this message?

A: This was a message that was meant to go out to a much broader constituency than ours alone. To that end, we expected that when we put something out on Black Friday in *The New York Times* and then backed that up with messaging in our retail stores, on our website and in a flight [of ads] on NYTimes.com, that we would have this very succinct, very sort of counterintuitive message out there.

For me personally, I knew it was effective when I went to visit my folks over Thanksgiving down in Florida, who live in a nice home on the golf course, and the next-door neighbor drove his golf cart over. I didn't tell anyone we were running this [campaign], and he had the ad in his hands and he looked at it and said, "You Patagonia guys sure are different." This is not one of our core customers. That is how I knew we had reached an audience that was very different than ours. And not that I was looking to acquire that particular customer: What I'm trying to do is to get the conversation and dialogue going to improve business [sustainability].

If there is a halo effect and it keeps Patagonia top of mind, we will take it. We are not a marketing company and I don't really consider myself to be a marketer. We very much don't use marketing as a vehicle to drive business. We use products as a vehicle to drive business. We use word of mouth, recommendations, public relations and, only as a last resort, a little bit of advertising to get our messages out there, and to be opinionated and have a point of view and, hopefully, one that is positive in future thinking.

Q: Were you concerned at all about sounding preachy or people dismissing the ad as the luxury of a company that sells high-end goods?

A: Yes and no. The concern was that if we don't walk our talk, if we don't live our communication, then we are actually just a marketing company after all, that we are actually full of s*#t and ultimately doing what the naysayers would accuse us of, and certainly did accuse us of, which is using this message to drive sales.

It is the forbidden fruit message. I didn't read this, but this is what I garnered from some of the social media that I was reading that was negative. Once you say: "Don't push the red button. Don't eat from the apple," man, you can't resist that forbidden fruit. That wasn't our intention at all. Our intention was to stop you in the sea of ads that said, "Discounts," and, "Off-price," and, "You can get more," and do it in the headline. Then if you read the body copy, which is extremely long and counterintuitive to what you would want in a newspaper especially on this particular day, you get this fuller, deeper story. And that is what really moves people.

People who were far against us, I didn't expect them to move towards the middle. The people who love us, I expected would write us and tell us how brilliant this was. We got that. It's the people in the middle who are open to ideas about how we shift business through consumption, through this idea of evolving capitalism and conscious consumption that we wanted to affect.

Q: You were just certified as a 'B Corporation'—a type of for-profit corporation in which the company's governing body can consider social or environmental objectives ahead of profits—but you still need to make sales. Were you concerned about how this campaign could affect your sales, and how did you convince your CEO and CFO to do this?

A: Of course, we are always worried about sales for Black Friday, especially because we are largely a fourth-quarter business. We make products for cold weather and that's what we are most known for. It is an incredibly important period of time for us, in which we will do up to 40 percent of our annual volume in two months alone, so if we falter, then yes, we are concerned.

But what we said is bullet-proof because it is what we believe in. It is the way we run our business. Every aspect of how we run Patagonia is really speaking to that ethos and it's the heart of our culture, so it wasn't difficult for the CEO or CFO to get on board once we sort of outlined the stroke of the campaign, the expected results, the action plan, the post-campaign and then, ultimately, the return that we can get from the level of dialogue we create either via public relations or social media and, of course, the interviews we are doing now. Since Black Friday, there has been an interview request coming in every day, and that is just from one ad in one newspaper, so the messaging is absolutely of strength and relevance—an eyebrow raiser. People want to know more about it and they are sure to get into it. They can hopefully discover more about our company and the way that we run our business so that we can inspire the other businesses to choose sustainability and not feel that that is a choice against profit.

Q: Patagonia has different goals and is a different company. Could other companies replicate this campaign?

A: If it is a marketing campaign, no. If it is a way they live their lives and do their business, absolutely.

Since we have to put it in a box here, this was not a marketing campaign. This is a message that we had been sending for decades, I mean literally for decades. We just hadn't put it in an amplified voice and stuck it in *The New York Times* on Black Friday. . . .

The key to the whole effort [is]: Put your money where your mouth is, or where your marketing dollars are, and support a model that is built around the concept of sustainability. That means you can't just apply it to your messaging or to a particular window of time. It has to be done 24 hours a day, 365 days a week.

For me, it's a challenge of, OK, we are a direct marketing company. We send out six catalogs. We send them out, roughly,

over 30 to 45 days. That is a tonnage of paper. How can I continue to deal with what direct marketing requires, which is direct communication in your mailbox, without increasing my paper count? How can I acquire more customers without increasing my paper count? That requires not just a catalog paper policy, but also a company-wide paper policy because if half the company is printing their horoscopes out on the printers and I am busting my hump trying to figure out how to increase our order base without actually increasing our paper, we are not walking the talk.

So again, it is putting everybody in the mix and having ownership not at the senior level, but at the staff level. At a company meeting, I want staff to stand up and say, "This is how we made our department paperless." That will inspire one other department to do that and that is what we are doing. As a result, we are getting much more refined in how we do our mailing and we work with 501(c)(3) nonprofits to ensure the paper we print is sustainably harvested. And to this day, we have not increased our paper usage by more than one pound in the last five years because this is what we focused on, but we have grown the company annually over the last few years by over 30 percent. . . .

It is not just enough to make good products anymore. There also has to be a message that people can buy into, that people feel they are a part of, that they can be solutions-based. That is what the communication efforts are really all about.

Q: What does your retail strategy look like—and given your environmental mindset, are you going to move away from catalogs?

A: We have going on about 100 retail stores on a global basis, a very robust e-commerce business and a website that has now shifted to become the centerpiece of what is going on at Patagonia anytime you want. The lights are always on at the website. It does not close like a retail store. You don't have to get it in your mailbox; it will come to you. You can get it via e-mail, RSS, however you want to get it.

We are shifting the catalog itself. The catalog can only represent, at any given time, maybe only 40 percent of what is available on the Patagonia line, so what we have done is we have shifted our thinking away from our catalog being the standalone vehicle—our soapbox, if you will—and stood up to say what was important to us: to the catalog being a push and offer vehicle to inspire you to go online or to go into brick-and-mortar stores.

So yes, our catalogs are shifting. Are they going to become extinct? Not in the next year, not in, maybe, the next two years. But we will slowly decrease our paper usage; we will slowly move people into the medium they are actually transacting on. Over 80 percent of people we send the paper catalog to buy online. If that is the way that people look at the catalog, we will build it along those models until the point that, hopefully, we can exit that arena completely. I am not sure we ever will. That is a little bit of a crystal ball I wouldn't feel comfortable pulling right now. But especially as a company that is known for their catalog, it is one of those things that I have to pay very close attention to and I have to honor how deeply the Patagonia catalog culture has been built.

Q: What percentage of your communication is direct marketing?

A: In terms of our distribution, we are 50 percent wholesale, so that is going to a reseller like REI, for instance, one of our bigger accounts, and 50 percent is direct. That would be through catalog, through social media, the e-mail program, e-commerce and what we do in terms of our retail stores. Probably 80 percent of our communication is direct marketing because of the fact that those businesses are mature and robust, and because we have such a big database of people that we can reach and a profound database of potential prospects. I have already got all the climbers I am going to get. . . . Now it is, How can I reach the people that we didn't reach previously through conventional mediums that are sport-specific, to find people who are aligned with our values, our goals of the company? . . .

[In our direct marketing,] 60 percent is product and 40 percent is messaging, environmental, photography, and all the rest of it. I have got a lot of freedom to be fairly robust, to have a story unfold over a catalog or e-mail, or a video or a podcast or whatever you may choose for the media to view it on.

We have one customer. We don't have a wholesale customer or brick-and-mortar customer, or a catalog customer. We have a Patagonia customer. Wherever they want to consume Patagonia, learn about Patagonia and understand Patagonia, we want to be ready and waiting for them on their terms. That is not a catalog strategy anymore. A catalog shows up in your box once a month, at best, and is disposable. Nowadays, we demand that companies give us their information when we want it. If that means 2 A.M. on Tuesday morning, then fine. That is when we have to be ready and willing to say: "How're you doing? Good morning. Let's talk."

Critical Thinking

1. Formulate your own definition for "conscious consumerism."

2. Summarize Patagonia's Common Thread Initiative.

3. In your opinion, what effect(s) will this initiative have on Patagonia's existing customers and competitors' customers?

Create Central

www.mhhe.com/createcentral

Internet References

Huffington Post
   http://www.huffingtonpost.com/tag/conscious-consumption/
Patagonia
   http://www.patagonia.com/us/common-threads/

KATHERINE LING is a freelance writer based in Fairfax, Va.

Katherine Ling, "Walking the Talk," *Marketing News*, March 15, 2012, pp. 24–28. Copyright © 2012 by American Marketing Association. All rights reserved. Used with permission.

Article   Prepared by: Nisreen N. Bahnan, *Salem State University*

Walmart Wants You to Believe Its Green Makeover Is Changing the World. Just One Hitch: China

Andy Kroll

Learning Outcomes

After reading this article, you will be able to:

- Comprehend the complex production and distribution network that mega-retailers are a primary part of.

- Examine the concept of sustainability, and how it relates to environmental, human resources, and consumer-relations practices.

- Analyze the important role that a giant retailer like Walmart plays in initiating shifts within the production, distribution and retail sectors.

On a warm, sticky winter morning, I waited nervously in a parking lot in Foshan, a city in southeastern China's smog-choked Pearl River delta, for a man I'd never met. His name was Mr. Ou, and he ran the sprawling factory in front of me, a jumble of offices, low-slung buildings, and warehouses. Though the factory was teeming with workers, a Subaru SUV and BMW coupe were the only cars in the lot. Drab, gray worker dormitories loomed nearby, and between them ran a dusty road that led to the factory. At last a young man emerged from an office building. He motioned for me to follow him in.

I settled onto a plush leather couch and absorbed the decor. Framed awards and certificates covered the walls. A shopping-cart-size wooden frog stood sentry in the center of the room. Ping golf clubs leaned against one wall; a Rolling Stones commemorative electric guitar gathered dust behind a chair. And there were grills: a small kettle grill on a desk, a brushed-steel

gas grill on the far side of the room, grills stacked atop other grills. This was Mr. Ou's trade: supplying Western retailers with the cooking apparatus of patio parties and Fourth of July bashes.

The young man closed the door. He took the chair to my right, lit a cigarette, and met my stare as if to say, *Let's get on with it.* Only then did I realize I was not talking to an assistant.

Mr. Ou had the good looks of a judge on one of those breathless Chinese talent shows. He wore a tailored blazer, an expensive-looking watch, polished leather shoes, and colorful striped socks. He asked why I'd come to China, why I cared about his factory. An American consultant, I said, had suggested I tour his operation, Foshan Juniu Metal Manufacturing, because Mr. Ou was part of a hallmark sustainability program launched by the company I had come to China to investigate—Walmart.

In October 2005, Walmart announced plans to transform itself into one of the greenest corporations in the world. Then-CEO Lee Scott called sustainability "essential to our future success as a retailer." The company has been especially vocal about shrinking its environmental footprint in China, its manufacturing hub. But do the facts on the ground match Walmart's rhetoric? This was the question that had brought me to Mr. Ou.

Mr. Ou dragged on his cigarette, mulling my questions. "Okay," he finally said. "I will tell you what you want to know."

He was 33 years old and came from a manufacturing family. His parents ran a factory making packaging for barbecue grills and then, in 1994, began producing the grills themselves. By 2004, when Mr. Ou took over from his parents, Walmart was a major customer. In 2008, Mr. Ou signed his operation up as one of 200 plants whose energy efficiency Walmart would seek to increase by 20 percent.

Mr. Ou said all this in a smoky rattle of a voice, but he perked up when he talked about this program. "As the biggest retailer in the world," he told me, "Walmart has a responsibility to do this." For the energy efficiency program, he submitted monthly reports to Walmart and met with a Walmart consultant about energy-saving equipment. But he had his doubts. While Walmart executives preached sustainability, its buyers pushed him to lower prices by 3 or 5 percent each year. Operating on the thinnest of margins and scrambling to keep up with Walmart's demands, he said, factories just don't have the time or capital to invest in green projects. "They will work the suppliers to death," he told me.

After our meeting, Mr. Ou's assistant, who looked slightly older than Mr. Ou, took me around the factory grounds, 25 acres in all. One- and two-story buildings lined the road, and a bilious-looking river cut through the property. When I asked, the assistant said its pollution came from other factories. We passed through a dark, ear-splittingly loud packaging facility where, amid stacks of Styrofoam blocks and plastic-wrapped metal parts, workers eyed us warily before turning back to the production line. Kingsford grill boxes reached high toward the ceiling, WALMART printed on the side.

Near the end of the tour, the assistant led me inside a hangar-like plant filled with the whine of heavy machinery. Workers

Walton's World from Small-Town Five-and-Dime to the Mother of All Megastores, How Walmart Conquered the World

1951: Sam Walton opens his first five-and-dime in Arkansas.

1985: *Forbes* reports that Walton, worth $2.8 billion, is the richest man in America.

1988: Some stores now feature oil change shops, banks, and salons.

1991: First foreign Walmart opens in Mexico City.

1992: President George H.W. Bush awards Walton the Medal of Freedom. Later that year, NBC *Dateline* reveals child labor at a Walmart supplier in Bangladesh.

1993: Walmart opens a prototype ecofriendly store in Kansas, featuring a man-made wetlands and a roof made of sustainably harvested timber. The company starts selling goods made in China.

1994: After the National Advertising Review Board warns that "Always the low price. Always." is misleading, Walmart changes slogan to "Always Low Prices. Always. Walmart."

1995: Iowa State University researchers find that five years after the opening of a

Walmart, nearby small-town stores see an average 25% decline in sales; they conclude that "smaller towns suffer the brunt of the discount mass merchandisers."

1996: Walmart opens its first store in China.

1998: A new Walton biography portrays a notorious Scrooge who got $5 haircuts and didn't tip his barber.

1999: Walmart becomes the largest private employer in the world.

2000: 123 US Walmarts are cited for 1,371 child labor violations, according to an internal Walmart audit.

June 2001: In what will become the largest civil rights class-action case against a private employer in US history, six female employees file a discrimination lawsuit against the company. The Supreme Court rejects class-action status for the suit in 2011, effectively killing the case.

December 2003: An anonymous blogger launches WalMart-Blows.com Its "Work for Wal-Mart? Need to vent?" forum garners 10,000 posts.

February 2004: The *Washington Post* reports that in China, where 80% of the company's suppliers are, Walmart's factory employees work up to 80 hours a week and make as little as $75 a month.

2005: A leaked memo reveals a Walmart HR exec's proposal to "attract a healthier workforce" to cut back or health care costs.

March 2005: Federal investigators find that Walmart's cleaning subcontractors hired 345 undocumented workers between 1998 and 2003.

October 2005: Walmart CEO Lee Scott says Walmart's goal is to be 100% powered by renewable energy, create zero waste, and "sell products that sustain our resources and environment." He doesn't say by when.

2006: Walmart hires PR firm Edelman to launch a campaign around initiatives like increased starting pay, a $4 flat fee for generic prescription drugs, and a bargain organic foods line.

2007: A report from the Environmental Investigation Agency finds that China

produces 84% of Walmart's wood products, a significant portion of which are sourced from illegal logging hot spots.

2008: Walmart rolls out a major initiative to reduce energy use and improve product safety in Chinese factories. It also changes its name from Wal-Mart to Walmart.

2009: An investigation by a Chinese labor watchdog group reveals that some Walmart suppliers created an "elaborate system to cheat Walmart audits."

February 2010: Walmart announces it will cut 20 million metric tons of emissions from its supply chain by 2015.

May 2010: Walmart agrees to pay $27.6 million after illegally dumping hazardous waste in 42 California counties.

January 2011: At the urging of Michelle Obama, Walmart pledges to eliminate trans fats from its packaged foods and reduce sodium and sugar by 25% and 10%, respectively.

2012: Walmart has 357 stores, 30,000 factories, and 96,800 workers in China, where 70% of the products it sells are made.—*Jaeah Lee* in jeans and T-shirts operated heavy presses, stamping metal sheets into grill lids. We sidled up to an unoccupied machine. Bits of metal glittered at its base like coins in a fountain. The assistant motioned for us to look closer, then pointed to a shoebox-size metal box affixed to one side that read "Mascot." When turned on, he proudly explained, this box slashed electricity usage. I had asked to see the factory's energy efficiency investments, and this was it.

Soon after, the assistant led me back to the parking lot. The tour was over. Mr. Ou gave me his card and told me to stay in touch.

It was never made clear to me how those energy-saving boxes exactly worked. What I did know was that Mr. Ou had welcomed me into his factory, served me tea, answered my questions, and let me snoop around. He seemed like a forward-thinking businessman with a strong belief in sustainability-exactly the right type to carry forward Walmart's vision for a leaner, greener supply chain in a country smothered by pollution.

Except, as far as Mr. Ou was concerned, that vision never came to life. And no one, he later told me, ever explained why.

Walmart's campaign to green everything from its break rooms to its global supply chain is one of the most publicized, and controversial, experiments in American retail. The company had made a halfhearted attempt in the 1980s and 1990s, with a few green products and ecofriendly stores. But this latest effort was different. It was sweeping, embracing every part of the company's business. It emanated directly from the CEO's office. And, perhaps most remarkably, some of Walmart's erstwhile critics in the environmental movement—the Environmental Defense Fund (EDF), Natural Resources Defense Council (NRDC), and World Wildlife Fund, among others—got on board. Former Sierra Club president Adam Werbach was hired to spread the green message among Walmart's 1.4 million US employees.

Almost seven years into the program, many environmentalists remain convinced that Walmart is serious about sustainability— and that its actions can have a major impact on the world economy because of the gravitational pull of its vast network of suppliers, customers, and employees. Walmart's environmental initiatives in China have been heralded—most recently by Orville Schell in *The Atlantic*—as a key force in spurring other corporations to embrace sound environmental practices. My reporting—more than a year of research that took me from Arkansas to China— suggests a more complex, less flattering story: Walmart has made laudable though modest progress on many of its goals. But with the global economic slowdown tugging at the company's profit margins, people involved with the environmental campaign say the momentum seems to be stalling or vanishing entirely.

Since launching its sustainability program, Walmart has pledged to eliminate waste, use only renewable energy, sell more organic produce, support small farmers, and slash its energy footprint. That's no easy task: Each second, 330 people buy something from one of Walmart's 8,970 stores worldwide. With 2.1 million workers, it is the world's largest private employer. Its carbon footprint—from its stores, distribution centers, company offices, corporate jets, and so on—totaled 21.4 million metric tons in 2010, more than that of half the world's countries, according to data Walmart provided to the Carbon Disclosure Project.

But that figure doesn't include Walmart's supply chain, a web of more than 100,000 suppliers from Tennessee to Turkey, Cambodia to Mexico. These companies fall largely into two categories: Some make house-brand products to Walmart specifications: Great Value (food), George (clothing), Mainstays (furniture). Then there are name-brand products, like Del Monte pineapples, Coleman tents, and Bic pens. Sometimes, a brand will make a Walmart-specific product; General Electric, for instance, sells kitchen appliances exclusive to Walmart and is subject to Walmart's factory regulations. But neither the house-brand nor name-brand suppliers necessarily produce the jeans, tents, or toothbrushes they sell to Walmart. That work is done by contractors and subcontractors, which include many unregulated "shadow" factories—and that's where some of the most carbon-heavy, polluting parts of the manufacturing process happen.

Counting all the suppliers, factories, mills, farms, and so on in its supply chain, Walmart estimates its total carbon footprint is closer to at least 200 million metric tons. And even that estimate doesn't include all of the companies Walmart does business with, such as its distribution trucking firms.

In the past, Walmart's outsize carbon footprint had made the company a favorite target of environmentalists. But in 2009, as hope for a congressional cap-and-trade deal evaporated and the Copenhagen climate talks ended in a stalemate, they began to see Walmart in a different light: If they could make the world's largest retailer greener, other businesses might follow suit, EDF had opened its own office near Walmart headquarters in Bentonville, Arkansas, embedding its employees in the "belly of the beast," as one staffer put it. "Even though they're a party of last resort, they're our only hope at the moment," said Linda Greer, an NRDC scientist who works with Walmart. "They have the potential to change the world."

Key word: *potential*. So far the company has made strides on only some of its goals. It says it has boosted its truck fleet's efficiency by 60 percent, eliminated hazardous materials from most electronics it sells, cut plastic bag use by more than 20 percent since 2007, and sold 466 million compact fluorescent lightbulbs in four years.

But interviews with key insiders and the company's own reports reveal that on some of its biggest promises, Walmart's results are underwhelming:

- At a glitzy Beijing confab in 2008, Walmart pledged to make Chinese suppliers agree to comply with labor and environmental laws and standards starting in January 2009. (All other suppliers were to comply by 2011.) As of its 2011 Global Responsibility Report, Walmart had no updates except to say that the compliance agreement "is being strengthened."

- Walmart committed to eliminate 25 percent of solid waste from its US stores by October 2008. In its 2011 responsibility report, Walmart said it had no data for 2005, 2006, and 2007. Instead, it touted a "waste-redirection" rate of 64 percent in the 2010 fiscal year.
- In 2008, Walmart pledged to boost energy efficiency by 20 percent per unit produced at 200 Chinese factories, including Mr. Ou's, by this year. In April 2011, it announced 119 factories had hit the target. Yet later that month, EDF, a crucial partner in China, left the program over Walmart's lack of cooperation, several sources told me. By year's end, the program was dormant.
- Walmart's goal to reduce greenhouse gas emissions by 20 percent at its stores and distribution centers worldwide by 2012 was half met by the time of the 2011 responsibility report.

And even where Walmart has made its goals, questions linger. The retailer says every supplier making private-label and non-name-brand goods has provided the name and location of every factory involved in making those products. Yet Walmart concedes that the use of murky subcontractors is widespread in China, Africa, the Middle East, and Bangladesh. Walmart also won't provide details about *how* it achieved its goal, whether suppliers were asked or compelled to share factory information, and whether any suppliers lost orders or were fired for unsatisfactory responses. My repeated attempts to get Walmart to answer specific questions yielded little in the way of hard data but plenty of PR speak. "We believe the sheer volume and ambition of our goals—and our annually reported progress—speak for themselves," a spokeswoman wrote me in one typical exchange.

That's why I decided to go see for myself.

Walmart began buying Chinese-made goods in 1993. The country's first supercenter opened three years later in Shenzhen. Today, the company directly employs 96,800 people in China and operates 357 Chinese stores. Walmart's supply chain includes some 30,000 Chinese factories, which produce an estimated 70 percent of all of the goods it sells. Walmart's global sourcing headquarters, the nerve center for its international operations, is also located in Shenzhen, a booming city on the southeastern coast.

In December 2010 I arrived in Foshan, a city in the heart of Guangdong province. Known as the "workshop of the world" and bordering Hong Kong, Guangdong is packed with factories that churn out Barbies and bras, tube socks and toilet brushes, iPhones and plasma TVs. The province's gross domestic product in 2010 was $690 billion, more than the GDP of Argentina, Saudi Arabia, or South Africa.

Walmart has connected other journalists with its suppliers and corporate officials in China in the past two years, but it had declined a half-dozen requests from me. And locating these sources on my own proved no easy task. The company closely guards all information about who makes its products. Aside from Mr. Ou, almost everyone connected to Walmart I met in China insisted I not use their real names for fear of being blackballed by Walmart and other employers.

Which is why I'll call the former Walmart factory auditor I met one Saturday night Michael Chao. Chao was in his mid-30s and spoke good English. We couldn't talk in public, he said, so we relocated to a friend's office a few blocks away.

Chao joined Walmart as an auditor in 2004 after two years at an independent auditing firm. He spent four years at Walmart, which, combined with his previous gig, was plenty long enough to understand how auditing in China *really* works.

Walmart helped spawn the supplier auditing industry. After a scathing NBC *Dateline* report in 1992 uncovered child labor at a Walmart supplier in Bangladesh, the company denied the allegations but then created a supplier code of conduct that, among other things, outlawed child and prison labor. Other big-name companies soon followed suit, and soon there was a market for companies that could police those firms. Today, Walmart's auditors inspect factories, meet with managers, scrutinize wage records, and interview individual workers to look for labor, health, and safety violations.

They have recently tried to keep an eye out for environmental issues as well, but it hasn't been easy, since the inspectors are already overtaxed. Auditing is a demanding job, Chao told me. Burnout is common. Factories often cook their books, keeping two sets of records—the real ones, and a clean version for the auditors. Managers coach employees to lie. And a passel of companies help suppliers fudge their numbers and pass compliance audits.

Sometimes the auditors themselves are corrupt, Chao said, willing to overlook violations in exchange for a *hongbao*—a bribe. (Hongbao means "red envelope," usually a bill-shaped sleeve filled with cash given as a gift at family celebrations.) Walmart, which has publicly acknowledged firing auditors for taking bribes, says it investigates all reports of corruption. But Chao told me that they can't catch all the crooked auditors.

Walmart hired a crop of young college graduates to replace auditors who were inured to corruption, but challenges remained. Like off-the-books subcontracting. In China, auditors typically see only "five-star" factories, so named for China's rating system for hotels and restaurants. These companies, he explained, obey the law, treat their workers fairly, pay decent wages, and ensure safe working conditions, by local standards. But Walmart and others often demand more than their five-star suppliers can produce, so a company scrambling to fill a massive order for, say, action figures will outsource to a shadow factory.

A shadow factory can be a mom-and-pop operation in someone's house, or it can be a full-fledged factory hidden on the same property as a five-star. Regulations don't apply inside a shadow factory, Chao said. Consultants and experts who've worked in China for decades say there are tens of thousands of shadow factories, and that up to 70 or even 80 percent of five-stars will outsource more than half of a given production order to shadow factories. At Walmart, Chao said, "We would look in the system which shows the [five-star] factory has only 300 people to handle an operation receiving massive production orders worth millions of dollars. How does it add up?"

Good auditors aren't blind to this, he noted. But they don't have time to hunt down all the shadow factories, and they feel pressure not to cause trouble or stop orders from being filled.

Chao recalled one case at Walmart when his boss received a confidential tip about a toy supplier outsourcing production to a strange location. Chao and a colleague staked out the supplier. When a truck emerged, they jumped into a waiting taxi and tailed it until the truck pulled into a prison. Upon further investigation, Chao confirmed that the factory was using inmate labor and got Walmart to pull its orders from the supplier.

He told me that story not to trumpet his or Walmart's detective skills—he said the auditors likely missed many more shadow factories than they caught—but to stress the slippery nature of the supply chain. Walmart's American brass, Chao said, doesn't have a complete enough understanding of Chinese manufacturing. "They have the basic concept, but the top management knows nothing about how to make it work" at the ground level, he said. "So they can say, 'Oh, a sustainability program,' but they can do nothing."

Chao isn't the only one to question Walmart's auditing. In 2009, the advocacy group China Labor Watch obtained documents from a Walmart packaging supplier on how to hide or adjust safety and environmental records; how workers should lie to auditors about wages, benefits, and working hours; and how to conceal a shadow factory. Another investigation by the group uncovered forced overtime, phony pay stubs, poor living conditions, and the use of hazardous chemicals at a Walmart shoe factory. Walmart-hired auditors had previously raised no concerns with either plant.

Li Qiang, China Labor Watch's executive director, told me that Walmart's auditing process has been plagued with fraud for years. In 2007, Li, who says he's met with Walmart officials numerous times, urged the retailer to scrap its corruption-riddled internal auditing program. Walmart followed his advice, but Li discovered that the problems hadn't disappeared. In November 2011, a lawsuit filed by Li's group against Intertek,

an international third-party auditing company, describes how in December 2009 an Intertek auditor took a bribe from a Dongguan toy factory while overlooking "extensive fraud" in pay and hours records. (An Intertek spokeswoman said the suit "has no merit" but declined to comment on specific allegations.) In its 2011 Global Responsibility Report, Walmart briefly hinted at this problem: "Lack of complete transparency to production practices [in China] has hindered our ability to implement meaningful change at the factory level."

Li said these problems were systemic. "If the fraud in the auditing system isn't solved," he told me, "I'm far from optimistic about Walmart's environmental programs."

Thirty years ago, Shenzhen was a drab fishing village on the South China Sea, a place so remote it didn't have a single traffic light. Then, as part of his economic reforms, Communist Party leader Deng Xiaopeng named Shenzhen the country's first "special economic zone," with laissez-faire trade policies and favorable manufacturing laws put in place to lure foreign investment. Shenzhen's economy exploded, its GDP climbing from $31 million in 1979 to $107.8 billion in 2007. Today Shenzhen is China's third-largest port city, packed with skyscrapers, nightclubs, and fancy hotels. Among the most luxurious is the Shangri-La, where, on any given morning, buyers for American retailers mill around the marble-floored lobby waiting for rides to factories. I sat down in the bar one Friday and ordered a cappuccino that arrived with the letters "S-L" spelled in froth.

I was there to meet Terry Foecke (pronounced FAKE-ee), a consultant spearheading Walmart's factory energy efficiency program in China. In a lobby full of Westerners, Foecke cut an unmistakable figure—thickly bearded, 6-foot-3, with a broad belly and hip square—framed glasses. He was an unlikely Walmart ally: a soft-spoken, almost professorial progressive who quoted George Bernard Shaw and told me he spoke out against runaway consumerism at his Unitarian church back home in Minnesota.

Foecke's actual employer was the Environmental Defense Fund, which in 2008 partnered with Walmart on the campaign to make factories more energy efficient. That degree of separation gave him the freedom to talk openly about implementing one of the retailer's most ambitious efforts: shrinking energy usage by 20 percent at 200 Chinese suppliers by 2012, the same program Mr. Ou had participated in. Foecke spent many days on the road, visiting factories and performing "rapid assessments"—two- or three-hour sweeps through a factory to pick out quick and easy ways to save energy and money. Foecke and his crack team of sleuths could find up to 60 percent in energy savings in a single visit, pulling down banks of lights that illuminated empty space or plugging leaky equipment.

Foecke wanted me to ride along on one of his assessments. But Walmart officials denied multiple requests to do so, and so

I had to settle for Foecke's colorful written accounts. Here he is walking through an aging factory that makes plastic Christmas trees and other fake flora:

"Then it was on to the plastic injection molders. Wow, I thought I had stumbled into Mr. Wizard's Wayback Machine and somebody dialed in ''1960.'' Wide-open hoppers (hard to keep the polymer dry that way; causes lot of rejects), leaking hydraulics bandaged up with rags; filthy motors everywhere, and more compressed air than I believe I have yet seen used. They have 50–60 smaller molders crammed into the space someone in [Minnesota] would use for a three-car garage, all actuated with compressed air instead of hydraulics, making bark and twigs and stems and such, sometimes even co-molding a stem onto a previously-made flower. P admitted later that the place made him jumpy, certified safety engineer that he is. The lack of safety guards and [emergency fail-safe] switches and doors and just plain space WAS impressive in a how-do-they-do-it? way. I got speared in the belly by an actuator, but in my defense the darn thing traveled a good foot into the manway."

But there were flaws with Foecke's program. Walmart said the participants in it were "top" suppliers, suggesting they had been chosen for their size. In fact, most of the 200 participating factories were simply those whose forward-thinking owners, like Mr. Ou, had volunteered, Foecke said. (And, of course, none of the 200 were shadow factories.) Also, the data in Foecke's program were self-reported. Foecke said he'd accepted Walmart's "inspire, not require" philosophy at the outset. Once Walmart expanded the program, he hoped it'd make energy metering mandatory. Otherwise, he explained, "the factories can say whatever they want, and when you have self-reported data it's built on sand. I said [to Walmart], 'You can do this for a while, but eventually cut the crap.'"

Yet two years into the program, well past the point where Foecke had expected it to be expanded dramatically, it was still stuck in the pilot phase. He'd seen similar hesitance on environmental issues at other companies, and that had usually spelled doom for energy efficiency programs. "It happens all the time," he said. "You go into big organizations, you get atomic decay, and unless there's something else there that drags it to the next level and starts integrating it, it becomes the flavor of the month."

A casual reader of the business pages could pinpoint the source of Walmart's hesitation. From 2009 to 2011, Walmart suffered seven straight quarters of declining sales in its US stores, a historic slump blamed on anemic job growth, weak demand, and high gas prices. Walmart responded by unveiling "It's Back," a plan to reclaim its original, bargain-seeking customer base by restocking 8,500 down-home products it had axed in an effort to declutter its shelves and class up its image. It also revived the popular "Action Alley," steeply discounted pallets of merchandise stacked up in the middle of the aisles.

"It's Back" left suppliers and environmental partners wondering if this doubling-down on its crusade to be the cheapest retailer around might come at the expense of sustainability.

One insider who watched this unfold was Michelle Mauthe Harvey, an expert and EDF staffer. In 2007, Harvey opened EDF's office in Bentonville, the Ozark country town that is home to Walmart's headquarters. Bentonville was the site of Sam Walton's first store, a five-and-dime that opened in 1951. In the decades that followed, Walmart transformed the town into a thriving international business hub. At least 750 companies that do business with Walmart have offices in the area, from Procter & Gamble to Levi Strauss to Dream Works. Cushy subdivisions ring the town, and both the median household income and average home value easily outpace the state average.

On a blisteringly hot summer day last June, I met Harvey over brisket and sweet tea at Whole Hog Café, a barbecue joint near the Walmart headquarters. Harvey is embedded inside Walmart, attending internal meetings and interacting with key players. She lauded Walmart for its ambitious goals but winced when I brought up "It's Back" and what it meant for sustainability. She said this roll-back initiative led some suppliers to think Walmart was stalling on sustainability as it grappled with slumping sales. "What's been concerning to us is the number of people who contact us and say, 'Is Walmart still interested in sustainability?'" She added, "There are still those [inside Walmart] who fall into the annoyed camp, who aren't entirely sure it's really necessary."

Consider Walmart's buyers, Harvey said, the people who negotiate with suppliers and help decide what makes it onto Walmart's shelves. If Walmart's sustainability ideal was to become reality, it needed to become part of buyers' day-to-day decision making, a criterion on which they were evaluated. For instance, would the buyers be encouraged to choose a T-shirt that costs a half cent more apiece because it used safer chemicals or was dyed at an environmentally friendly mill? When Walmart embraces that notion, Harvey said, "that's when sustainability is really embedded."

"Is it there yet?" I asked.

"It's not there yet."

After nearly a year of my asking for an interview with a company official in Bentonville about the sustainability program, Walmart finally put me in touch with Jim Stanway, a rumpled-looking Brit who worked in the energy sector before joining Walmart in the late 1990s to help trim its energy bills. We met in a small conference room at the Sam Walton Development Center, accompanied by a Walmart flack who took notes throughout the interview.

A man who admits he's "morbidly attracted by complexity," Stanway was Walmart's point man in working with the Carbon Disclosure Project to calculate that Walmart's carbon footprint was greater than that of many industrialized countries. Stanway is now leading the campaign to cut 20 million metric tons of greenhouse gas emissions from Walmart's supply chain by 2015.

Stanway rattled off his success stories, including uniting the fractious dairy industry behind using low-carbon cattle feed and methane digesters and selling Hollywood on the virtues of slimmer DVD packaging. A little plastic here, some cardboard there, and you're talking millions of dollars in savings. Not only did suppliers see their costs shrink, so did customers. "We want to show things where we can deliver customer value on price *and* quality, and lower costs for suppliers," Stanway said.

I'd hoped to ask Stanway about China, but the flack, who insisted on vetting all interview questions days beforehand, ruled out those questions, routing them to Walmart China. Despite four more requests, I never heard back.

Linda Greer is a sharp-witted, veteran scientist and director of the public health program at the Natural Resources Defense Council. She spoke to me about a program she started in 2007 called "Clean by Design," which has brought together companies like Walmart, Gap, Nike, and H&M to develop a set of best practices for Chinese dye and finishing mills, one of the most energy-intensive sectors in the apparel industry.

Greer told me in 2010 that she'd turned to Walmart and other private companies for lack of other options. "We really couldn't count on the Chinese environmental department to even come close to catching up on this in my lifetime," she said. "The private sector stands alone, being the only functioning additional party over there." She was no Walmart cheerleader but believed the company was making a sincere effort. "They've made a lot of ambitious promises, many of which were maybe naive in terms of how hard they are to implement."

But when I checked in with her again last fall, her guarded optimism had given way to discouragement. She and her team had spent a year and a half assembling 10 best practices to reduce water, chemical, and energy use at the mills; their suggested repairs and upgrades paid for themselves in eight months' time and, in some cases, saved energy use by 25 to 30 percent. The next step was putting the guidelines into practice, showcasing their benefits to lure other mills into the program. She asked the corporate partners for the names of four or five mills. Nike, Gap, and the others came through. Walmart gave her only one viable factory.

Greer was bitterly disappointed. "They're not even up at the plate swinging at those balls," she told me. (Walmart says it "continues to believe in—and promote" Greer's program but gave no specifics as to how.)

An energy efficiency consultant who also works with Walmart (and requested anonymity; I'll call him Martin) echoed those observations. He said there was overwhelming support for Walmart to succeed in China, given the ripple effect that would have in Chinese commerce. Yet 2011, he told me, was widely seen as a disappointing year. "The word on the street in China is: 'Where is Walmart?'" he said. "Because we haven't seen them continue to move forward in 2011."

Martin brought up a major Walmart supplier, a network of factories making name-brand products. (He asked that I not reveal the brand, but it's a household name.) Like Mr. Ou once did, this supplier submitted scorecards on energy and water use to Walmart. The retailer's response: silence. Martin said the supplier admitted to him that the data was "total crap," but it never heard from Walmart one way or another. Martin summed up the supplier's attitude toward Walmart scorecards like this: "Walmart sets a new target, everybody gets all excited, runs around for six months, and then everything kind of slows down and the wheels fall off."

Eight months after my first conversation with Terry Foecke, I caught up with him again in Minnesota. Seeing little appetite from Walmart to expand the factory efficiency program, he'd ditched it to start his own energy consulting business. Foecke sounded more befuddled than bitter—he'd always seen Walmart's factory project as a small but important first step. "It was key that they expand the program—that's what we put on the table" in the beginning, he said. "Until they're willing to do that, it's not quite greenwashing, but it's very close."

Mr. Ou witnessed the demise of Foecke's program firsthand. When I reconnected with him last winter, he said Walmart had stopped asking him for reports on Juniu's energy usage. No one told him why. As far as he could tell, Walmart had canceled the program. Mr. Ou said he'd not lost his appetite for energy efficiency but admitted it was more difficult to make progress without Walmart's pressure and expertise. "I spent a lot of time and energy," he said. "It really is a pity that Walmart stopped the program." (Walmart says it's still finishing the pilot phase of the program.)

If there is any silver lining to Walmart's wavering on sustainability in China, it's that other major retailers have made significant progress. Foecke's current clients include IKEA and Levi's, companies that he said took a different approach to suppliers, building more durable relationships. It wasn't a perfect model—IKEA has issues with shadow factories, too—but he was allowed to walk into factories, suggest changes, and speed up the sustainability process.

Foecke still credits Walmart for nudging other companies, and he told me he would work with them again. But he remained somewhat discouraged by what he'd seen. "I really do think they're very distracted by the weakening economy, and they don't want to spend any money on anything right now," he told me.

The NRDC's Greer said Walmart's partners had every right to be critical of the company. "I would say we, the environmental community, have been enormously patient . . . We've not only been patiently waiting, we've been actively helping." She went on, "At this point, we don't see that they're trying." When Walmart fell short on her Chinese mill program as part of its goal to cut 20 million metric tons of greenhouse gas emissions from its supply chain, she says, "I thought, 'There they go again.' It breeds cynicism. Is this just a PR effort, or is this something they're serious about?"

Critical Thinking

1. Drawing from the article, formulate your own definition for the term "sustainability."

2. In your opinion, are sustainability and affordability always mutually exclusive?

3. With a group of peers from your class, analyze the important role(s) that a giant retailer like Walmart plays in initiating shifts within the production, distribution, and retail sectors.

Create Central

www.mhhe.com/createcentral

Internet References

AlterNet
http://www.alternet.org/rss/breaking_news/98778/walmart_suppliers_in_china_charged_with_rights_abuses

China Labor Watch
https://www.chinalaborwatch.org/pro/proshow-120.html

International Institute for Sustainable Development
http://www.iisd.org/business/

Network for Business Sustainability
http://nbs.net/

Andy Kroll, "Walmart Wants You to Believe its Green Makeover Is Changing the World. Just One Hitch: China," *Mother Jones*, March/April 2012. Copyright © 2012 by Mother Jones. All rights reserved. Used with permission.

Article   Prepared by: Nisreen N. Bahnan, *Salem State University*

It's More Than Green to Be Keen

At Keen, sustainability incorporates the whole person and the society they live within.

Carol A. Finnegan, Eric M. Olson, and Stanley F. Slater

Learning Outcomes

After reading this article, you will be able to:

- Recognize the role played by corporate social responsibility in positioning a brand and designing a marketing mix.

- Analyze Keen HybridLife, the positioning effort implemented by Keen.

Does the world really need yet another shoe company? From ultra casual Crocs to ultra chic Manolo Blahniks, it would seem that this ultra-competitive $19.4 billion market (according to sustainableindustries.com) is flooded with designs for every age, taste and activity. But for the six-year-old footwear brand Keen, the answer appears to be a resounding yes. From its start-up in 2003, Keen products are now sold in more than 2,000 retail outlets worldwide. Commensurate with this, the company has seen revenues consistently grow—$20 million in 2004, to $60 million in 2006 to more than $120 million in 2007 (according to an August 8, 2008 article in the *San Francisco Times*). The key to its initial success was its innovative product design; the phenomenal growth is due to its product line and company values of product innovation and sustainability, which are redefining the outdoors and giving back to the community and environment. Early on, Keen challenged itself as a company to work toward being a company that cared about the surrounding world, both socially and environmentally. Keen began by looking at its product designs to incorporate sustainability values. It created the Ventura, a sneaker-styled shoe that was vegan. The company also repurposed materials from its footwear manufacturing process to create its bag line, and introduced a line of bags made from recycled rice bags called the Harvest line. When designing its

showroom in Portland, Ore., and its tradeshow booth, it challenged the designers to incorporate sustainable materials. It changed its shoe boxes and hang tags to be made from 100% recyclable materials. Keen considered each and every one of these steps part of its "Hybrid.think" philosophy of rethinking what is possible as a company with a conscious.

During its first year of business, the company also cancelled its marketing dollars, contributing the funds to the December 2003 Tsunami effort and setting up an ongoing giving program called Hybrid.Care.

But for Keen, it is not sufficient to just make products or implement business practices that have minimal impact upon the environment and donate to social issues. Through its products and charitable efforts, Keen seeks to enhance the physical and spiritual existence of consumers and in so doing, enhance society as well (an ambitious set of goals for a simple shoe company). Keen has sought a wider definition of sustainability, one that incorporates the whole person and the society they live within.

To do so, Keen introduced Keen HybridLife in 2006. More than just an advertising tag line, Keen HybridLife is the company's brand positioning and the embodiment of its philosophy of living a balanced and sustainable life around three core values. Keen has incorporated this philosophy into a brand tag line "Create. Play. Care. It's a way of life. We call it HybridLife" in order to attract creative thinkers, outdoor lovers, and social or environmental activists alike to its global community.

Keen articulates these three values:

Create

Create possibilities and express your vision of what is possible. Lead change and solve environmental or social issues in a new, creative way by actively engaging in the outdoors. Be motivated and awed by what is possible.

Play

Embrace the outdoors in its entirety through active participation. Reimage the outdoors as any place without a ceiling. Believe that the far edge of one place is really just the beginning of somewhere else.

Care

Engage with causes that make a positive difference around social causes and the environment through the outdoor experience. Make each choice large and small a considered one.

Kicking off their HybridLife campaign in 2006, Keen unveiled a print campaign asking customers, "How are you living a HybridLife?" Consumers sent in pictures and stories, documenting their lifestyles, and became engaged in the Keen community as a result.

So who is living the HybridLife? Keen started out serving avid outdoors-minded people in their mid-30s who live in the Pacific Northwest, with an innovative protected toe sandal called the Newport. (Think a more rugged Teva.) By the second season, Keen introduced closed-toe footwear for hiking and trail running, as well as outdoor-inspired casual footwear for both men and women. Today, the only segment not explicitly targeted is the fashion-fickle teenage market. Consequently, the company's customer base has also broadened beyond hardcore outdoors consumers to include customers "inspired by the outdoors."

As part of the Keen HybridLife campaign, the Keen marketing team implemented Stand in 2007, a marketing program to inspire consumers to think about how they could incorporate sustainability into their life. The company awarded a total of $150,000 in grant money, including three $25,000 grand prizes to creative and committed individuals who had a new idea or were implementing programs that would contribute to the sustainability effort in some tangible way. The campaign was advertised during the second half of 2007, awards were announced in April of 2008 and the winners were honored at the Stand Festival in Portland, Ore. in July 2008.

Keen continues to inspire consumers to live a Keen Hybrid Life, and to make a difference in the world around them. One example of how individuals can make a big difference is the 1 kg More program started by Zhihai Zhu in China. Several years ago, he started leading expeditions into poverty-stricken areas asking volunteers to carry in a mere 1 kg of paper, pencils or books. While the items were small items, the impact on the lives of the children of this devastated area was large. He encourages other travelers to do the same. After the devastating earthquake in Yunnan Province in May 2008, he set up children's libraries within the tent cities—where more than 4 million people will live for the next one to two years, while their homes are rebuilt. The libraries provide an outlet for the children during this time. Keen is currently developing programs to support his efforts.

Keen HybridLife is also internally directed at Keen employees who continuously challenge themselves to live by these values. Starting with small measures such as changing the printer default from color to black and white, encouraging and paying employees to take off time for volunteering, or creating a "Green Team" to identify opportunities to become more environmentally friendly, Keen employees have taken it as their responsibility to ensure the company holds true to its own message. As an example, several Keen employees spent two weeks in China in July 2008, distributing free shoes to residents of Yunnan Province after many of them lost their worldly possessions, in addition to their loved ones in the great earthquake.

So how does the HybridLife philosophy define the Keen brand? Following an aspirational branding strategy, managers sought to create marketing campaigns analogous to Nike's "Just Do It" campaign. The goal of the Keen campaign is to inspire people to follow their passion and live a balanced life. Given that 60% of its consumers own two or more pairs of its shoes/sandals, it seems fair to say that Keen is getting its message across to consumers.

Rollouts of new product lines embody this philosophy as well—from design to proliferation. Playing an active project management role, Keen outsources product concepts to a group of its independent designers. Seasonal briefings and market visits are clearly balanced by a strong brand concept and understanding of core customers. Staff members then compile the marketing information, and communicate with designers through detailed product briefs and storyboards. In a period of about nine months, marketers and designers cycle through multiple prototype samples before pre-lines are shared with key accounts for feedback, along with the storyboards. Retailers may offer suggestions on key product features, such as colors and materials, based on their specific consumer needs. Well-received designs are subsequently adopted and scheduled for production runs.

The Commuter, a new cycling shoe due out in Fall 2008, exemplifies the process. Given the economic downturn, headquarters staff noticed that there was an uptick in bicycle commuting—not only in the Portland area, but across the United States. Observing that commuting customers tended to wear the Keen Newport sandal, Keen gathered a group to ask usage questions. From those early conversations, a new cycling shoe—and category—was developed. Because the new shoe fit a need and was able to pass a basic branding litmus test, the Commuter was developed as the first shoe in a new product category. This new product promotes personal health and supports customers' efforts to improve their social surroundings, through reduced car traffic and emissions.

Product pricing is driven on a value proposition rooted in quality, durability and comfort. Keen products are priced at the higher end of the mass market business. While it is difficult to assess the degree to which consumers are willing to pay a premium for products—which they perceive as high quality, comfortable, long lasting, and with certain environmentally friendly features—clearly, Keen has been able to position its products as having premium quality. The fact that Keen sales continue to grow dramatically, while less expensive competitive products abound, suggests that the firm's target market appreciates the quality and style of the products—as well as the values for which they stand.

In choosing distributors, Keen selects partners that match its target market and have similar values. Although some overlap between distributors exists, Keen managers adjust variety and selection based upon the distributors' customers. For example, REI and Nordstrom's offer a somewhat different shoe mix and color selection, because their customers are looking for somewhat different styles. The firm also provides retailers opportunities for product training and support via its eight regional field service representatives. To support its retail partners, it has an account marketing program, with annual planning calendars and electronic exchanges of marketing communication materials. Over time, Keen strives to build trust with its retail partners, so that retailers are willing to take a risk on new products, such as The Commuter. By including retailers in the pre-line stage, Keen offers signs of trust in its partners that it hopes will be reciprocated at product rollout.

One of Keen's biggest challenges is to communicate the brand's core values in a clear and understandable way, to elicit an emotional response from global consumers. As a small company, Keen spends its marketing budget cautiously in print media, online social networks, events like the campus tours, and in-store displays. The largest spend is in print and online marketing medias, which consumes about a quarter of the budget. Keen targets the health and fitness conscious, outdoors enthusiasts and people who are socially and environmentally motivated. Accordingly, the firm places ads in magazines and works with online partners who are true to Keen's core brand values and lifestyle. Because the company has a highly regarded product, it is able to merit attention in independently rated buyer guides and other outlets, such as ABC.com and the daytime talk show Ellen. Much of the promotional activities are designed to drive customers to the company's website.

While Keen has been highly successful in North America, believing that the Keen HybridLife holds universal appeal, the company now seeks a global presence. To that end, Keen has developed a process of standardizing its global brand positioning and creative look on its international Web sites and communication channels. In the early days, national Web sites were developed on a country-by-country basis, but not necessarily replicating the look, feel and functionality of the brand site. The marketing team also has worked on standardizing all communication tools, and provides country offices with a brand guidebook that outlines the positioning and provides creative and copy direction. Local adaptations would include choosing which non-governmental organization partners should be recognized for its giving back programs, and plugging the most popular national products into the communication tools.

The sales numbers clearly demonstrate that Keen has identified a heretofore unfilled market niche. While initial market success was largely due to product innovation, the idea of a capped-toe sandal is not one that can easily be protected from competitors. Indeed competitors such as Teva have now come out with their own capped-toed sandals. Consequently, the long-term success of Keen will largely be dependent upon the position the firm and its products hold in the minds of consumers. Keen has taken a pioneering position in the industry, by aligning itself and its products with the issue of living a balanced life and incorporating sustainability in its broadest sense. It now remains to be seen if efforts to build a distinctive brand are strong enough to overcome competitors' attempts to hijack Keen's HybridLife message.

Critical Thinking

1. In your opinion, what is the key to Keen's initial success and future phenomenal growth?
2. In your own words summarize Keen HybridLife, the company's brand position.

Create Central

www.mhhe.com/createcentral

Internet References

BSR
   http://www.bsr.org/
CSR Wire
   http://www.csrwire.com/directory
Keen Footwear
   http://www.keenfootwear.com/us/en/

Carol A. Finnegan; Eric M. Olson; Stanley F. Slater, "It's More than Green to be Keen," *Marketing Management,* September/October 2009. Copyright © 2009 by American Marketing Association. All rights reserved. Used with permission.

Unit 2

UNIT

Prepared by: Nisreen N. Bahnan, *Salem State University*

Research, Markets, and Consumer Behavior

"It is not the strongest of the species that survives, nor the most intelligent that survives. It is the one that is most adaptable to change."

— Charles Darwin

If marketing activities were all we knew about an individual, we would know a great deal. By tracing these daily activities over only a short period of time, we could probably guess rather accurately that person's tastes, understand much of his or her system of personal values, and learn quite a bit about how he or she deals with the world.

In a sense, this is a key to successful marketing management: tracing a market's activities and understanding its behavior. However, in spite of the increasing sophistication of market research techniques, this task is not easy. Today, a new society is evolving out of the changing lifestyles of Americans, and these divergent lifestyles have put great pressure on the marketer who hopes to identify and profitably reach a target market. At the same time, however, each change in consumer behavior leads to new marketing opportunities. According to James White, President and CEO of Jamba Juice: *"the best leaders and the best companies will leverage and exploit diversity to help make their organizations more relevant and sustainable. Their workforce will view the world differently. They will come up with better solutions and be more effective in the market by seeing the opportunities that others in the industry do not see."*

The writings in this unit were selected to provide information and insight into emerging trends in thought and practice within the areas of research and targeting.

Within the *Market Research* subsection, the common theme is the recent explosion of social and mobile media. This results in a wealth of online data, flexibility and ease of electronic data collection, and a more receptive audience, all of which have fast-tracked the research evolution.

The focus of the *Markets and Demographics* subsection is diversity. In the words of President Jimmy Carter: "We have become not a melting pot but a beautiful mosaic. Different people, different beliefs, different yearnings, different hopes, different dreams." The readings examine the importance of demographic and psychographic data, economic forces, and age considerations in making better marketing decisions. We look at an illustration of content analysis—where media reflects reality—that of an ever-growing demographic, cultural and social diversity with the U.S. Consumer packaged goods companies invest significant resources in consumer research to better embrace the heterogeneity of the market and the impact that heterogeneity has on consumers' shopping behavior. Articles profile specific segments such as the intriguing Millennial generation, with its growing influence and importance to marketers.

The articles in the final subsection tackle the ill-defined topic of *consumer behavior* and psychology, namely the role of emotion in purchase and consumption behavior. The common premise across the three articles is that consumers are incapable or unwilling to lucidly communicate their reasons for choosing a certain brand. In some cases, preferences and purchases may be linked to consumers' physiology and perception, and thus may be fickle and transient, as Apple's Steve Jobs so aptly stated: "You can't just ask customers what they want and then try to give that to them. By the time you get it built, they'll want something new."

Article   Prepared by: Nisreen N. Bahnan, *Salem State University*

Why Traditional Market Research Is a Waste of Time

DR GAVIN SYMANOWITZ

Learning Outcomes

After reading this article, you will be able to:

- Identify potential problems and limitations associated with using traditional market research.

- Analyze the reasons behind these limitations and formulate ideas for alternative approaches to research.

When marketer Dietrich Mateschitz visited Thailand 30 years ago, he discovered the benefits of a syrupy tonic drink sold in pharmacies as an energy booster. He approached Chaleo Yoovidhya, owner of the tonic drink company, with the idea of introducing the drink to the West. It would have to change though, to appeal to Western tastes. While he kept the main ingredients intact, Mateschitz carbonated the drink and packaged it in a slim blue and silver can. He also changed the name from the original Krating Daeng (translated from Thai as "red water buffalo") to the more familiar Red Bull.

He then did some market research to test the concept. The results were catastrophic. "People didn't believe the taste, the logo, the brand name," he chuckles. "I'd never before experienced such a disaster." Mateschitz ignored the market research and set up offices in the Austrian town of Fuschl.

Fast forward three decades and Red Bull has been a spectacular success story. Today it sells upwards of 5 bn cans annually across 165 countries, and employs over 8000 people. Mateschitz's wealth is estimated at $7 bn, making him one of the wealthiest people in Austria. Along the way, the drink that "gives you wings" has created an entirely new category in the global beverage market: the energy drink.

This is not the first time that market research has got it completely wrong. When Coca-Cola started experiencing a slump in sales in the early 1980s, it wanted to know why. According to the softdrink giant's research, the main factor affecting the decline was taste. So they set about concocting a new formulation that was sweeter than the original flavour. Then it embarked on a massive market research exercise, conducting 200 000 blind taste tests. Over half of the subjects preferred the new formulation to the original flavour and to competitor Pepsi. On the strength of these results, Coke withdrew the current flavour from the market and introduced New Coke. The results were disastrous. People hated it. The brand was eventually withdrawn as customers demanded that 'Classic' Coke be returned to the shelves. New Coke has gone down in history as one of the most spectacular new product failures of all time. By extension, it's also one of the most spectacular market research failures of all time.

So Why Does Market Research Get It Wrong So Often?

There is an old joke about the accountant who was being interviewed for a job. "What is two plus two?" asks the interviewer. The accountant leans across the desk and replies in a low voice: "How much do you want it to be?"

The problem with most market research is that it can often be interpreted in the way we want it to be. Our natural tendency is to look at survey results in a way that appears to be consistent with our prior beliefs. This well-known psychological trap is called the confirmation bias. So as the data rolls in, we shout out things like "Yes, I knew it!" or "See, I told you so!" even when there is no objective evidence to support our position. Very few market research exercises begin from a point of neutral investigation; inevitably the research has been commissioned to confirm a particular point of view (such as the attractiveness of a new product idea). In many cases, huge sums have already been paid on product development and there is a strong need to justify this expenditure and continue down the product development path. As David Ogilvy, the father of advertising, once said: "Some people use research like a drunkard uses a lamppost: for support, not illumination."

In fact, the questionnaire is often designed to lead respondents to answer in a particular direction. Sometimes this is deliberate (and hence unethical) and sometimes it stems from ignorance. For example, suppose you were conducting an opinion poll on what people think about abortion. If you were a religious group conducting the research and wanted to bias the results in your favour, you might ask "Are you in favour of the right to life?" On the other hand, if you were an NGO representing the interests of young single mothers you might bias the results in the other direction by asking "Are you in favour of giving people the choice when it comes to their bodies?" In both cases, the natural answer is "yes". In fact, people's natural tendency is to say what they think the interviewer wants to hear anyway.

Another problem with traditional market research is that there is usually a basic underlying premise, which is not questioned. For example, suppose a bank has decided to deliver its cheque books in a fancy new chequebook holder. It might ask potential customers questions such as "Would you prefer it in a red or black color?" or "How many compartments would you like in your new cheque-book holder?" or even "How much more often will you use your cheque book because of the fancy new cheque-book holder?" Of course, if customers don't want a cheque-book in the first place, then none of these questions matter.

Many people would be surprised to discover that there is a science behind questionnaire construction and sampling design (I should know, I used to teach it to university statistics students). Just because anyone can come up with a questionnaire, it doesn't mean that they should. With the rise in popularity of online survey sites, and easy access to online networks, it is incredibly easy to slap together a quick survey to get market feedback. As one indicator of this worrying trend, I often get invited to participate in research conducted by MBA students for their dissertation. These are conducted under the auspices of business schools that are fiercely protective of their reputations, and yet the quality of the questionnaires is usually incredibly poor. These are our future business leaders, so little wonder there is such a lack of respect for proper questionnaire design and the need to avoid biased samples in the broader business environment.

The Biggest Problem of All

The biggest problem with traditional market research is the fact that it is unavoidably artificial. We pose hypothetical scenarios and ask people how they think they would react. We ask questions such as "If we introduced X, how often would you visit the store?" or "How much extra would you spend if we offered a discount of X?"

In reality, people's purchasing decisions are incredibly complex and it rarely comes down to a single factor such as price. We simply cannot divorce branding elements, emotional cues and belief structures from the decision-making process in a real environment. People might like to think they'll behave in a certain way in a certain environment but the reality is usually quite different. So when they answer our market research question in a particular way, they may actually believe their answer, even if this proves to be very different from how they behave when the product is actually launched.

Current market research conventions actually exacerbate the problem. For example, it is regarded as poor form to reveal the name of the sponsoring brand when conducting a market research exercise. The interviewer will typically say that they are conducting the research on behalf of "a large telecoms company." In reality, whether the new offering is to be launched by Vodacom or MTN or Cell C or Telkom will have a material impact on how people feel about the offering. It should definitely form part of the questionnaire. When asked why they persist with this silly convention, market research companies typically answer that it is for scientific validity. They don't realise it's exactly the opposite.

How Can We Do It Better?

If the biggest problem with the market research is that it is artificial, the way to do it properly is to create a realistic environment instead. Instead of asking people if they would buy a certain product, rather present them with a real-life version of the product and ask them to take out their wallets. This is the acid test—as they say, "money talks, BS walks."

One potential criticism of this approach is that the company would need to go through the full product development process just to be able to present the respondent with the product in real life. Five years ago this may have been true but not today. The incredible rise in rapid prototyping techniques such as 3D printing have revolutionized what is possible. Consider the photograph of a pap cooker, produced by local product development specialists Ideanav.

Imagine seeing this in a glossy home products magazine and then being presented with the opportunity to buy it for Rs. 250. Would you phone the number in the advert to place your order? We could test this in a live environment and get a really accurate picture of what customers in the target market thought about the product and whether they would be willing to buy it.

Would it surprise you to know that the product doesn't actually exist? That the picture above was created using advanced photoshopping techniques to create a realistic representation of what the product could look like if it was eventually produced? Ideanav did actually create a working prototype using a 3D printer for a few thousand rand, to test the product in a live environment. The results of this market research costs very little but gives incredibly useful insights into the potential success (or otherwise) of the proposed product.

If you have a new product or service idea, can you create an environment to test your idea as realistically as possible? Can you scale it down (perhaps with a small subset of customers or with a limited-feature working prototype) so that potential customers can get a realistic feel for your new product or service? Can you get them to pay real cash for your product or service—even if they only discover later that it is not yet available? This is the way to do effective market research.

We've also seen the recent explosion of crowd-funding websites, where innovators can propose a new product idea along with a request for a certain amount of funding to make their dream a reality. Consumers who like the idea can pledge a certain amount (usually a few dollars) and then receive certain benefits such as a discount when the item is eventually produced. It's still early days, but the crowdfunding model has the potential to revolutionize financing for new products. However, the model is particularly powerful for another reason, which is often glossed over. If 5 000 people think your idea is a good one—and are prepared to put their hard-earned money behind it—then that's a pretty good signal that there will be good demand for the product when it's launched. You don't need to do market research to validate the idea, it's built into the process.

When done properly, market research can be an incredibly valuable tool, proving invaluable insights. However, when done badly, it can be incredibly dangerous, leading to all the wrong conclusions. The German rocket scientist Wernher von Braun said: "Research is what I'm doing when I don't know what I'm doing." Make sure that doesn't happen when it comes to your next big idea.

Critical Thinking

1. In your own words, explain what is meant by confirmation bias in market research.
2. List and discuss some other potential problems with traditional research.
3. Given all the limitations of traditional research, brainstorm some alternative methods for companies to gather data for use in decision-making and strategy-setting.

Create Central

www.mhhe.com/createcentral

Internet References

ESOMAR World Research
http://www.esomar.org/index.php
Marketing Minds Research
http://www.marketingmindsresearch.com/case_study.html
Marketing Research Association
http://www.marketingresearch.org/

Gavin Symanowitz, "Why Traditional Market Research is a Waste of Time," *Finweek*, March 6, 2014. Copyright © 2014 by Finweek. All rights reserved. Used with permission.

Article   Prepared by: Nisreen N. Bahnan, *Salem State University*

Closer to the Truth

Online surveys, focus groups and other digitally driven research methods by which you actively compile customer data now are supported by passive, observational data collection methods such as behavioral tracking. Use the full arsenal to hone in on your target.

MOLLY SOAT

Learning Outcomes

After reading this article, you will be able to:

- Recognize that there are various approaches to collecting consumer data through marketing research.

- Distinguish between passively-compiled and actively compiled online consumer data.

- Compare the advantages and disadvantages of using these two approaches to online data collection.

Online research has been in the crosshairs for some time. First it was the quality of online samples: Many question whether these people are who they say they are and are giving their honest feedback. Now the marketplace's attention has moved on to the value—and virtue—of online behavioral tracking.

In this era of big data, scraping the Web for information is almost standard practice, but the question is, how valuable is this passively compiled data compared with the consumer information and insights that researchers compile actively through traditional surveys and focus groups? You shouldn't use one method to the exclusion of the other, of course, but how much weight should you give to the readily available consumer data proliferating online? The consensus is that passively compiled data certainly can help you get closer to the truth regarding consumer behaviors, but it could—and probably should—represent a smaller piece of the research pie than the industry chatter and seemingly endless media attention would lead you to believe.

Through the Looking Glass

Data compiled from tracking consumers' online behaviors anonymously—which sites they visit, how long they linger, what they search for and buy, and so on—allows marketers to flesh out general customer data by adding a fly-on-the-wall perspective to self-reported insights, experts say. "Where survey research is a great way to find out the 'why' and the 'how,' behavioral tracking lets you find out the 'how much' and the 'how often' and the 'where,'" says Gina Sverdlov, market research analyst at Cambridge, Mass.-based Forrester Research Inc. and author of Forrester's recently released report called "Combining Survey Research and Behavioral Tracking Creates Deeper Insights."

Sherrill Mane, senior vice president of research, analytics and measurement at the Interactive Advertising Bureau (IAB), a New York-based member association that is a proponent of behavioral tracking and targeting, concurs. Passively compiled data gathered through behavior tracking is chiefly a "form of enrichment," she says, "because there is always a gap between what consumers tell you they think, what consumers tell you they intend to do and what consumers actually do."

Online behavioral tracking eliminates the age-old recall problem that often skews survey results. Consumers may remember that they "liked" a company on Facebook when they're asked in a survey, but they'd have a tough time remembering the dates, times and frequency of their "likes." "Behavioral tracking really provides that granularity and details that people won't necessarily recall," Forrester's Sverdlov says.

Plus, passively compiled data is not subject to survey bias. Many people can interpret a survey question differently, there by skewing the resulting data. Survey data and focus groups also cause consumers to change their answers based on "social desirability," which is the tendency for respondents to adapt their responses to make them sound better rather than simply being straight forward. "In the old days of research . . . you didn't have technology that was capable of collecting all of this information. You would try to devise multi-methodologies for one study so you could cross-check because you always know that there are things like social desirability," Mane says. "When you have data that looks at how people actually behave and you know how to put the pieces together, you can find where there are missing links in the various data sets and learn how to interpret them so you can make better decisions."

Not all behavioral tracking is the anonymously compiled data collected via cookies embedded on consumers' PCs. There are also large-scale, opt-in tracking programs. Boston-based Compete Inc. gathers digital data for corporate clients including Carlson Rezidor Hotel Group and Hyundai. Michael Perlman, vice president of agency and publisher solutions at Compete, explains that the ability to track thousands of consumers online allows marketers to get a comprehensive view of consumer behavior that traverses all demographics. "Looking at the behavior and then looking at thousands of users, and taking averages and looking at a whole market, you really start to get insight into consumer behavior," he says.

"By looking at consumer behavior online, you can understand performance of past campaigns, you can successfully plan future media campaigns and you can inform site-design decisions. . . . By understanding what's resonating with consumers and how they're engaging and using your particular properties, you can really drive a lot of interesting and useful insight that's actionable."

Despite the fact that consumers opt into Compete's tracking program and therefore are aware that their online behaviors are being observed, Perlman says that the social desirability bias doesn't affect the results. "Our panel is solarge at 2 million people and, for the most part, it's very unobtrusive to the user as far as us being able to get our data," he says. "It's not interrupting their browser activity at all, so we're not concerned about [social desirability bias]."

Behavioral tracking provides you with customer data in real time, adds Joe Bugajski, managing vice president of Web, mobile and application development at Stamford, Conn.-based research firm Gartner Inc.

"We can learn [a consumer's] response to the way we present ourselves. We can learn about their beliefs concerning us or our products, or our management or the company as a whole, so that we can learn in ways that we really couldn't get before without a serious amount of expenditures. We can . . . make adjustments on the fly," he says.

No Holy Grail

While it is generally believed that more data is better data, Andrea Matwyshyn, assistant professor of legal studies and business ethics at the University of Pennsylvania's Wharton School, warns that more isn't always more when it comes to behavioral data. It's better to be selective, she says. "Thinking through not only the goal of national data aggregation, but the goal of strategic data aggregation, and thinking about the downsides of over-collection, that's the one message that sometimes gets lost in the discussion around marketing, particularly in the context of behavioral advertising."

Further, Matwyshyn says, "The context is sort of absent in standard behavioral tracking, and when context is imagined by the marketer to provide a broader understanding for themselves in terms of how they might leverage that information, that's also where consumers start to become annoyed with marketers because they see preferences being imputed to them that don't reflect the reality of what their preferences are."

Larry Ponemon, director of the Traverse City, Mich.-based Ponemon Institute, a research center and consulting firm focused on information-security policy—who's familiar with not only the inherent privacy concerns when compiling online data, but also the rationale for compiling such data in the first place—points out that while behavioral data can be "good enough" to support on-the-fly marketing decisions, you should keep in mind that it most likely isn't the most reliable resource. "Marketers need to have information quickly that can actually come to the right person and so I would say that's probably the No. 1 advantage: the ability to get a profile sufficiently and easily, and that's pretty accurate . . . without having to do exorbitant things and having fancy models in-house. . . . The data that you collect may not be as accurate, but it can be good enough for what you're trying to deliver," he says. To ensure the quality of the behavioral data gathered, Ponemon says, make sure that the information comes from a reliable source and includes a time stamp or other verifiable identification, and that the information is collected with the consent of the consumer as often as possible to avoid potential privacy issues down the road.

Mixing with the Tried and True

When it comes to the "why" of a consumer's behavior online, actively compiled data is still the best method for researching attitude, sentiment and motivation. "When you do behavioral tracking, you can't get everything. You can get their online behavior—what websites they're visiting, what they're buying online, how much time they're spending on Facebook—but you can't get things like their sentiments and attitudes, you can't get their market share, you can't get a profile of what consumers want," Forrester's Sverdlov says.

Actively compiled online research also is the only way to conduct prelaunch research. "If you're a company that's launching a new product that doesn't exist yet, there's no behavioral data to track. Marketers can use some quantitative techniques such as conjoint analysis or purchase driver analysis to test product features and optimize a hypothetical product, pricing and marketing messaging prior to market launch so there by they would maximize the company's chances of success prior to going to market," Sverdlov says.

Ideally, marketers can combine passively and actively compiled data to get the fullest picture of consumers' behaviors online. With social media, marketers now are able to not only engage with consumers, but also get real-time feedback without infringing on privacy issues or potentially bothering the consumer with time-consuming survey requests. Researchers are increasingly using sentiment analysis to augment their market research—that is, "the extraction of beliefs about people, products and organizations that traverse through Twitter, that go onto Facebook, that show up in other [social] media," Gartner's Bugajski explains.

Online chat functionalities are a relatively new research tool, as well. Matwyshyn lauds the increasingly popular tool as a balance between actively and passively compiled consumer data. "One trend that I've noticed increasing online is the immediate gratification of a chat vehicle for consumers. . . . That kind of an interaction, which can give feedback immediately in terms of what's accessible and successful about the site and what consumers are having trouble with, that's a win-win because it focuses the consumer in trying to complete a transaction and it gives feedback . . . and the consumer feels like it's not invasive; the consumer feels like it's helpful."

Brad MacDonald, the Brussels, Belgium based Carlson Rezidor Hotel Group's senior director of customer strategy, analytics and partner marketing in the U.S., has been tracking and studying the behavior of the hotel chain's online customers for the past three years. Carlson uses a combination of in-house and out sourced data-aggregation methods, mainly tracking the Web traffic into, around and out of the Carlson booking site. "We've taken customer profiles for people who use the Web heavily, for people who don't use the Web heavily, people with different brand preferences, and we've designed some surveys around [those profiles]." MacDonald supplements the data that he gathers through behavioral tracking and other online observations with insights compiled from surveys, he says, to find out the "why" behind the "what," as Forrester's Sverdlov would say.

Behavioral tracking is just one piece—albeit an important piece—of an ever evolving digital research pie, the IAB's Mane says. "The human capacity for having emotional connections, assimilating information, acting on information, is far more complex than one data set or the other, so you're always going to need combinations, but they're going to become more and more innovative—the way that you use data, the way that you speak to consumers, the way that you listen to consumers," she says. "We didn't have ways to *listen* to consumers before digital media, social media."

Adds Bugajski, "The more we can take some of these other sources of information such as sentiment analysis, quick-stream analyses, interactions with the users in a chat session, the more that we can extract value from those and combine that with our traditional marketing data, the more robust a solution we can build to deliver our products to the market."

Survey data can get you only so far. Adding data gleaned from observing Web users in action gets you closer to your target, so take aim with as many research methods as you can muster.

Critical Thinking

1. List and discuss the advantages and disadvantages of passively-compiled online behavioral tracking.

2. Do you agree with the main premise of the article that combining both passively compiled and actively compiled data is the most effective for consumer research? Justify your response.

3. In your opinion, what are some ethical concerns with collecting and using passively-compiled online behavioral tracking?

Create Central

www.mhhe.com/createcentral

Internet References

Electronic Frontier Foundation
  https://www.eff.org/issues/online-behavioral-tracking
Electronic Privacy Information Center
  http://epic.org/

Molly Soat, "Closer to the Truth," *Marketing News*, June 30, 2012, pp. 15–17. Copyright © 2012 by American Marketing Association. All rights reserved. Used with permission.

Article   Prepared by: Nisreen N. Bahnan, *Salem State University*

Respect Your Elders

Digital marketing techniques might be flashy and young, but conventional marketing strategies haven't lost their impact. The ideal modern marketing mix makes room for both.

Tom Stein and Tim Devaney

Learning Outcomes

After reading this article, you will be able to:

- Define and understand digital marketing strategies.

- Compare traditional (conventional) promotional and digital marketing techniques and strategies.

- Recognize that the best approach to promotion includes both traditional and digital marketing techniques.

Once the cool but unnecessary add-on to most companies' marketing strategies, digital marketing now leads the charge, and offline strategies, tactics and channels often complement marketers' increasingly Web- and mobile-focused efforts. The tide has officially turned, and if you're not incorporating blogs, social networks, search advertising, QR codes, geo-targeted promotions and the like into your marketing strategy, you're unapologetically behind the times and at risk of generating ineffective marketing initiatives—or so it would seem.

As the American Marketing Association and countless trade groups and business publications the world over have reported, all companies should at least have an online presence and invest in regular search marketing and social marketing efforts, but the demise of conventional, offline marketing strategies and tactics has been greatly exaggerated. Traditional techniques such as print advertising and direct mail still work—and work well—and many successful marketing strategies today have found the right balance between those traditional techniques and their flashier digital counterparts.

Face Time Beats Facebook

A November 2011 survey by Constant Contact Inc., a Waltham, Mass.-based firm that specializes in helping small businesses with their e-mail marketing, online surveys and events, shows that while most small businesses now market online and many are embracing social media, they also remain committed to more conventional methods. Eighty-one percent of small-business executives who responded to the survey said that they use Facebook and other social sites for marketing, and the same percentage reported that they also use good, old-fashioned face time. And while 66 percent invest in online advertising, 71 percent still invest in print ads.

Meanwhile, on the receiving end, customers say that social media is one of the least effective ways for a business to gain their loyalty, according to a November 2011 survey by Stamford, Conn.-based customer communications management firm Pitney Bowes Inc. that polled customers in the United States and United Kingdom. Just 18 percent of survey respondents said that interaction with a business via Facebook, Twitter or some other social network would make them more likely to buy from the business again, and for small businesses, that number drops to 15 percent. The most effective ways to engender customer loyalty, according to the survey, are offering customers home delivery options and arming them with the ability to choose which communication channel through which they'd prefer to connect with your company.

In with the Old

Old-school methods are still a vital tool in marketers' kits—and might be even more effective now. Mike Sprouse, president

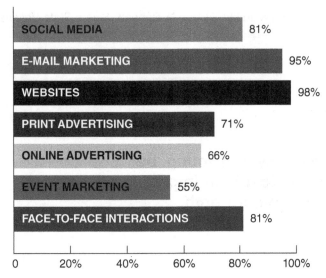

SOCIAL MEDIA	81%
E-MAIL MARKETING	95%
WEBSITES	98%
PRINT ADVERTISING	71%
ONLINE ADVERTISING	66%
EVENT MARKETING	55%
FACE-TO-FACE INTERACTIONS	81%

0   20%   40%   60%   80%   100%

The modern marketing mix.   Percentage of respondents who report using the tactic/channel

Source: The Fall 2011 Attitudes and Outlook Survey by Constant Contact Inc. polled 1,972 mostly United States-based respondents across a range of small businesses in both business-to-business and business-to-consumer industries.

and CEO of Sprouse Marketing Group, a full-service firm with clients such as Salesforce.com and Yahoo, and author of *The Greatness Gap,* says that if the herd is zigging to social marketing, savvy businesses should zag toward traditional media such as TV and print. "If 95 percent of marketers go one way, I want to be among the 5 percent going the other," he says. "Mail volume is down, but people still get—and open—mail, so why wouldn't I want to have my mail piece in someone's mailbox with, say, three other pieces, as opposed to years ago when it was with 10 other pieces? The old-school channels haven't disappeared; they're just not in vogue. But smart marketers know how to leverage that."

David Langton, principal and co-founder of New York-based communications design firm Langton Cherubino Group Ltd. and co-author of *Visual Marketing: 99 Proven Ways for Small Businesses to Market with Images and Design,* says that there's a story in his book about a building contractor who mailed postcards of his work to a list of prospects. Years later, his card was still generating new business. "People held onto that postcard," Langton says. "They put it on the fridge or stuck it in a book. Traditional marketing has stronger staying power than the ephemeral digital work we're bombarded with. It's easier to keep a postcard and view it multiple times than the e-mails and banner ads we swat away every day."

In fact, one survey found that consumers consider online advertising to be twice as annoying as offline ads. In a survey for

the 2010 digital marketing show ad:tech London, respondents called traditional advertising more informative, entertaining and necessary than online, with 69 percent saying that traditional advertising was relevant to them, compared with just 45 percent for online.

It's All about Balance

Of course, any business that relies too heavily on old-school marketing tactics risks looking, well, old-school. Coupled with the fact that online marketing has proven to be effective, this means that marketers should find a balance between new and old.

Most small businesses know this. The aforementioned survey by Constant Contact reports that 65 percent of small businesses use social media tools in conjunction with other forms of marketing. Offline campaigns that might otherwise look stodgy—a door hanger, a windshield flyer—can be energized with a QR code and URLs for your Facebook and Twitter accounts. Word of mouth, widely considered to be the most powerful form of advertising, gets a digital boost when satisfied customers share their experiences online in consumer-generated reviews and blog posts.

Even some businesses that operate entirely online are rediscovering the power of offline marketing. Fan Bi, co-founder of Blank Label, a Boston-based e-commerce retailer that lets customers design their own dress shirts, says that his company tried Facebook—and he wasn't impressed.

"We spent an hour a day thinking up engaging messages to post on our page," he says. "We were getting thousands of likes, but we weren't really seeing any customers come through Facebook."

Traditional marketing tactics have been much more effective, Bi says. He and his partners call and write to reporters and editors to pitch their story directly, and Blank Label has so far been featured in *The New York Times, Bloomberg Businessweek, Fast Company* and *Forbes.* Each time a story has run in a print publication, Blank Label has experienced a jump in sales.

"It's funny," Bi says. "Most people think old-school marketing is dying and social media is the wave of the future. In reality, without old-fashioned media relations and PR, we'd never have been able to grow our business so quickly."

Critical Thinking

1. The United States Baby Boomer cohort is significant in size and purchasing power. With a small group of peers, conduct some research on baby boomers and generate a profile of this cohort.

2. Summarize the article's main premise in regards to digital marketing techniques.

Create Central

www.mhhe.com/createcentral

Internet References

Social Media Today

http://socialmediatoday.com/

Social Media Week

http://socialmediaweek.org/

TOM STEIN and **TIM DEVANEY** are freelance writers based in Palo Alto, Calif.

Tom Stein; Tim Devaney, "Respect Your Elders," *Marketing News,* April 30, 2012, pp. 20–21. Copyright © 2012 by American Marketing Association. All rights reserved. Used with permission.

Article

Prepared by: Nisreen N. Bahnan, *Salem State University*

Do You Have a Millennial Marketing Strategy?

The Millennial generation is larger than the Baby Boomers and three times bigger than Generation X. Understanding their needs, tastes and behaviors will impact your business.

JEFF FROMM

Learning Outcomes

After reading this article, you will be able to:

- Understand the impact of demographics on marketing trends and practices.

- Identify the different generational cohorts in the U.S.

- Identify distinctive characteristics of the Millennial generation.

To determine the most important trend affecting your future sales growth, there's no need to look further than the up-and-coming Millennial generation.

Millennials, ages 18–34, represent about 25 percent of the U.S. population. They are entering your stores, your restaurants and your work force, in many cases for the first time. They represent about $200 billion in direct purchasing power and $500 billion in indirect spending due to their influence on older generations.

Kansas City ad agency Barkley, in partnership with Service Management Group and The Boston Consulting Group, recently completed a research study among 4,000 Millennials and 1,025 adults in a contrast group. The research results are presented in "American Millennials: Deciphering The Enigma Generation." It's a far-reaching study with more 3,500,000 data points that reveals insights that will definitely have an impact on franchisors and franchisees in 2012 and beyond.

Millennials are 2.5 Times More Likely to Be Early Adopters of Technology

If your company is in the restaurant or retail sectors and hasn't built its go-forward technology strategy and woven it into a customer journey or experience design, it might be best to hit the panic button now.

Millennials report using a variety of technology tools before, during and after they dine and shop. According to Forrester Research, the rate of smart phone proliferation is expected to continue to increase in 2012.

This generation expects mobile-friendly websites, Facebook presence, quick responses to tweets and substantive rewards for having the most check-ins on Foursquare or Gowalla. If your organization doesn't have a strong digital and technology strategy in place, it risks losing the Millennial consumer spend.

A great example of integrating technology into your experience design is LIVESTRONG Sporting Park in Kansas City. They have QR Codes on all 20,000 seats for quick check-in and personalization on the Sporting Club's own social network before during and after soccer matches. Now that's taking a position on customizing the experience for each and every guest.

Millennials Watch Saturday Night Live Sunday on Hulu

Television isn't dead. Like their older counterparts, Millennials are consuming lots of TV, but they watch it differently. They aren't as likely to DVR or Tivo their favorite shows. When they're not watching live TV, they are much more likely to watch shows on Hulu—mainly on their laptops—to the tune of a shocking 42 percent. Integrating non-traditional media into your marketing mix in a relevant way absolutely makes sense.

Not only do Millennials catch their favorite shows digitally, 58 percent of them share video content with their friends. This is not a life-stage trend. This generation is digital at the core.

Millennials Seek Peer Affirmation and Advice

Perhaps because of their need to share and to find commonalities, 70 percent of Millennials reported feeling more excited when their friends agreed with them about where to shop, eat and play—and, of course, they connect with these friends online. Only 48 percent of adults were as heavily influenced by their friends and colleagues. Whether due to their youth or as an indirect result of growing up in the social media age, Millennials yearn for information from their peers. Social scientists tell us that social pressure is a significant influencing factor on human behavior. For 18–34 year olds, this phenomenon seems especially true.

Franchisors looking to market to Millennials should not shy away from social media out of concern about its inherent risks. Whatever platform your company chooses, social media enables the conversation and their participation which is crucial. It should be the eyes and ears into the Millennial generation to learn what's being said to whom, when and why. And yes, if done authentically, social media should also be your franchise's voice.

Millennials Crave Adventure

One topic of the conversation might be your most recent exploit. This doesn't mean fraternity-style drinking games. It's about your physical and intellectual journeys and accomplishments. The large majority of Millennials, 70 percent, want to visit every continent in their lifetime. Fewer than half of adults report that goal.

This craving for adventure isn't just based on a desire to be citizens of the world. Millennials crave more adventure in their daily lives. This can translate into your restaurant in terms of exotic flavors or your retail store in terms of unique experiences.

Restaurant Marketers: Do You Have a Snacking Day-Part Strategy?

Not only do Millennials report a desire for adventure, they think life should be fun. Whether shopping, dining out or immersed in their mobile devices, Millennials prefer the music turned up and the atmosphere casual.

If you want to pick up more shares of the stomach with Millennials, think outside of your traditional day-part strategies because the opportunities abound in snacking. Millennials crave snacking opportunities, and are more than twice as likely as older people to seek them out mid-morning, mid-afternoon and late at night. When Barkley worked with Sonic Corporation to introduce the Sonic Happy Hour, which offers half-price fountain drinks and slushes every day from 2 p.m. to 4 p.m., they found that it drove material sales growth and during a fringe part of the day for most restaurant marketers.

Retail Marketers: Your Associates Will Play a Critical Role

If your business is a retail franchise, your leaders already know that its sales associates are one of the first representatives of your brand. The aforementioned Millennials research reveals that franchises would be smart to hire them as walking, talking mannequins. When female Millennials were asked a series of questions about where they purchase a fashion brand, it became clear that if your store associates don't know the trends and don't look the part, Millennials will not be spending their money in your stores.

Associates should wear your brand's apparel (or use your product) and be genuinely enthusiastic about it. Due to their love of brands and tendency to seek out peer reviews and source information, Millennials can spot a fake before they've even entered your doors. Combine that astuteness with their skepticism of corporations and it's clear that carefully hiring and training your sales associates is time and money well-spent.

Since the Millennial generation is larger than the Baby Boomers and three times bigger than Generation X, your understanding of their needs, tastes and behaviors will clearly shape who wins the greatest share of wallet.

Critical Thinking

1. "The Millennial generation is larger than the Baby Boomers and three times bigger than Generation X." With a small group of peers, conduct some research on Millennials and generate a profile of this cohort.

2. In what way is the current generation of Millennials (people aged 18–34) of today different than previous generations of this age cohort?

Create Central

www.mhhe.com/createcentral

Internet References

Pew Research Center
    http://www.pewresearch.org/2009/12/10/the-millennials/

United States Census Bureau
    http://www.census.gov/

Jeff Fromm, "Do You Have a Millennial Marketing Strategy?" *Franchising World*, September 2011. Copyright © 2011 by International Franchise Association. All rights reserved. Used with permission.

Article

Prepared by: Nisreen N. Bahnan, *Salem State University*

Targeting Demographics in Beverage Marketing

Identifying preferences of the most influential groups in the nation.

STEPHANIE HILDEBRANDT

Learning Outcomes

After reading this article, you will be able to:

- Comprehend the impact of demographics on marketing strategies, particularly for consumer packaged goods (CPG) companies.

- Gain familiarity with the growing Hispanic segment in the U.S.

- Gain exposure to other demographic segments of growing importance to companies in CPG industry.

The united states received the name "the melting pot" in the 18th century by welcoming a diverse mixture of people into the country and melding them into one common culture. However, some would prefer to use the metaphor of a mosaic or salad bowl, which represents a number of different cultures yet retains the distinctions between them. Likewise, many consumer packaged goods (CPG) companies invest a lot of time and research into learning about their consumers and how their ethnicities, genders, values and geographic locations impact their shopping decisions. As a result, companies have the opportunity to strengthen their marketing programs to better reach these consumers.

The marketing preferences for some of these demographics reflect the general population, but other groups stand out from the crowd. For instance, Hispanics are the fastest-growing consumer group in the United States, making up 16 percent of the population, Chicago-based SymphonyIRI Group reports. The segment grew 43 percent in the last 10 years, spends nearly

8 percent more on CPGs than any other race, and is expected to hold $1.3 trillion in purchasing power this year, the market research firm adds.

"Hispanic consumers are a key growth segment, with buying power increasing 50 percent through 2015," said Kris Licht, partner, consumer practice at McKinsey & Co., Colorado Springs, Colo., in a statement. According to the 2012 Customer and Management Channel Survey compiled by McKinsey & Co., New York-based Nielsen and the Washington, D.C.-based Grocery Manufacturers Association, the top-performing CPG companies in their categories are three times more likely to invest in high-growth retail channels and the Hispanic market.

Acknowledging the Micro-Segments

However, it's important to note that Hispanic consumers should not be lumped into one large group.

"To connect with Hispanic shoppers and develop meaningful, lasting relationships, it is critical that marketers approach Hispanic shoppers with unique, targeted marketing strategies that celebrate the many micro-segments that exist within the Hispanic marketplace," said Staci Covkin, principal of consumer and shopper insights for SymphonyIRI and author of "Diverse and Distinct: The Hispanic Population Delivers Numerous Segments and Opportunities—and an Exceptionally Fast-Growing Market," in a statement. Findings from the publication are based on a detailed set of reports that empower CPG marketers to compare the shopping and purchasing habits and attitudes of unacculturated and bicultural Hispanics to those of more acculturated Hispanic households, as well as to the non-Hispanic population, the market research firm says.

The Hispanic population is diverse, and each segment has distinct methods of engaging with, reacting to and building relationships with CPG brands, SymphonyIRI says. Therefore, companies should recognize and respond to this diversity by accounting for factors such as country of origin, age and life stage. According to the report, manufacturers and retailers should know that Hispanics spend 20 percent more in club stores and 36 percent more in mass merchandise outlets than the general population. Additionally, Hispanic consumers place a strong emphasis on family and nutrition. They often prefer to cook from scratch, and it also is common for entire families to shop together, which means that children can be strong purchase influencers, the market research firm notes.

Product Preferences

Although Hispanics purchase brands in a wide variety of categories, there are a few beverage categories that are more popular among Hispanics than other demographics. According to Chicago-based market research firm Mintel, Hispanics are the most likely of any race to consume sports drinks, with 56 percent reporting such compared with 38 percent of Caucasian consumers, 50 percent of African-American consumers and 39 percent of Asian consumers drinking sports drinks. The popularity of sports drinks among Hispanic consumers is driven by the relative youth of the race as well as the high number of these consumers that perform manual labor jobs where sports drinks prove beneficial, the market research firm reports.

In the alcohol market, beer is most poplar among Hispanics, Mintel notes. Hispanics drink 6 percent more imported beer than any other ethnicity. Additionally, they make up the largest group of tequila drinkers in the United States. More than 27 percent of Hispanics drink tequila, which is the highest percentage for any ethnic group, according to the market research firm. On the other side of the spectrum, wine is the least favorite alcohol beverage among Hispanics, with 23 percent drinking wine compared to 33 percent of the total population.

"Many U.S. Hispanics, particularly Mexicans, have not been exposed to wine in their home country, so there isn't a wine-drinking culture or tradition," Leylha Ahuile, senior multicultural analyst at Mintel, said in a statement. "However, we expect this to change in the coming years as it is already on the rise. Between 2005 and 2010, the number of glasses of wine consumed by Hispanics per month increased by nearly 50 percent. Many of these Hispanic wine consumers are second or third generation, and their level of acculturation is impacting their wine consumption habits."

When it comes to marketing to this group, all media outlets and dual language communication are important, Mintel says.

According to a Mintel report, 36 percent of Hispanics find TV commercials interesting, and 38 percent arrange their schedules around TV programs.

Laurie Demeritt, president of The Hartman Group, Bellevue, Wash., adds that some Hispanic consumers prefer to have Spanish language on the package; however, in most cases, Hispanics are not as concerned with the language on the packaging as they are with media advertising, such as TV commercials and print ads, representing their physical features.

"We know that qualitatively there is some preference among certain Hispanic consumers to have Spanish on the package, but frankly, what we've found is that, in many cases, what they were saying around advertising was not so much that 'I want it to be in Spanish' per se, but 'I want to see people like me portrayed in some of the media advertising,' Demeritt explains. "It was kind of a more subtle cue that I think is an interesting one."

Nevertheless, many CPG brands feature Spanish language on products targeted at Hispanics. For instance, Global Trade Bridge Corp., New York, introduced Rica juice drinks to the U.S. market this year. Similarly, Andale! Energy Drink Co. LLC, Bakersfield, Calif., launched its same-named beverage in California this year. Both products feature Spanish language on the packaging.

Last month, White Plains, N.Y.-based Heineken USA Inc. launched Tecate Michelada, an authentic ready-to-drink beer mix that follows the traditional michelada recipe.

"Beer mixes are growing in popularity among Mexican consumers in the U.S. and have shown sustainable growth over the past three years," said Felix Palau, vice president of marketing for Tecate, in a statement. "This new product line is perfect for consumers that feel like having a beer that has a little something extra and is ready to be enjoyed on the spot."

To promote the launch of the new product, the brand partnered with creative agency Olabuenaga Chemistri to develop an out-of-home advertising campaign for select U.S. markets.

"The transit shelters and bulletins, for example, boldly celebrate the authenticity and full flavor of Tecate Michelada by showcasing the 16-ounce can surrounded by the key ingredients that make up its complex profile: cerveza, spices, lime and salt," Palau explains. "It was also important for us to develop specific [point-of-sale] (POS) elements for our in-store marketing efforts across the western and central regions of the U.S."

The brand collaborated with Dieste to develop POS materials, including floor and cooler decals, wobblers, shelf strips and a suction cup holder that enables retailers to display individual cans inside coolers, she says. All of the advertising and POS materials feature English and Spanish text to target the brand's consumer base of Hispanic men living in the United States, she adds.

"CPG companies that win with Hispanics focused on tailored products and marketing, created better in-store experiences with retailers, and increased Hispanic-focused resources and capabilities," McKinsey & Co.'s Licht said in a statement.

Getting Digital

When it comes to digital media, there are several groups—including Hispanics—that are highly influenced. Hispanic and African-American consumers are more likely to research and purchase products online than other races, The Hartman Group's Demeritt says. The general population searches online for items at a rate of 28 percent, whereas the rate for African-Americans goes up to 44 percent, and the rate for Hispanics is 36 percent, she adds.

"Our guess is that, especially for the Hispanic consumers, there may be products that they've traditionally used that are more based on cultural or historical reasons that they may not know if they can find it at a mainstream grocery store, so they're more likely to be looking for it online," Demeritt explains.

Hispanic consumers also are significantly more likely to indicate that Facebook and Twitter might be ways to connect with them, she says. Approximately 36 percent of Hispanics say Facebook would be a good way for companies to connect with them, and 12 percent say Twitter is a good way to reach them. Although these numbers aren't large, they are statistically higher than what the general population says, she reports.

African-American consumers also indicate that Facebook and Twitter are good ways to connect with them but also include email and text messaging, Demeritt says. Fifty percent of the general population says email is a good way for companies to connect with them, whereas 62 percent of African-Americans see email as a good communication vehicle, she explains.

"This is showing for some of the new media [that] there is a likelihood that both Hispanic and African-American consumers are more likely to consider those good vehicles than the general population and, in particular, Caucasian consumers," Demeritt says.

Similarly, millennial consumers—between the ages of 18 and 29—are highly likely to rely on social media for insight and opinions; however, they prefer traditional retail stores for making purchases, according to a report by RedPrairie Corp., Atlanta. Despite this preference for in-store purchases, the report notes the need for retailers and manufacturers to be present everywhere, including online, via quick-response codes at retail, mobile apps, social media and other channels.

"When it comes to trying to satisfy millennials, the bottom line for brands is adaptability," said David Bruno, director of corporate messaging at RedPrairie, in a statement. "One minute they want to shop and compare online and via every social networking site available, and the next they want to purchase in-store. Retailers essentially need to provide "endless aisle" capabilities in every channel and location. When marketing to

millennials, retailers and brands must strike a balance between personalizing the shopping experience via individualized product information and not overwhelming or overstepping perceived boundaries of privacy. It's a challenge to meet these seemingly conflicting expectations, but with the right technology and integration in place, it's achievable."

Driving Innovation

Although Hispanic consumers are the fastest-growing group in the United States, millennials make up the largest generation next to baby boomers and are responsible for driving most of the innovation in the beverage industry, according to Chicago-based Technomic Inc. By 2018, millennial consumers will all reach legal drinking age in the United States, and they're already making their mark on the adult beverage market, the company says. Millennial consumers are responsible for driving trends such as craft beer, boutique spirits and sweeter flavor profiles in wine, it explains. They consume domestic light beer, hard ciders, cocktails, red wine blends and Moscato wines more often than older consumers, the company adds.

According to Technomic, this generation is more likely to try new drinks than members of any other generation in both on- and off-premise locations.

"Millennials are absolutely driving some of the biggest trends in adult beverage and will continue to do so for the next few years," said David Henkes, vice president at Technomic and leader of its adult beverage practice, in a statement. "We do see, however, that this is not a homogenous group. Due to its sheer size and inherent diversity, beverage professionals from suppliers and marketers to retailers and restaurateurs must be very strategic in engaging millennia's in terms of adult beverage occasions and consumption."

For instance, teaching millennials about new brands, flavors and cocktails at on-premise locations is more important than ever for the younger generation, Henkes explains.

"When you're talking about new flavors, part of it is just building variety into your menu, part of it is perhaps sampling, part of it could be flights and having, an alluring back story to your cocktail menu—things that make your drink list and your drink selections more interesting and give millennials a reason to experiment, because they are much more likely to experiment than some of the other generations," Henkes says.

Furthermore, because they're much more social media savvy than past generations, it's also important for operators to have a social media marketing strategy in order to reach them, he says.

New Consumer Segment

In addition to prominent consumer groups including Hispanics and millennials, a new consumer segment has been identified.

The "heartland" consumer group is made up of 60 percent of U.S. consumers and is underserved and overlooked by most brands, according to Paul Jankowski, chief strategist at consumer engagement agency Access Brand Strategies, Brentwood, Tenn., and author of "How to Speak American."

"Many branding decision-makers disregard the cultural nuances of the new heartland and fail to create campaigns that 'speak American,' or are culturally relevant to this segment," Jankowski said in a statement. "A lot of agencies and clients apply a one-size-fits-all strategy because they don't know this segment and, in many cases, are afraid to immerse themselves in a culture that's foreign to them."

New heartland consumers reside in the Midwest, Southwest and parts of the Southeast and are bound together by a core set of values including faith (not religion), community and family, he explains.

"Beverage brands need to be very cognizant of how they communicate with the new heartland," Jankowski says. ". . . [T]here's certain cultural nuances that make the way you message very important and how you can create measurable results, so I would just keep those in mind—those cultural nuances. I would make sure you understand that the new heartland is an amalgamation of several cultures, but again, the core value piece plays in there, so you've got to be culturally relevant."

PepsiCo, Purchase, N.Y., aligned itself with celebrity personalities to help tell its story and appeal to new heartland consumers. For example, the company enlisted Grammy award-winning trio Lady Antebellum to represent Lipton's "Drink Positive" ad campaign. The band is featured in national TV spots that highlight 100 percent Natural Lipton Iced Tea and new Lipton Tea & Honey iced tea mixes. Additionally, Lady Antebellum and Lipton created behind-the-tour webisodes, which feature the band engaging in a series of challenges to determine which member knows his or her bandmates best. The campaign also includes a Facebook sweepstakes as well as print, radio, digital and retail integrations.

"Lady Antebellum is the voice of the new heartland, home to generations of Lipton lovers," said Marc Hanson, brand director for Lipton, in a statement. "They were the perfect match to represent the positive spirit of the Lipton brand and bring the campaign to life."

Critical Thinking

1. In your opinion, why do most consumer packaged goods (CPG) companies pay such close attention to the Hispanic micro-culture?

2. Create a descriptive profile for the new consumer segment, "Heartland," introduced in this article.

3. With a group of peers from your class, suggest some marketing rules for companies that may ensure brand acceptance by the "heartland" segment?

Create Central

www.mhhe.com/createcentral

Internet References

Access Brand Strategies
http://accessheartland.com/

AHAA: The Voice of Hispanic Marketing
http://www.ahaa.org/default.asp?contentID=12

Beverage Daily
http://www.beveragedaily.com/

Nielsen
http://www.nielsen.com/us/en/reports/2012/state-of-the-hispanic-consumer-the-hispanic-market-imperative.html

Stephanie Hilderbrandt, "Targeting Demographics in Beverage Marketing," *Beverage Industry*, October 2012. Copyright © 2012 by Beverage Industry. All rights reserved. Used with permission.

Ad Campaigns are Finally Reflecting Diversity of U.S.: But Why Did It Take So Long to Recognize Socially Liberal Shift? by Natalie Zmuda

87

Article   Prepared by: Nisreen N. Bahnan, *Salem State University*

Ad Campaigns are Finally Reflecting Diversity of U.S.

But Why Did It Take So Long to Recognize Socially Liberal Shift?

NATALIE ZMUDA

Learning Outcomes

After reading this article, you will be able to:

- Identify major recent societal changes in America.

- Understand the role that advertising plays in reflecting and enforcing diversity in the population.

- Analyze the opportunities and risks that companies face when they utilize potentially controversial advertising campaigns.

Tim Mahoney saw the potential for trouble. As part of Chevrolet's "Find New Roads" campaign, the brand's chief marketing officer helped create a commercial that would break on the Sochi Olympics featuring family vignettes, including gay and interracial couples. The theme: "The new us."

Before greenlighting the spot, Mr. Mahoney reviewed the Commonwealth-created campaign with senior executives and several hundred local marketing associations. The automaker's communications teams were also prepped to respond to negative feedback. "The dealers acknowledged it might upset some people," said Mr. Mahoney. "But fundamentally they also get its about expanding the desirability of Chevrolet and bringing more people in."

Ultimately, he said, the message was to "reaffirm that Chevrolet is a new company with a new way of thinking. . . . It's an acknowledgement that America has changed."

While America has grown more socially liberal, it's taken Madison Avenue some time to reflect that reality. Pop culture typically sets the boundaries of social conversation, said Jason Chambers, author of "Madison Avenue and the Color Line" and professor at the University of Illinois. Advertising has proved to be the last frontier when it comes to reflecting societal changes. "There is a natural hesitancy to speak to where [consumers] are rather than lead them where they should go, because what if they say, 'no'?" said Mr. Chambers.

According to U.S. Census data from 2010, one in 10—or 5.4 million—opposite-sex couples are interracial, a 28% rise since 2000. According to the data, the number of same-sex-couple households in the U.S. was 646,000, up 9% from 2000.

That may explain why it's only within the past year that mass marketers have been embracing inclusiveness in mass-market campaigns, marked by big splashes from the likes of Coca-Cola, General Mills and Chevy on advertising's biggest stages. Coke created a gorgeous pastiche of diverse faces singing "America the Beautiful" in a host of languages. Big G reunited the mixed-race parents of Gracie, the endearing young star of its Cheerios commercial, for the Super Bowl. They join Gap Inc.'s Banana Republic, Procter & Gamble's Swiffer and Guinness, all of which have used more diverse casting in recent weeks.

Room for Progress

Marketing experts say this is the moment that historians and social commentators will likely declare a tipping point for advertising enlightenment in the years to come. But, in truth, adland is late to the game, and plenty of progress is still to be made.

The country has shifted quite a bit in a more socially liberal direction, even in the past two to three years. But in some ways we're still where we were in the 1970s when we started with integrated advertising," said Mr. Chambers.

He said the Cheerios ads are reminiscent of some of the first racially integrated ads, where different races were present but didn't necessarily interact. In the first ad, he notes the couple is shown in different rooms, while in the second ad, they are standing several feet apart and only exchange a look. "You never see the parents in close proximity. They don't have that level of social intimacy."

Likewise, J.C. Penney made headlines and won over some consumers in 2012 with its unwavering support of spokeswoman Ellen DeGeneres, who is openly gay, in the face of protests from One Million Moms. But that didn't mean it showed Ms. DeGeneres kissing another woman in a national ad.

To be fair, advertisers have been dipping their toes in these waters for years. But the move has been from progressive and niche companies rather than those that target the mainstream middle. Brands from United Colors of Benetton to Expedia have widely featured interracial couples or gay couples in print, digital and outdoor ads. "Gay vague" ads were not unusual in the 1990s, for example. One that was widely discussed was Volkswagen's 1997 "Da da da" spot that showed two men in a car but wasn't explicit about their relationship.

The difference now is scale. "Big brands have woken up to the realization that at least part of the Republican Party woke up to in 2012, which is that young Americans across the board value diversity and organizations or brands that explicitly affirm their acceptance of diversity," said David Rogers, professor of digital marketing at Columbia University's business school.

Good for Business?

Why has it taken so long? Once-skittish advertisers are realizing it's good for business. A scroll through Chevrolet's Facebook page, for example, reveals consumers have been jumping to the brand's defense against derogatory comments.

According to YouGov BrandIndex, perception of Chevrolet has skyrocketed with the LGBT community, as has purchase consideration. Buzz among 18- to 34-year-olds is also on the rise (though not purchase consideration). And a disproportionately high number of people viewing Chevrolet's anthem ad said they would recommend the brand, according to Advertising Benchmark Index, an ad-tracking firm.

"It's probably a good business decision, over time," said Lars Perner, University of Southern California's Marshall School of Business, noting that gay and lesbian consumers, on average, tend to have higher incomes.

Still, the overriding takeaway from these campaigns was not about the great taste of Coke or the health benefits of Cheerios. It was that Coca-Cola and the cereal brand are diverse and accepting. "People seem to have decided diversity can be used as a statement. It's an interesting shift," said Jaime Prieto, president-global brand at Ogilvy. "I would recommend [this strategy] as a way to be an authentic brand in today's environment."

These brand values are also playing out in the political arena. Late last month companies including Apple, Salesforce.com and Target publicly (and successfully) pressured Arizona Gov. Jan Brewer to veto the state's measure that would allow businesses to discriminate against gays and lesbians on religious grounds.

But while the inclusiveness showcased in recent ads may have cast a halo over certain brands, it's also been polarizing and generally didn't drive consumers to take action, said Garry Getto, president at Advertising Benchmark Index.

"Just because the majority are siding with the brand, doesn't necessarily mean they're supporting the brand with their pocketbooks," said Ted Marzilli, CEO at YouGov BrandIndex.

And for most brands that's the calculation: not what they could gain, but what they risk losing.

"There are still plenty of very, very conservative clients who wouldn't want to be out front," Mr. Prieto said.

More to Come—Slowly

Even the brands being lauded for their bravery when it comes to diverse casts are hesitant to talk candidly about their approach. Several brands contacted for this article declined to make executives available for interviews, preferring to provide statements and let the ads speak for themselves. "Cheerios knows there are many kinds of families and we celebrate them all," said Doug Martin, marketing manager for Cheerios, in a statement.

Mr. Chambers paraphrased a quote from his book, noting "the businessman doesn't want to antagonize anybody, even the bigots." In other words: "I don't think anybody wants to put their foot in their mouth," he said. A Coca-Cola spokeswoman said in a statement: "We believe 'It's Beautiful' is a great example of the magic that makes our country so special, and a powerful message that spreads optimism, promotes inclusion and celebrates humanity—values that are core to Coca-Cola."

They may not be making a lot of noise about it, but more and more marketers are seeking out diverse faces for their ads—albeit slowly. Francene Selkirk, the casting director behind Cheerios' interracial family, said she's seen an uptick in requests for blended casts and mixed-ethnicity models. "This is what the world is like nowadays. I'm disappointed I don't see more of it in advertising," she said.

One ironic side effect of this mainstreaming of ad diversity could be a drag on multicultural agencies. This total-market

Ad Campaigns are Finally Reflecting Diversity of U.S.: But Why Did It Take So Long to Recognize Socially Liberal Shift? by Natalie Zmuda

89

approach "is a new trend that appears to be gaining in trac-tion," said Bill Duggan, group exec VP at the Association of National Advertisers. "A big point of friction or discussion here has to do with ad agencies. More 'general-market' agencies are doing this type of work. As a result, that is a threat to the more 'traditional' multicultural agencies, although some of those agencies are doing this type of work too and viewing it as an opportunity."

Mr. Chambers, for one, is curious to see where the indus-try is in four to six months, as well as what marketers do as part of their "normal" marketing cadence. "We've had a couple of big-splash moments—Super Bowl and Olympics. Any time we have things like that, marketers and advertisers are always willing to do things a little bit differently to stand out more," he said. "Let's get into a new quarter, get into new iterations of advertising from those marketers and see what we have."

Mr. Mahoney said he feels Chevrolet has "opened the door now. . . . We have to continue to execute on it. New work has to follow this work. Otherwise it's like, 'Oh, they tried that.'"

Critical Thinking

1. Do you agree with the following statement from the article: "advertising has proved to be the last frontier when it comes to reflecting societal changes"?

2. In your opinion, what are some of these recent societal changes?

3. Discuss the examples, provided in the article, of brands that have incorporated these societal changes into their advertis-ing, and suggest similar examples of other brands that, in your opinion, have done the same.

Create Central

www.mhhe.com/createcentral

Internet References

Diversity Central
  http://www.diversitycentral.com/
United States Census Bureau
  http://www.census.gov/

Natalie Zmuda, "Ad Campaigns Are Finally Reflecting Diversity of U.S.," *Advertising Age,* March 2014. Copyright © 2014 by Crain Communications, Inc. All rights reserved. Used with permission.

Article   Prepared by: Nisreen N. Bahnan, *Salem State University*

Can More Information Be a Bad Thing?

Despite the best efforts of researchers, consumer decisions will always have subjective components.

ROBERT S. DUBOFF

Learning Outcomes

After reading this article, you will be able to:

- Acknowledge a different approach to the deeply-engrained, left-brain "facts lead us to the best option" paradigm in decision-making situations.

- Recognize ways that decision makers may be subconsciously biased when making choices.

The basic paradigm is so engrained in our business culture that it is rarely even stated explicitly: To make marketing decisions, we amass facts and, using our best judgment and experience, we opt for the alternative that the available information favors. This is implicit in every market research brief and proposal; it is a given for any task force charged with deciding on a path forward on an issue.

The "facts lead us to the best option" approach can also be easily inferred from every press release or other explanation of a decision. Only Steve Jobs (and a few others) have had the temerity to explain a course of action as being based on his or her own instinct. And even he, while eschewing much market research with consumers, often alluded to data that supported Apple's decision.

It has not always been so. In Plato's days, there was the Philosopher King, who, uniquely, could discern reality in the mists and make decisions based on judgment and, perhaps, his own experience.

Most people likely feel our evolved model is a better one: Use all our resources to gather as much information as possible, and then (perhaps using a decision tree or a set of criteria) go where the data lead. And yet a growing set of discoveries is now calling this very left-brain, logical approach into question.

A New Paradigm

Before discussing the evidence that threatens the rule of reason for decisions, I want to clarify the focus. "Decisionmaking" is an extremely broad term of reference, including the trivial and the personal, as well as the life-changing and bet-your-company calls. I will focus here on business marketing decisions of some importance made by an individual or small team.

Also, there are decisions that clearly depend on future acts/reactions of humans (e.g., hiring, new product launch) vs. those more focused on inanimate objects (e.g., where to locate a plant or to invest capital). The latter are more about mathematics, so the former will be the focus here. For our purposes, we will be thinking in the context of important marketing decisions that involve future human actions. The core thesis is that the assumed, if not stated, paradigm is flawed in practice, except for a very few cases. While good decision-making means deliberating and selecting the best option after gathering sufficient information is a Platonic ideal, I believe that better decisions can be made by embracing these facts:

- "Information" is rarely truly factual and, where it purports to predict the future actions of people, is never valid, even if produced with skill and objectivity (neither of which is always present).
- Regardless of how they may feel or describe themselves, decision makers are not objective beings willing to rationally choose whatever option the information might indicate.

My thesis is supported with evidence from behavioral economics, neurophysiology and, I hope, common sense. Of course, I accept that a reader who firmly believes in the sanctity of well-developed numbers and his or her own objectivity will never fully accept this and might well stop reading here.

For those still open to thinking about the best ways to make marketing decisions, let me suggest a new paradigm and then provide the evidence indicating that this may be a better route than current practice, which is to say and act as we are following the ideal rational paradigm.

Preconceptions Play a Role

Assume we have to decide whether to introduce a new brand, one in a category that already exists.

We have invested a great deal based on research that depicted an unmet need in this mass market. We have 12 months or so before we need to decide to go ahead or not. Let us further assume that the payoff will be in the tens of millions of profit per year if we can become the second or third in market share.

Before we commission market research, we get the three decision makers together and ask each one what he or she would decide today if they had to decide, and why. If they all agree, we ask them to name a key lieutenant or two that they trust to play the other side—to marshal the best arguments against the current choice.

At the same time, we question them about their degree of confidence and their concerns. We ask them about what information might change their minds. We probe them about how their current preferred decision would make them feel. Do they have any qualms? We ask how they feel about the investment made so far.

At this point, we might conclude that it is highly unlikely that their minds will change and make the decision today, thereby getting a head start and saving all the money that would have been spent producing information. In my experience, if the decision maker(s) on the go/no go launch are the same as those who authorized the spending on development so far, it is likely they will go ahead. I have always read the new Coke launch decision this way, despite all the ex post facto justification that (flawed) consumer taste tests drove the decision.

Or, if it seems there is really an openness to going in a different direction, we might launch the "best arguments against" and/or gather (only) any information that could hit at their concerns and qualms.

In this case, we would likely engage third parties respected by these decision makers, in essence, a mutually agreed upon arbiter.

There are other concepts that might help, but the key prescription is to get the decision maker(s) to acknowledge the role of their preconceptions and preferences rather than the current practice of (intentionally or not) pretending there is a totally fact-based decision to be made.

Why is this approach better?

Briefly

- Recognize the influence of non-objective factors when designing research.
- Acknowledge the right brain's important function in consumer decision-making.
- Remember that information is not always truly factual.

First and foremost, there is now voluminous evidence that all of us are influenced by non-rational factors when we make decisions. Too often, decision makers use information only for affirmation.

Even worse, we are often not aware that we are doing is or being influenced. *Thinking, Fast and Slow* by Daniel Kahneman is the latest of a long line of research-based books that show the impact of factors such as anchoring, selective perception, cognitive dissonance and the like.

Second, a related, pernicious mental factor is frame of reference. Too often, people do not position their product broadly enough, the classic marketing myopia. Most recently, this has seen RIM ignore the iPhone to its peril.

The Innovator's Dilemma is a subset of this. Companies, especially first-mover technology companies, see their core product and customer base as the key universe. They focus so heavily on meeting short-term enhancements (versions 2.0, etc.) that they miss someone else redefining the category.

Third, the information that decision makers receive is often filtered, if not tainted, in an attempt to support the views of the decision maker and often to seek his/her favor. The *now known to be erroneous information* given to President George W. Bush that indicated there were weapons of mass destruction in Iraq is a prime example of this.

Fourth, even without a filter, the most common source of information about how the market will likely react to a new product is market research. This information is increasingly suspect because of at least three factors:

- It is nigh impossible to get a sample representative of any large universe (except one's own customers if a business is lucky enough that customers need or want to register with them).
- There are simply no good lists of all the cell phone numbers from which to randomly select.
- There is no online panel with a truly representative group of members who can be selected (vs. them opting in) for a given study.

These factors add to the age-old problem that consumers will often lie about key issues (their past purchasing behavior, for example).

Even with a representative sample telling the truth as they know it, there are still erroneous responses due to the same factors that influence decision makers. What people were doing before the survey, what words they were hearing, whom they last talked to about the topic, and so on., could all influence responses such that the answers do not represent how that respondent really feels or thinks, much less how they will act.

Related to this is that, unless the survey picks up their knowledge about the topic, it cannot allow researchers to play out scenarios as new facts or factors emerge or current ones become known between the time of the survey and the time the respondents are able to buy the new product.

Even with a good sample and truthful respondents and no unconscious influences, there is a fundamental flaw that decision makers and researchers have accepted only by suspending disbelief. As Steve Jobs stated, consumers simply cannot reliably tell us how they will respond to something they don't readily recognize. In our example, we are not talking about an iPod in MP3 days or an iPad before tablets.

But any new brand that purports to be different/better in a new way cannot really be understood by a consumer, can it? At some level we know this, and yet research is still the most accepted and likely best way to get some estimate, some number to grasp. If we like the number, we allow our disbelief to dissipate. If we don't like the number, maybe we rejigger it or simply reject the research.

Research shows that playing French music correlates with boosted sales of French wine in the same store where, during the playing of German music, German wine sales increase. Could you capture this in a survey? The point is not to stop doing surveys, but rather to focus any research on questions that (1) respondents can answer accurately and (2) might have an impact on the actual decision maker.

When Research Works

In the hypothetical new product launch mentioned earlier, if decision makers are truly concerned about whether enough people will buy the new product, the research could focus on what the "ideal" product in the category would do and measure each existing product against the ideal on the specific attributes. The research could also talk to retailers and distributors to get their expert perspective on the category. This would make it easier to understand the market and how best to promote the new brands. Other options exist as well.

Ways Decision Makers May Be Subconsciously (or Not) Biased

- **Anchoring:** Influence of initial information on the topic.
- **Cognitive Dissonance:** Tendency to eliminate/lessen any possible contradictions by rationalizing toward the stronger feeling (e.g., explaining away statements of or charges against a favored politician).
- **Recency:** Relying more on the latest or last information received.
- **Priming:** Influence of even disconnected words or other input heard before a decision (i.e., French music in a liquor store correlates with heightened purchase of French wines).
- **Selective Perception:** Accepting information that comes from a source you deem reliable and/ or confirms instinct, while filtering out contradictory data.

How does the ad agency feel? Would they rather have the account of the current leader in the category or this new brand? Do they have ideas about how to message about it?

Finally, it is always good practice to run reaction tests—focus groups with valued customers to pilot the decision to learn if there are dramatic and, especially, unanticipated reactions to the favored decision.

If nothing else, this kind of testing would protect against a decision from the gut that flies in the face of customers.

There are also techniques such as Delphi panels and lead users that have proven far more prescient than more normal surveys, no matter how well-crafted. [See sidebar below for further explanation.] Delphis and lead users research don't pretend to be "reliable" in the statistical sense; they are not projectable to the marketplace.

However, they may be more "valid," the other test of research, in that they can portray a picture of the evolving marketplace that is likely to be more true than surveys representative of the current consumers.

To summarize, most decisions are not made in a truly objective, information-based manner. While decisions can be based on data, they all have subjective components. Where the gut lines up with the brain, the decision is relatively easy. Where it doesn't, emotion often rules.

Research Techniques That Work

Some research methods are not based on the simplest paradigm of asking direct questions about what respondents will do in the future and then projecting their responses to the universe of interest.

Lead user analysis, developed by Professor Von Hippel of MIT, is predicated on the assumption that people who are most in need of the product or service (e.g., in B-to-B, the buyers for whom your product is essential; in B-to-C, airline travel or alarm clocks for a frequent business flyer) will provide the most valid and thoughtful information. Even more valid data can be gathered by observing how they use the product because often they will have made adaptations that could presage what other people or companies might want to do if you offered those enhancements.

This core concept has been amended by others to extend into early adopters as, literally, "lead users" whose decision about whether to buy or recommend your product will determine whether others will see it and/or think enough of it to try it.

Another premise is akin to the wisdom of crowds. The Delphi research technique utilizes a set of experts in diverse fields who are asked the likelihood of various well-thought-out and researched scenarios (or more simply, the likelihood of X people buying Y product). The results are tabulated and then the experts, after seeing how others voted, opine again. If consensus grows, the marketer's confidence grows.

This technique was invented by the Rand Corporation in the wake of World War II and is credited with the development of the Marshall Plan. It has since been successfully used to help several companies decide whether or not to invest in emerging technologies.

My final argument is the most fact-based. The track record on marketing decisions is pretty poor, particularly in the area of new products. Estimates of the failure rate range from 60 percent to 90 percent. Think of all the wasted time and money. Wouldn't it be better to acknowledge the role of the right brain on decisions and, rather than hiding it and seeming to use bad research and/or filtering it, legitimize the gut instinct and the influences of the past and use that as the starting point for more focused research and discussions?

Even if that only works half the time, it's better than our current decision-making performance.

Critical Thinking

1. According to the article, is decision-making a rational and scientific process?

2. List some reasons why decision-makers may be subconsciously biased.

3. Discuss a recent decision-making experience that had subjective components.

Create Central

www.mhhe.com/createcentral

Internet References

Changing Minds
http://changingminds.org/explanations/theories/anchoring_adjustment.htm

Consumer Psychologist
http://www.consumerpsychologist.com/

Decision Making Confidence
http://www.decision-making-confidence.com/

ROBERT S. DUBOFF is CEO of HawkPartners, a Cambridge, Mass., consultancy that works at the intersection of marketing and marketing research. He may be reached at Rob.Duboff@hawkpartners.com

---

Robert S. Duboff, "Can More Information Be a Bad Thing?" *Marketing Management,* Summer 2012, pp. 25–29. Copyright © 2012 by American Marketing Association. All rights reserved. Used with permission.

Article Prepared by: Nisreen N. Bahnan, *Salem State University*

Our Brands, Ourselves

The Power of Attachment

LAURENCE VINCENT

Learning Outcomes

After reading this article, you will be able to:

- Understand the concepts of brand narratives and brand attachments.

- Differentiate between different types of brand relationships that consumers may develop (extension of self-concept, prominence in daily use, avoidance, etc . . .)

You'd never guess that the green-eyed teenager in the photo was a fugitive. The boy in the self-portrait that buzzed around the world's media that day in 2009 stared up at you wearing Apple earbuds, resting his head on a knapsack in a patch of brush. You could have easily mistaken him for a Boy Scout. This was Colton Harris-Moore, an 18-year-old runaway who eluded authorities for over two years when he embarked on an adventurous crime spree that resulted in over one hundred cases of theft, burglary, and criminal trespassing. The world knew him as "the Barefoot Bandit," a name he earned after a surveillance video caught him pilfering without shoes. He must have approved of the brand name because he began drawing chalk footprints on the floors of his victims.

Like many people, I became fascinated with the Barefoot Bandit because his story seemed like something only Hollywood could invent. He ran away from home, survived on his own in the woods for weeks at a time, burglarized affluent communities, flaunted legal authorities using a catchy alter ego, and stole a few planes to venture from the remotest corner of the Pacific Northwest to a tropical island in the Caribbean. But not everyone loved Harris-Moore. The residents of the towns and communities where he committed his crimes despised him. Harris-Moore damaged property, robbed people of their

valuables, and violated a lot of people's sense of security. Some who knew him when he was young pitied him, describing him as a socially challenged kid from a battered home who loved animals and was infatuated with airplanes.

Then there were the millions of people around the world who made the Barefoot Bandit into a folk hero. A Facebook fan page created about him attracted nearly fifty thousand followers, with fans likening him to a modern-day Jesse James. "He's the right criminal at the right time," said Zack Sestak, the self-appointed head of Harris-Moore's fan club. "Executives are getting billion-dollar bonuses, and . . . the normal people, everyday people, people who are struggling to pay their bills—they see someone like Colton taking on the system, and they say 'All right!'"

I found it a little odd that so many people identified with Harris-Moore. A cottage business developed with entrepreneurs selling T-shirts and novelty items bearing his likeness. Music videos appeared on YouTube celebrating his adventure and urging him to "fly on." It seemed especially odd because there was no indication that Harris-Moore would have approved of any of it. After he was captured, he refused to grant interviews, appeared shy in front of news cameras, and frequently asked the media to go away. He is said to have sold the rights to his life story only as a means to repay his victims.

It struck me that the Barefoot Bandit was an interesting example of a force that gives branding so much potential power: *attachment*. When people become attached to brands, their attachment changes their behavior. Though I can't say for sure that Colton Harris-Moore began his life of crime because he was attached to brands, his story is littered with some of the most prestigious brands in our culture.

There's more to it than that, however. The story of the Barefoot Bandit provides a compelling glimpse at why there's a growing backlash against brands. Looking at Harris-Moore and the people who were drawn to his story during his run from the law, it's tempting to suggest that branding has led us completely astray from moral values. Indeed, this has been the central argument of Adbusters, the anticonsumerist organization of activists who stage demonstrations and mount campaigns to convince the public to reject advertising and media because they lead people to focus too much on using external rewards to develop a sense of personal identity. I believe there is ample truth in their argument: Branding, marketing, and media are often misused in irresponsible and unsustainable ways—ways that overpromise on the value that can actually be delivered; ways that manipulate by appealing to our most shallow, image-driven vulnerabilities; and ways that define brands as substitutes for human relationships.

That said, I believe that brands can play a valuable role in our culture—and that those of us who have the privilege of guiding brands have a responsibility to understand the impact they can exert on a consumer's individual identity.

How J. Crew Do You Look?

Brand attachment measures how much consumers (or any members of a brand audience, for that matter) view the brand as an extension of themselves. This differs quite a bit from measures of brand attitudes. When we measure attitudes, we mostly aim to gauge how much people like a brand. In contrast, attachment measures how much people will say that a brand is like them—they identify with a brand because it reflects their values and resembles the way they see themselves.

Harley-Davidson loyalists wouldn't be caught dead on another bike. While they'll certainly tell you they like the Harley brand, their loyalty runs deeper than their attitudes. They're loyal because Harley is as much a part of their identity as their body—maybe more so.

I've known Hollywood agents who don't feel they're legitimate until they own a genuine Armani suit and drive a luxury German car. There are guitar players who will sacrifice all their worldly possessions in pursuit of becoming a rock star, except for one: their Gibson Les Paul solid-body guitar. I've met auto mechanics who don't feel they can do their job as well without access to Snap-on tools, and chefs who carry their own Wüsthof knives from job to job. In each instance, the possessions and the brands that make them special are part of the consumer's self-concept.

We can measure brand attachment in two ways. First, we can measure the degree to which a brand reflects a person's self-concept, whether it's "like me" or "the opposite of me." You have to measure more than self-concept, though. After all, even though a particular brand skews toward my sense of self, it might not be relevant to me at this moment in time. For example, I might tell you that a TAG Heuer watch is a lot like me, but

I don't think about TAG Heuer watches much. I don't own one, and I don't intend to buy one anytime soon. Although I find the watches beautiful and I'm inspired by their craftsmanship, I'm in no hurry to spend that much money on a timepiece. It's not as relevant as other needs.

Relevance, then, determines how much your audience actually has use for your-brand. It determines how prominent the brand is in daily life. When you hear someone say, "I want to look very J. Crew tomorrow," the brand is being employed in speech in a way that makes it useful and instrumental to our thinking. These are the prominent brands.

The brands that are truly extensions of us are the most relevant and the most connected to our self-concept; we go to great lengths to keep them in our lives. In contrast, there are brands for which we have nothing but disdain; instead of being sacred, these brands are profane. I had a colleague who could not stand Ed Hardy apparel. What I found ironic about his behavior was how often he referenced Ed Hardy in his conversations. If we met someone on the street who seemed a little too flashy, my friend would say something like, "Can you believe that Ed Hardy hipster?" The brand even showed up in a client presentation he delivered about what *not* to do with a brand. Ed Hardy was so prominent in my friend's thoughts that he regularly introduced it as a point of reference even though it was the antithesis of his identity.

And most brands—including many of those we come across daily—just don't factor into our decision process much. We neither think of them all that much nor do we really see them as a reflection of ourselves. Our behavior around them is mostly a force of habit, a consequence of price sensitivities, or a matter of convenience.

It's worth our time to understand how consumers collectively attach a brand to their self-concept because that attachment proves to be one of the best drivers of relevance. Relevance is strongly correlated to brand preference. While it's commonplace for companies to measure preference—how much consumers prefer their brand to competitive alternatives—they should invest as much energy explaining *why* consumers prefer their brand.

What We Want to Be

Brand attachment doesn't materialize in a vacuum, of course—history is often a factor, though many advertisers consider nostalgia a dangerous third rail. Brands such as Coca-Cola and Ford have more than a century of rich history that can provoke strong affections and positive feelings. The danger is that a consumer will think the brand is dated if it is too closely associated with the past. Would an association with Ford's Model T really help more consumers create a stronger attachment to today's Mustang? Probably not. However, Chrysler launched a very effective rebranding campaign in 2011 that struck a great balance. When "Imported from Detroit" debuted during the Super Bowl, with rapper Eminem (a Detroit native) driving a newly designed Chrysler 200 against images of the Motor City, the brand tapped its history and its present day to create strong, authentic attachment.

But while our history undoubtedly influences our sense of self, most of us are predisposed to look forward, not back. Nearly two out of three people say they think about themselves "in the future a great deal of the time or all the time." And when thinking of themselves in the future, people say that they more often imagine a positive outcome than a negative one by a ratio of four to one. Our hopes and dreams live in the domain of our possible selves; most of us believe we can become whoever we want to be.

The trouble starts when we allow nagging probabilities to temper our aspirations. The dreamer inside us constantly wrestles with the realist, and that gap between what we *aspire* to be and what we think we'll *probably* be influences our brand behavior. In fact, we become so attached to many of our possessions and brands because they create the illusion that our aspirations are one step closer to reality.

Let me illustrate with a puzzling phenomenon. When economic times are tough, why do consumers skimp on staples like diapers and spend a little more on brand-name cosmetics? Many makers of luxury goods such as handbags, shoes, and cosmetics have posted record sales while consumer staples such as batteries, bleach, and diapers have suffered staggering declines. I think that the trend reveals the influential power of our possible selves: We want to have brands in our life that connect us with our aspirations in spite of the probabilities. We might never be able to afford a $10,000 necklace from Tiffany, but for $175 we can carry a Tiffany keychain with us everywhere we go.

According to his mother, when Colton Harris-Moore was about 15 and living in a dilapidated trailer on the outskirts of town, he made collages of things he wished to be or to have. A 2010 CBS profile showed one of these collages, filled with brand names such as Cadillac, Armani, and Discover Card alongside photos of airplanes. The planes drew most viewers' attention: Growing up, Harris-Moore had said that he wanted to be a pilot—and he got his wish. During his time as a fugitive, he stole and piloted five planes; investigators believe he learned how to fly by watching an instructional DVD purchased with a stolen credit card and by studying a flight manual stolen from an unlocked aircraft. His first time in the sky was the day he took off in a stolen single-engine plane from an airfield on Washington state's Orcas Island. He flew through harrowingly gusty winds over the Cascade mountain range before crash-landing in a field. Miraculously, he walked away—and repeated this crazy stunt four more times. To say that he was driven by aspiration seems an understatement.

When Harris-Moore flew those planes, they were important instruments in bringing his possible self to life. Aspiration is a powerful force. While you may be unwilling to risk your life in such a daring way to accomplish your own aspirational goals, you probably are prepared to take risks and invest in selected activities that give you a sense that you are making your aspirations a reality. Some of the brands to which we are most strongly attached are the ones that we literally use as instruments in our activities to fulfill aspirational goals.

Sales of prestige cooking appliances such as Viking ranges and KitchenAid mixers have steadily risen in correlation with the growth of the Food Network. There are millions of aspiring home chefs all around the world who are willing to pay a premium for a Viking range because it authentically serves their aspirations to be great cooks. It doesn't matter that many of them never prepare anything more difficult than macaroni and cheese. Once they have this brand in their life, they don't want to be separated from it. Many Viking owners insist on taking them along when they buy a new home. The act of using this brand brings an aspiration to life because of its instrumental value.

Indeed, you can tell a lot about the degree to which consumers are attached to a brand by taking it away from them. Although we're willing to suffer a substitute for an ordinary brand on occasion, we can experience separation anxiety when denied a brand to which we're genuinely attached. Early in my career, I worked with an executive who drank Diet Coke, and only Diet Coke, all day long. When she was scheduled to travel to Paris for a meeting, she brought a six-pack of Diet Coke in her carry-on bag because she feared Air France wouldn't serve it. That's separation anxiety.

When we are truly attached to a brand, we're willing to make compromises in our other consumer behaviors in order to keep that brand in our life. I met a talented young photographer who had moved out of his parents' house for the first time to live on his own. He worked a lot of unrelated jobs to pay his rent and ate ramen and spaghetti for just about every meal. He spent most of his money on his camera gear. He was a Nikon shooter, and he owned a professional-level camera body and a few expensive lenses. Yet Nikon wasn't his top brand attachment, as I realized when I asked if his expensive Beats by Dr. Dre studio headphones had been a gift. He told me he had just bought them. In fact, they were his second pair—he had forfeited savings designated for upgrading his camera kit so that he could buy the new headphones. Music inspired his photography, he told me, and he couldn't imagine listening to music on anything other than his Beats.

Comfort From Closeness

In the same way that you can measure brand attachment by how anxious a consumer becomes when the brand is taken away, we can measure how much comfort and satisfaction consumers report as a result of having the brand in their possession or in close proximity. The more consumers view the brand as an extension of their own identity, the more they want the brand nearby.

You might not have the budget to stock your wine shelf with Opus One, but having one bottle in the collection is enough to validate your aspiration that you are a wine connoisseur. You might purposefully put off opening that bottle because it's worth more to you on your shelf than in your belly.

The recent reemergence of the Moleskine brand of high-end journals and day planners is another example. The brand goes to market as the notebook used by "Vincent van Gogh, Pablo Picasso, Ernest Hemingway, and Bruce Chatwin." It is a brand that had faded into obscurity until reimagined as more than a pad of paper. Today, it is used by many professionals who keep it close because it is one of many "indispensable creative tools that help define who we are, identifying us wherever we are in the world."

Which brings me back to the Barefoot Bandit. It's dangerous to play armchair psychologist and speculate on Colton Harris-Moore's motives. But I found the nature of many of his crimes striking. Most burglars break into a home, steal what they can sell, and leave as quickly as they can. Harris-Moore broke into homes and then made himself comfortable—he took showers, ate meals, and slept in the empty beds. While many of Harris-Moore's suspected crimes included theft of cash and illegal use of credit cards, he is also believed to have kept some of the items he stole. In his now-famous self-portrait, he is wearing a Mercedes-Benz branded polo shirt. When he was captured in the Bahamas, he was carrying a Walther PPK handgun in his backpack. It's not the greatest weapon for a fugitive, but it was the gun that James Bond used. Living on the run, Harris-Moore couldn't take a lot with him, but the few things he did take seemed to have brand significance. Perhaps they provided a sense of comfort; perhaps the mere possession of the brands made the risk-taking worthwhile.

Regardless of Harris-Moore's deeds and motives, humans have a history of imbuing possessions with so much meaning that we want them close at all times. Whether it's the lucky rabbit's foot we must have in our pocket or the personal artifacts we find buried with the ancients, it's in our nature to view some of our possessions as essential parts of ourselves. What's changed is how we've transferred that meaning from objects to brands. After working on various smartphone branding projects, I've noticed a clear dividing line in early adopters. There is always a segment who must have the latest gadget, regardless of the brand affiliation. For them, the comfort comes from the newness of the device itself. In fact, these fickle early adopters are also known as "first droppers," because they are usually the first segment to move on to a new technology. But there's another, growing segment who wants the newest device from

their preferred brand. This segment even defends and rationalizes poorly designed devices—to them, it's the brand in their pocket, not the object itself.

On Display

There is perhaps no stronger sign of attachment than consumers' willingness to show off a brand. When a brand connects strongly with our self-concept, we often want to use it as a way to signal who we are to the rest of the world. Historically, the degree to which we're willing to wear brands comes in waves. During the 1980s, brand display was critical to conspicuous consumption; people enjoyed draping themselves with brand identities, creating odd tapestries reminiscent of NASCAR uniforms. Around the millennium, distaste for displaying labels spawned a backlash movement. But the wearable brand never went away completely—it simply became more discreet. Whether used to show others you have status and style, as you might when carrying a signature Louis Vuitton handbag, or to display your commitment to quality, as you might with a Mont-blanc pen, we're often attached to brands because they help us project our identity to the rest of the world.

Sometimes this leads to problems for the brand's maker. A colleague recently told me that fashion brand Bebe was considering whether to discontinue production of its logo T-shirts, available online and in most stores for about $20 to $30. It was rumored that some Bebe executives were troubled to see housekeepers and nannies in local neighborhoods wearing Bebe T-shirts in the performance of their duties. They were worried that the brand would be perceived as less special because it was so accessible that you might find it on someone who was pushing a stroller or cleaning windows.

CEO Manny Mashouf had publicly stated that his goal was to position Bebe as a fashion icon worthy of premium pricing. In an investor call in 2010, he cited this goal as his rationale for partnering with public personalities such as Kim Kardashian, who he believed provided the brand with celebrity cachet. Many of the women wearing the Bebe logo T-shirt might indeed identify with the brand's sex-object image. Unfortunately, while many of these women consider themselves stylish, sexy, and sophisticated, they probably can't afford many of the products in Bebe's line. The comfortably priced logo T-shirt allows them to possess the Bebe brand and present themselves to the world as part of its culture.

When consumers use brands to display their sense of self, they make a statement about their relationship with the rest of the world. A brand can help consumers demonstrate how much they wish to fit in (as in the Bebe example), or it can help them signal how much they want to stand out.

When your consumer audience celebrates interdependence—that we're all connected and that the more we work with others, the higher the benefit—your brand serves as a common bond. However, some consumers attach themselves to a brand because they see it as a symbol of disruption; they see it and themselves as iconoclasts out to overturn traditions. The brand demonstrates how they don't follow anyone's rules, nor do they care whether they are accepted into the mainstream. When Alexander McQueen's fashion lines first debuted, they shocked the fashion elite. McQueen built a name for himself by creating provocative styles such as low-rise pants, dubbed "bumsters," and staged fashion shows with controversial names such as "Highland Rape." The early followers of McQueen's fashion lines wanted to stand out. They took delight in his creative approaches to design, and they saw his brand as a form of rebellion—an opportunity to signal their autonomy and fierce independence.

Do You Drive a Bentley?

It may not be so surprising that consumers buy and use brands to shape their self-concepts. But can a brand be part of a consumer's identity when the consumer doesn't even possess it? The answer, of course, is yes. It's common to find consumers who identify with brands they have never owned or used. Think of the number of car aficionados who identify with the Ferrari, Maserati, or Bentley brands. Most of them haven't even sat in one of those vehicles, let alone owned one. The same is true for fashionistas who identify with Chanel, Prada, and Dolce & Gabbana.

When brands that resonate with our identity are hard to possess, we compensate in other ways. In the real world, it is often true that we are what we buy. Online, we are what we post. And on social-media sites such as Facebook, Tumblr, YouTube, and Twitter, all you have to do is click the "Like" button or tell people you're following a brand. There's almost no risk. Every time you include a brand in your social stream, you're signaling to your world that this is what you stand for.

Which brings me back again to the Barefoot Bandit. Why would thousands of people choose to identify with a notorious fugitive and an alleged criminal? The easy answer to the question is that our culture has a history of glorifying outlaws. We've had naughty brands (*Playboy*), irreverent brands (Virgin), tricksters (AXE), and outright hostile characters (think of Apple's sometimes-maddening, sometimes-endearing "take it or leave it" approach to new product introduction). But dismissing Harris-Moore's Facebook fan base as nothing more than a love of antiheroes misses the point.

Consumers who liked the Barefoot Bandit on Facebook were engaged in at least one identity-affirming activity. Some clicked the "Like" button because when they came across Harris-Moore's story, something inside them identified with him.

Whether they admired his flagrant challenge to law enforcement or saw him as the free spirit they'd like to be, they said, "That's great. Fly on!"

The other possibility is that they liked his fan page because they wanted to signal to their circle of friends and acquaintances that their own personal brand is aligned with the brand of the Barefoot Bandit. Aidin Stephens, an entrepreneur who profited from Harris-Moore's run from the law by selling T-shirts bearing his likeness, said he rooted for the Barefoot Bandit because "being good doesn't really get you very far. It's a kind of a sucker's swindle. . . . [W]hether he's a mastermind or not, he was obviously never going to have the kind of opportunities that some people might have to have a Mercedes or to be a pilot." Stevens proved his argument every time someone paid him $15 for a "Momma Tried: Colton Harris-Moore" T-shirt.

The story of the Barefoot Bandit (who, in January, was sentenced to six and a half years in prison) is an allegory about the pervasiveness of brands in our lives. It is possible that Colton Harris-Moore attached so much meaning to brands that he elected to possess them the only way he knew how—to steal them. It seems likely that the meaning of some of those brands emboldened him to engage in extraordinarily risky behavior, literally putting his life on the line. Along the way, he defined a brand of his own, creating a brand mark and establishing an identity that influenced others. And in perhaps the most striking lesson, his brand became a link to people all over the world—people disinclined to criminality. Instead, they saw a part of themselves in his brand, and they used a nonrisky channel (the online universe) to associate with his equity.

Brands are a part of the consumer narrative, and you must strive to understand what it means thematically to the narrative your consumers are trying to activate. For many of the great brands, this meaning was accidental at best. As we attach more and more meaning to our brands, it's worth your time to understand the compelling context your brand provides to the consumers who will make it their own.

When celebrities fall from grace, as they do from time to time, they often say that they never asked to be role models. But whether it's a star, an athlete, or a politician, the public is rarely sympathetic to this argument. The fact of the matter is that once you enjoy the benefits of celebrity, you have an obligation to serve your fans if you want to sustain your relationship with them. Increasingly, those fans want you to be a role model. They want you to prove them right for aspiring to be like you and for attaching you to a part of themselves.

Brands must live by the same obligation. It is simply insufficient to ignore this new social contract. If your brand enjoys high levels of attachment, you have an obligation to live up to what you promise. If not, you risk becoming irrelevant or—even worse—reviled and outcast.

Critical Thinking

1. "When people become attached to brands, their attachment changes their behavior." Can you relate to this statement? Discuss, drawing from your own consumption experience.

2. Brands are a part of the consumer narrative, and within this narrative some brands are sacred and others are profane. Elaborate this idea, including examples of brands that fall into each of these two categories.

3. The article states that "branding, marketing, and media are often misused in irresponsible and unsustainable ways-ways that overpromise on the value that can actually be delivered; ways that manipulate by appealing to our most shallow, image-driven vulnerabilities; and ways that define brands as substitutes for human relationships." With a group of peers from your class, debate the ethical implications of branding strategies.

Create Central

www.mhhe.com/createcentral

Internet References

Brand Strategy Insider
http://www.brandingstrategyinsider.com/

Prophet
http://www.prophet.com/home

Excerpted/Adapted by permission of the publisher, from Brand Real by Laurence Vincent © 2012 Laurence Vincent, AMACOM division of American Management Association International, New York, NY. All rights reserved. www.amacombooks.org

Unit 3

UNIT

Prepared by: Nisreen N. Bahnan, *Salem State University*

Developing and Implementing Marketing Strategies

"Without strategy, execution is aimless, without execution, strategy is useless."

— Morris Chang, CEO of Taiwan Semiconductor Manufacturing Co.

"**T**he marketing organization," Philip Kotler once said, "will have to redefine its role from managing customer interactions to integrating and managing all the company's customer-facing processes." The development and implementation of integrated strategies is considerably complex, and much of this complexity is due to changes in the environment within which managers must operate. Strategies that fail to heed the social, political, and economic forces of society have little chance of success over the long run. The selections in this unit provide a wide-ranging discussion of how marketing professionals and companies interpret and employ various marketing strategies today. The articles are grouped in four sections, each dealing with one of the main strategy areas: product, pricing, distribution, and promotion.

Product Strategy

Product strategy is the core component of overall marketing strategy. The product itself guides further strategy decisions necessary to achieve marketplace success. Successful marketing strategy recognizes the power of effective branding and the need for continuous innovation.

The famous Peter Drucker once stated that "suppliers and especially manufacturers have market power because they have information about a product or a service that the customer does not, and cannot have, and does not need if he can trust the brand. This explains the profitability of brands." Some of the articles in this subsection discuss branding strategy, focusing on the success of the most trusted brands in the U.S. and emerging

markets. Selections also address the role of innovative technology as the driving force behind product development, as Steve Jobs noted: "Innovation distinguishes between a leader and a follower." The issue of technology is examined in the ever-growing digital applications sector, presenting valuable knowledge every small business should have before going mobile.

Pricing Strategy

Few elements of the total strategy of the "marketing mix" demand so much managerial and social attention as pricing. There is a good deal of public misunderstanding about the ability of marketing managers to control prices and even greater misunderstanding about how pricing policies are determined. The selections in this subsection suggest new pricing strategies that enable companies to create shared value with customers, and address pricing practices for companies that target less affluent consumers residing in low-income emerging markets.

Distribution Strategy

For many enterprises, the largest marketing costs result from closing the gap in space and time between producer and consumer. In no other area of marketing is efficiency so eagerly sought. Physical distribution seems to be the one area where significant cost savings can be achieved.

The costs of physical distribution are tied closely with decisions made about the number, the size, and the diversity of marketing intermediaries between producer and consumer, as is illustrated in some of the articles in this section. Other selections present thought-provoking arguments that the current American marketing distribution model is dysfunctional, and small and medium-sized businesses operate under a misconceived ideology of producing and selling.

Promotion Strategy

The basic objectives of promotion are to inform, persuade, or remind the consumer to buy a firm's product or pay for the firm's service. Advertising is the most obvious promotional activity. However, in terms of cost-effectiveness, advertising has been playing second fiddle to social and digital media marketing. As Wendy Clark, Senior VP of Integrated Marketing at Coca-Cola put it: "if your plans don't include mobile, your plans are not finished." The purpose of this subsection is to expose marketers to emerging social and mobile trends, including online communities and blogs, and to educate them on how to enlist this new medium to enhance their brand and better engage their customers.

Article   Prepared by: Nisreen N. Bahnan, *Salem State University*

Tapping the Untapped

Marketers can learn from product preferences that are simply linked to consumers' physiology.

Diana Derval

Learning Outcomes

After reading this article, you will be able to:

- Define the term "sensory perception."

- Recognize sensory perception as a novel, and more effective basis for consumer segmentation.

- Ascertain the potential and promise of this emerging scientific approach to marketing research and strategy.

Product preferences are closely linked to our physiology: nearsighted people are relaxed by blue, and testosterone-driven women prefer fruity scents, for example. Brands, therefore, can use physiological knowledge to predict consumers' preferences and design the right sensory mix.

Sensory Perception

Sensory perception is an untapped strategic resource that has a direct impact on purchasing decisions. Everything from shape, color, texture, smell, and taste can attract or repulse consumers. Variations in sensory perception are huge among individuals: some people hear the same sound four-times louder, or feel the same fabric 12-times softer than others do. The success stories of beauty retailer Sephora, Domino's Pizza and Pleo pet dinosaurs illustrate how grabbing the opportunity of sensory perception analysis at an early stage can help marketers with:

- increasing the innovation hit rate,
- identifying local and emerging markets; and
- increasing sales.

Pleo Reborn

Pleo is an example of using scientific market research to win new markets. After the International Consumer Electronics Show in Las Vegas, Innvo Labs Corp. took the show at the Gulf Information Technology Exhibition consumer electronics shopping extravaganza in Dubai with the new Pleo RB (reborn). The robotic companion pet is back with more sensors to interact with the environment: shaking when it's too cold, answering to its name, asking for food and appreciating hugs.

The original Pleo, launched in green for the U.S. and European markets, didn't appeal as much to the Chinese and Hong Kong markets. Innvo Labs wondered about which color to choose for Pleo Reborn.

Derek Dotson, CEO of Innvo Labs, confirms that traditional market research gives little help: "When we asked our customer base which color they prefer, many of them said red, others blue, and some green."

Luckily, scientific research can help. You might wonder what science has to do with attractive colors. Well, according to the laws of physics, each color has a different refraction: blue and violet, for instance, will hit the front of our eyeball, whereas red and yellow will hit the back of our eyeball. The focal point of the eye [is] where all color waves meet after passing the lens.

The twist is that the exact location of the focal point varies depending on an individual's physiology, and determines his or her favorite colors:

- Nearsighted people focus light in front of the retina; viewing blue is effortless for them. To perceive red, they must tense their ocular muscles.

- Farsighted people have a shorter eyeball, and the F point is beyond the retina. Viewing red is effortless for them. To perceive blue, they must tense their ocular muscles.

Briefly

- Product preferences are directly linked to the millions of sensors monitoring our bodies and brains.
- Segmenting consumers based on their sensory perception is more powerful than grouping them by revenue or age.
- When in the same context, consumers who have an identical Hormonal Quotient® make the same purchasing decisions.

China, including Hong Kong, happens to have the largest population of nearsighted people in the world, with 400 million individuals—33 percent of the Chinese population and more than 60 percent of the Chinese youth. So brands targeting young Chinese shoppers can use blue as a relaxing color and red as an exciting one. When targeting Australians, the vast majority of whom are farsighted, it is the contrary: blue will be an exciting color and red a relaxing one.

Innvo Labs successfully introduced to Hong Kong its Pleo Reborn—in blue, of course.

The Hormonal Quotient®

As we saw from the Pleo case, segmenting consumers based on their sensory perception makes a lot more sense than grouping them by revenue or age. And it enables brands to design the right products and services for each target group and local market.

An interesting finding is that product preferences are directly linked to the millions of sensors monitoring our bodies and brains. The number and distribution of these sensors are greatly influenced by prenatal hormones so that it is possible to predict favorite colors, tastes, scents, shapes, textures, and sounds—almost from the womb.

Some people, for instance, hear high-pitch sounds four times louder than others. If they switch to an electric car, these super-amplifiers are more likely to enjoy a Chevrolet Volt than a Nissan Leaf, just because noise diagrams confirm that the Nissan Leaf engine generates high frequency noises that are extremely annoying to sensitive super-amplifiers' ears.

In many animal species, there are several types of males and several types of females with specific behaviors and preferences. These gender polymorphisms are directly linked to the influence of prenatal hormones.

Among side-blotched lizards, for instance, orange-throated males—exposed to higher levels of prenatal testosterone—are dating several females at the same time and do not perceive stress. Meanwhile, blue-throated males have a smaller territory and are monogamous.

Based on thousands of measurements in more than 25 countries, Chicago-based DervalResearch identified eight gender polymorphisms in humans—the Hormonal Quotient®—so that shoppers with the same HQ profile show very similar preferences in terms of colors, shapes, scents, tastes, textures, and sounds. For instance, women with a testosterone-driven HQ are more likely to prefer fruity to floral scents—always good to know for a beauty retailer like Sephora, or for men who haven't given up on offering perfumes.

Furthermore, women with a testosterone-driven HQ are also more likely to be sensitive to chemicals, so the safe areas for these super-inhalers would be air, food and mates' scents. That's good to know if you are a hotel planning to spread synthetic fragrances in the lobby, or a shop intending to burn incense throughout the day. If these women are in your target, you might end up repulsing the consumers you wanted to attract.

The Domino's Pizza Case

Domino's Pizza and Pizza Hut decided to penetrate a complex market with many local disparities (a bit like in the United States): France. Both brands have a very strong network of outlets, but the distribution on the map is very different, with Pizza Hut concentrated on the biggest cities and Domino's Pizza present also toward the Atlantic coast. So which of these pizza brands is the No. 1 in France, and why?

Interestingly, when referencing more research, it's found that consumers more likely to eat pizza are concentrated in the big cities and toward the Atlantic coast. Domino's Pizza clearly became the No. 1 pizza player in France by opening outlets in the right catchment areas, taste-wise.

Integrating a sensory approach at an early stage of a business plan is highly beneficial, but the initiative can come from research and development, product marketing, process innovation, brand management, business development, or the consumer experience teams. What really matters is to be ready to look at one's own products from a new and more scientific angle.

Sensory perception can be used to:

- design the ideal consumer experience for a given target group (a fruity scent for testosterone-driven women) or geographical area (a blue Pleo for the Chinese market); or
- identify the most profitable market opportunity or geographical area for a given product or service—like the French Atlantic coast for Domino's Pizzas.

SENSORY QUIZ PROPOSED BY DERVALRESEARCH

Are You More Into?

		(a)	(b)
1.	**TASTE**	(a) strong black coffee	(b) tea or coffee with milk
2.	**SMELL**	(a) flower scent	(b) fruit scent
3.	**SOUND**	(a) pop music	(b) other music genres
4.	**VISION**	(a) ▇▇▇▇▇▇	(b) ▇▇▇▇
5.	**TOUCH**	(a) cotton	(b) silk

Your Sensory Profile:

		Answer (A)	Answer (B)
1.	**TASTE**	You are not very sensitive to bitterness and can eat almost anything.	You are sensitive to bitterness and more picky on food.
2.	**SMELL**	You enjoy most scents and essential oils.	You are sensitive to synthetic fragrances and prefer natural scents.
3.	**SOUND**	You struggle following a conversation with background noise.	You prefer bass sounds to high pitch noises.
4.	**VISION**	You see well far away and are relaxed by colors like red or orange.	You see better close-up and are relaxed by colors like blue or purple.
5.	**TOUCH**	You are irritated by certain fabrics and very sensitive to temperature changes.	You enjoy all sorts of fabrics and pay more attention to the clothing style.

An Exact Science

The promise of this scientific approach to marketing is huge: no more gambling, endless surveys, evening focus groups or pricey brain scans. Brands just need to identify the sensory profiles of their target consumers once.

Marketers can then make decisions for each new product and service, based on reliable scientific observations. The time and budget saver is that people with the same sensory profile, in the same context, behave in the same way. Brands can team up with experts in behavioral neuroendocrinology, who understand the impact of hormones on the body and the brain, to develop the products and services that consumers want. This field of research is growing fast: more than 500 scientific articles have been published over the past two years about hormones and behavior, with marketing applications from segmentation to positioning. Consumers will greatly benefit from a sensory-friendly brand experience.

Critical Thinking

1. Define the term "Sensory Perception."
2. Discuss how the Pleo Reborn is a good example of effective scientific market research.
3. Do you agree with the premise that "segmenting consumers based on their sensory perceptions is more powerful than grouping them by revenue or age?"

Create Central

www.mhhe.com/createcentral

Internet References

Brain Facts
http://www.brainfacts.org/
Brain Games
http://braingames.nationalgeographic.com/episode/0/
Neuromarketing
http://www.neurosciencemarketing.com/blog/

DIANA DERVAL is president and research director of DervalResearch, an international market research firm specializing in human perception and behavior, inventor of the Hormonal Quotient® and author of *The Right Sensory Mix: Targeting Consumer Product Development Scientifically* (Springer, 2010), a finalist of the Berry-AMA award for best marketing book 2011. She may be reached at Diana@derval-research.com.

Diana Derval, "Tapping the Untapped," *Marketing Management*, Spring 2012, p. 24–27. Copyright © 2012 by American Marketing Association. All rights reserved. Used with permission.

Article

Prepared by: Nisreen N. Bahnan, *Salem State University*

The CMO and the Future of Marketing

Tomorrow's CMOs will need a broader skill set to survive and thrive.

GEORGE S. DAY AND ROBERT MALCOLM

Learning Outcomes

After reading this article, you will be able to:

- Define the role of the Chief Marketing Officer (CMO) within an organization.

- Discuss the driving forces, discussed in the article, that shape the role of an organization's CMO.

How will the roles, responsibilities, and influence of the chief marketing officer evolve in the future? The answers will emerge from the interplay of three driving forces and the unique features of each company's strategy and legacy. These three driving forces include the predictable trends in the marketplaces, the changing role of the C-suite, and uncertainty about the economic climate and organizational design in the future.

The impact of the three driving forces on the job of the CMO will be amplified by the unrealistic expectations of the chief executive officer and the rest of the leadership team about what a CMO can accomplish . . . and the lack of preparation of a majority of candidates for this job.

The average tenure of a CMO is about three years, and is unlikely to be much longer in the future. Yet some CMOs will rise to the intensifying challenge, and earn a "seat at the table." These "whole-brain" marketing leaders will ground their decisions in analytic realities, while painting a realistic vision for the company that bridges today and the future. They will excel at the five priority actions needed to navigate escalating complexity and uncertainty:

- act as the visionary for the future of the company;
- build adaptive marketing capabilities;
- win the war for marketing talent;
- tighten the alignment with sales; and
- take accountability for the returns on marketing spending.

Forces Shaping Marketing's Future

When thinking about the future in an era of accelerating change, five years is a long time. To appreciate how much can happen in five years, think back to 2007. Facebook and Twitter were barely on the horizon, e-books hardly existed, clouds were still something in the sky and the credit bubble that triggered the financial meltdown was still expanding. We can be sure that five years from now in 2017 there will be equally dramatic surprises; we are uncertain about these shocks and events. At the same time, there are a number of predictable trends that CMOs can prepare for with some confidence.

The Evolving C-Level

A recent analysis of C-level jobs concluded that once people reached the C-level, the skills and functional mastery that got them there matter less than their leadership skills and general business acumen. The chief information officer, chief technology officer, or CMO who thrives as a member of the senior leadership team will be a team player who can lead without rank and has built an organization that earns the respect of the rest of the business. The skills that are increasingly in favor are strong communication, willingness to partner, and strategic thinking. Successful members of the management team will advise the CEO on key decisions and strategic choices, but offer their own well-informed insights.

For CMOs to thrive and survive in a collaborative C-suite, they will have to adopt a general management mindset and earn the respect of the others with fact-based analyses. They will be accountable for the brand strategy, driving the organic growth agenda and positioning the business for the future. As the acknowledged voice of the customer and consumer, they will ensure the strategy is built and executed from the outside in. They can no longer be passive service providers, content to oversee market insight activities, coordinate relationships with key marketing partners, and ensure compliance "reasonably" with brand guidelines.

Predictable Marketplace Trends

The second set of driving forces has been the subject of many analyses in our purpose here is to highlight a few trends to make the basic point that marketing in the future will be increasingly complex, and will change at a faster rate than most companies can handle. Consider the interplay of the following trends:

- demographic shifts;
- connected and empowered consumers;
- new technologies enabling micro-targeting;
- the rise of global markets in China, India, Brazil and Indonesia;
- new media (cinema, video, sponsorship, direct mail, SMS, Internet, social, etc.); and
- channels of distribution becoming complex ecosystems of networked partners.

> **"The best possible solutions come only from a combination of rational analysis based on the nature of things, and imaginative reintegration of all the different items into a new pattern, using non-linear brain power."**
>
> —*Kenichi Ohmae* "The Mind of the Strategist"

The predictable consequences of these trends, which we have already experienced, will surely accelerate to make markets more complex and fragmented. There will be a continuing shift in power to consumers and a proliferation of media and channels—all at the same time that plummeting communication costs and diffused manufacturing technologies enable new, low-cost competitors to enter from anywhere in the world. These trends have exciting (and scary) prospects for marketers who will be expected to be creative and tech-savvy global thinkers and results-oriented leaders.

Living with Uncertainty

What will the future bring? This question is hard to answer because of many uncertainties where the outcome is not known with any confidence. What will the price of oil be? The geopolitical climate? The regulatory requirements? These are material, but to a group of CMOs brought together by the American Marketing Association, the two uncertainties that were most informative and potentially influential were the system-wide resources available to marketing and the dominant organizational models. These two critical uncertainties were each reduced to a single spectrum with the credible extreme states at each pole (as seen in Figure 1).

These two axes were crossed to form a 2×2 matrix, with four different quadrants of uncertainty. Each quadrant portrays a plausible, alternative hypothesis, or scenario about how the environment might unfold, and highlights the risks and opportunities to the organization—or, in this case, to the function of marketing within the firm.

These scenarios let marketers "learn from the future." They can rehearse the future to avoid surprises by breaking through the illusion of certainty. Unlike traditional strategic planning, which presumes there is a likely answer to a strategic issue, scenario learning considers multiple futures. It meets the needs of marketers for plans, capabilities, and organization models that are robust across the scenarios, so the organization is prepared for whatever the future will bring.

The "best-case" scenario is that system-wide resources are plentiful and we stay with the traditional closed model. The most challenging scenario for marketers is scarce resources and open network, because this is likely to subordinate the role and influence of marketing.

The reason for uncertainty is that the traditional organization model has shown an amazing level of adaptability. On the other hand, there is considerable evidence that companies that

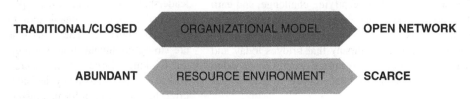

Figure 1   Most potentially influential uncertainties

have a network structure are more nimble and will win the market battle. Companies such as Cisco Systems Inc. or Li & Fung Ltd. are organizing as a network structure to leverage and gain more resources. The best place to see open networks in action is the area of open innovation or innovation networks. However, at this stage, we cannot be certain whether this model will prevail or will be another management fad, because alliances and joint ventures have not had a very successful track record.

The second area of uncertainty relates to the availability of resources. Will they be abundant or scarce? If you read The *Wall Street Journal*, the *Financial Times*, or *The New York Times*, the mood swings are quite abrupt. It could well be that we are going to face a persistently weak economic climate with shrinking profits. One of the consequences is that there will be many more price wars, intense competition and people will manage for the short run. In that environment, marketing almost invariably is on the defensive. However, if resources are perceived to be abundant, the marketers can take the offensive and partner with sales—and there is grounds for optimism.

CMO Challenges

How will the "whole-brain" marketing leader become an influential member of the C-suite and ensure the organization stays ahead of the myriad driving forces that shape the future? First and foremost, they will advocate outside-in thinking that starts with the market when designing strategies, rather than the other way around. Winning strategies will be viewed through a customer value lens and illuminated by deep market insights. Second, they will embrace the dual challenge of building a world-class marketing function that can anticipate and act on the driving forces of change. From our CMO experience and work with dozens of CMOs, there are five priority actions that stand out.

> **"Winning strategies will be viewed through a customer value lens and illuminated by deep market insights"**

Acting as the Visionary for the Future of the Organization

Adaptive organizations continuously scan for opportunities in markets, competitive white spaces, and changing customer needs. They win by seeing sooner than their rivals. This will take an experimental mindset, a willingness to learn quickly from mistakes, and identifying, testing, and deploying new models.

Increasingly, the CMO will be the person leading a function that is adept at monitoring markets and extracting insights for future growth. When Kim Feil, Walgreens CMO, learned from her research group that some consumers viewed the retailer as a convenience store with a pharmacy on the back wall, she saw both a problem and an opportunity. At her urging, the company began to reposition itself as a premium healthcare brand, by showcasing its wellness offerings and walk-in clinic.

Building Adaptive Marketing Capabilities

The CMO of the future must wear many hats and embrace sometimes competing, even contradictory, forces both within and outside the organization. Among the most challenging is the need to deliver business results today, while "creating" the business of tomorrow. Both are essential to a healthy business (and a successful CMO), but require very different marketing processes, skills and capabilities

Delivering today requires more proven, predictable and repeatable tools, skills and processes. It is a bit more left- than right-brained. You are in delivery mode more than planning mode. The marketing capabilities required are developing and executing repeatable models, simplification, executional discipline, rigorous measurement, and decisive action. Convergence, focus, and delivery with a more short-term mindset is required. The CMO who does not master these capabilities and build them in the organization will not likely get the chance to spend much time on the longer-term challenges and opportunities.

"Creating" the business of tomorrow is equally critical and, longer term, the CMOs who do not master these primary sources of knowledge, expertise and ultimate success. With the digital-technology-led transformation in communication, it is the "future generation" who has the great knowledge, understanding

---

Briefly

- The CMO's future role will be determined by the interplay of three driving forces: the predictable trends in their marketplaces, the changing role of the C-suite, and uncertainty about the economic climate and organizational design in the future.
- For CMOs to thrive and survive in a collaborative C-suite, they will have to adopt a general management mindset and earn the respect of the others with fact-based analyses.
- It is the job of the CMO to continue finding ways to make the organization more efficient—not just the marketing spend.

Q/A

Robert Malcolm Elaborates on His Article with George S. Day, Discussing the Role and Expectations of CMOs Today

Q. What is the background of the incoming CMOs? Is their experience appropriate? What kind of experience would be appropriate?

A. The background of incoming CMOs is as varied as the role and responsibilities of CMOs: there is no standard CMO role profile and the educational and work experience preparation of CMOs varies wildly.

Not surprisingly, a critical issue at the root of the relatively low success rate and short tenure of CMOs is the mismatch between expectations and the ability to deliver the expectations. Sometimes, this is a function of misalignment of expectations and resources within the business and sometimes, it is a misalignment in the expectations and the capability of the CMO. David Aaker, vice chairman of the global marketing consultancy Prophet, has identified five broad classifications of CMO roles: facilitator, consultant, service provider, strategic partner, and strategic captain. For the CMO whose job expectation lies primarily in the area of providing marketing services, specific experience in this area—but not necessarily in [profit-and-loss] management, cross-functional leadership, strategy, or business transformation—would be sufficient. For the strategic captain—who leads the strategic direction of the entity, has a core responsibility to deliver profitable growth, drives the resource allocation decisions, and owns the effectiveness and return on marketing spending—there is a very different set of experiences and capabilities required. The key is to match the role and the experiences/capabilities, and this is too often done poorly.

Today's CMOs, unlike their CFO counterparts for the most part, come from a wide experience and educational base. Some have an educational background in marketing, many, if not most, do not. Some come out of marketing functional roles, but many also come from sales or strategy roles. Some even come from the agency side. Some have grown up in very strong marketing functional training companies, where marketing has a central role and is dedicated to the training of future marketing leaders—companies like Procter & Gamble, Coca-Cola, Unilever, Diageo, General Mills, etc. Many come from companies in which there is minimal training, and where marketing plays a secondary or supportive role. By contrast, most CFOs have a strong finance education and functional training track record. As the role is similar, and many of the deliverables are determined by strict financial and accounting reporting and regulations, there is more homogeneity in experience and preparation than for CMOs.

Q. Do companies discourage the needed working style (e.g., collaboration) by the way they operate and promote people into other C-level roles?

A. In my experience, silos exist more as a result of historical organizational and reward structures—rather than as a conscious effort to discourage collaboration. Oftentimes, functional structures and rewards inadvertently create conflict, even competition. For marketing, this is most often the case vis-à-vis the sales function. But it can also show up in the relationship with the finance function. Every effective CMO I know works diligently to build understanding of and confidence in the marketing function, what it does and how it contributes to creating enterprise value. They open up the function, rather than close it down or protect it. Less-successful CMOs do not always recognize the broader leadership and collaboration imperative, and thus stay more isolated within the function.

Q. Do the kind of people that are needed actually exist in large enough numbers? If the average tenure of CMOs is due to this problem, then should companies keep trying the same tactics and expect a different outcome? Maybe the role needs to be redesigned.

A. The answer lies in that last statement: each company needs to design the right role for their business; these will not be uniform. The CMO needs to have the right skills, experience, and culture fit for the properly scoped role. Critically, the role needs to be set up for success, and this is not often done. In many cases, a CEO will have an expectation for the CMO to achieve things that the organization is not structured, resourced, or culturally aligned to achieve. CMOs who finds themselves in this situation and cannot change these things to allow for success, are set up for failure—and failure pretty quickly. Turning to the first question, my experience is there are not enough CMOs who have the combination of talent, experience, and leadership skills to do many of the large transformational CMO roles in the largest corporations. The key challenge is to develop the functional mastery and the "total business leadership" pedigree that cannot only deliver the needed marketing outputs, but influence the broader organization so that it gets the best results out of its marketing. More CMOs fail on the "total business leadership" dimension than another.

and comfort of the new digital and social-marketing applications. Indeed, they are the digital "natives" for whom Facebook, social networks, tweets, and blogs are "just the way we live."

The adaptive organization will recognize the value in getting the best out of the "immigrant and native" digital marketers, and will neither be stuck in the past, nor discard all the institutional knowledge and experience in jumping to a completely new model of marketing. Despite what many pundits would have us believe, the fundamentals of marketing strategy and consumer behavior have not been repealed. The adaptive organization will study the changes, understand how the consumer "consumes influence" with the new marketing technologies, will challenge old models and tactics and experiment with new ones. They will figure out what works in the new digital environment for their business and customer and evolve their models and practices. They will neither totally abandon the past, nor completely adopt the latest digital fad.

Tightening the Alignment with Sales

Too often, there is an adversarial Mars vs. Venus coloration to the relationship of sales and marketing. It has historically been rooted in mutual incomprehension of the other's role, different time horizons and divergent goals and incentives. Typically the two functions occupied separate silos, and one function had more power than the other, depending on the industry.

The traditional lines between marketing and sales are blurring. Key account managers serving large, powerful customers are engaged in long-run marketing strategy and brand development. Meanwhile, the number of possible points of contact with customers and consumers has been increasing exponentially, with social media, interactivity, and mobility demanding closer coordination. Increasingly, CEOs are looking for a single point of contact with all market-facing activities, who can take responsibility for the value proposition, innovation, marketing, and sales across all platforms. Many companies have responded with a new combined role of chief commercial officer. This combined function ensures closer internal and external alignment, by using the Internet to coordinate all marketing and sales activities—from customer-service reps responding to complaints on blogs to systems for tracking sales calls and consumer web behavior.

Taking Accountability for the Returns on Marketing Spending

There is no foreseeable future where marketing won't have to demonstrate that it can earn acceptable returns on marketing investments. While there is admittedly a fair amount of craft (even art) in effective marketing, the discipline at its core, exists to create value for the enterprise. The CMO who doesn't understand this, embrace it and build marketing culture and

capability around value creation through the performance of its marketing investment, will not survive. Key to this is recognizing that this is not a contradiction with the creative side of marketing. As Bill Bernbach, one of the agency creative giants of the 20th century put it: "Properly practiced creativity MUST result in greater sales more economically achieved."

In our experience, once a CMO has embraced the dual responsibilities of creative and accountable delivery, there are several core priorities. The first is the mindset—adopting the mindset of the general manager or CEO, not the creative CMO. The marketing function exists to deliver increased enterprise value in the short-, medium- and long-term. And it does so by owning both the numerator and denominator of the "value equation"— optimizing the ability of marketing to generate top-line growth (the numerator) and reducing the cost of delivering that growth (the denominator). The CMO needs to adopt this mindset and create a marketing culture that fully embraces it. He or she needs to role model the desired values and behavior, and embrace the core metrics and measurements—not avoid them.

Second is the importance of building a strong relationship with the chief financial officer and the financial function. The successful CMO understands the financial model for the business, how economic profits are generated and the expectations of the CFO. More importantly, the CFO and finance function have resources that every CMO should use to improve the marketing value equation. Finally, a CFO who knows and trusts his CMO is an indispensable ally when there are tough judgment calls to be made.

Third, in order to deliver improved enterprise value, you need to know how marketing "works" for your business. How does it create value? What are the specific growth levers and how do you best employ them? Here, you must get past the assumptions or general marketing beliefs and truly know your business. You have to be ready to pull the plug on things that don't work, and consistently reallocate funds to the drivers of more value. This also means an obsession with the efficiency of marketing—and the entire organization.

Fourth, be obsessed with improving the efficiency of marketing, eliminating the "dogs," and making the "stars" more efficient. This is not the job of the procurement department, although they can certainly help. It is the job of the CMO. And, it includes always finding how to make the organization more efficient—not just the marketing spend.

Critical Thinking

1. With a small group of peers from your class, draft a job description for a CMO.

2. List and summarize the three driving forces, discussed in the article, that shape the role of an organization's CMO.

Create Central

www.mhhe.com/createcentral

Internet References

America's Job Exchange
http://www.americasjobexchange.com/chief-marketing-officer-job-description

Chief Marketing Officer Council
http://www.cmocouncil.org/

McKinsey and Company
http://www.mckinsey.com/insights/marketing_sales/the_evolving_role_of_the_cmo

The CMO Survey
http://www.cmosurvey.org/

GEORGE S. DAY is the Geoffrey T. Boisi Professor, professor of marketing and co-director of the Mack Center for Technological Innovation at the Wharton School of the University of Pennsylvania. **ROBERT MALCOLM** is a lecturer in marketing at The Wharton School at the University of Pennsylvania, has held senior marketing and general management positions at Procter & Gamble, and was the chief marketing and sales officer at Diageo. They may be reached at DayG@wharton.upenn.edu and RMalc@wharton.upenn.edu, respectively.

George S. Day; Robert Malcolm, "The CMO and the Future of Marketing," *Marketing Management*, Spring 2012, p. 34–43. Copyright © 2012 by American Marketing Association. All rights reserved. Used with permission.

Article   Prepared by: Nisreen N. Bahnan, *Salem State University*

Lessons in App Building

JENNIFER WANG

Learning Outcomes

After reading this article, you will be able to:

- List and explain the steps in the New Product Development Process for technology products.

- Identify particular challenges faced by application developers to develop and market their offerings.

The winners: angry Birds, fart generators, doodles. The losers: almost everyone else.

Thanks to fairy-tale success stories, "app-preneurs" abound. But the truth is that most apps lose 76 percent of their consumers after the first three months of use—which means that even in the unlikely event your product is chosen from among the daily App Store deluge, any ad or freemium revenue streams would dry up quickly.

So how do you build an app that will attract loyal users, one that's strong enough to support a profitable company? To find out, we went behind the scenes at Los Angeles-based inMarket, the development firm responsible for CheckPoints, a free shopping app that allows users to check in at more than one million retailers to earn discounts toward goods—essentially digitizing paper coupons, bridging online and offline commerce.

Todd DiPaola, president of inMarket, and his brother Mark, CEO, sold their El Segundo, Calif.-based marketing agency Vantage Media in 2002 for roughly $150 million and used those proceeds to develop CheckPoints, which launched in late 2010. Now they're gearing up for a sequel app, List Bliss—this time, backed by a team of 20 and some lessons from "a month of hard knocks."

What they learned on the first go-round was that rushing the development process can lead to a buggy product. "Check-Points encountered difficulty with a few bonus features we wanted to add at the launch," Todd DiPaola says. "We wound up removing them until a later version when we could give it the focus it needed.

"Building an app is like building a house," he adds. "You need to put time into thinking about what the rooms are going to look like before you start building." That attention to detail has paid off: the inMarket network has more than 20 million users.

With the launch of List Bliss, inMarket is offering a user-friendly tool for creating grocery lists. It's the first in a suite of planned apps aimed at simplifying mobile shopping. The app allows users to scan bar codes to add items to their lists; it also keeps track of ingredients already in their pantries, enables sharing of lists with family and friends for more efficient trips to the store and incorporates coupons and product reviews. It costs nothing to sign up; an ad-free premium subscription version is $1.99 per month.

"With List Bliss, we've made it a point to keep the feature set focused, so any launch bugs can be corrected easily," DiPaola says. "We have a ton of new features in store for our users a few weeks after launch, but right now our priority is to make a rock-solid version 1.0."

Here's how a critical weekly progress meeting at inMarket went down, along with general tips for businesses to keep in mind for their own app-development processes. But the most important piece of advice may also be the most obvious: as DiPaola says, "It should just work."

For six weeks, Todd DiPaola and his team—vice president of technology Kiran Rao, vice president of production Ricky Juarez and three other development staffers—have been brainstorming. They've checked out the competition, evaluating the features in existing list apps, and they believe they have come up with a product that will appeal to their target market: the Midwestern mom, a "fresh" smartphone user who doesn't even know she needs a better shopping list. The point of today's meeting—at inMarket's bright, cozy office on hip Abbot Kinney Boulevard in L.A.'s Venice district—is to boil the List

Bliss design down to the absolute essentials. "Great apps," DiPaola contends, "aren't bloated."

The login page is a cartoon cow pasture with a nerdy but cute mascot named Mr. Listo, whose purpose is to add "sparkle" to the app. (This worked well with Mr. CheckPoints, who's so beloved, his fans have requested toys and stuffed animals in his image.) Mr. Listo will show up in animations while List Bliss elements are loading; say, chillin' and sipping a drink as items are crossed off the grocery list.

First on the agenda is user sign-up. The process for Facebook and e-mail logins gets the OK from the team. But a proposed one-step Register and Subscribe button is nixed; the developers figure that even if 10 percent of users want the premium version, the 90 percent who would want only a free version might see the option as a roadblock and get turned off or confused.

Lesson learned: The fewer registration buttons, the better. Impatient users will look for any excuse to back out of downloading an app.

The home screen has three proposed feature buttons: grocery List, Pantry Inventory, and History. But some on the team think not enough people will use History to justify the effort and expense it would take to build it. However, shelving it for a future release or premium feature is a possibility.

"It's a cool feature, but let's see if users want it," Juarez suggests. "If they do, we'll add it, and it will show them that we're improving the app and listening to them."

Lesson learned: Watch out for feature creep. A great app is designed with a specific set of purposes in mind, and when you add unnecessary items, you dilute that functionality.

The heart of the product, the Grocery List, went through many iterations as the team considered potential uses. "There were, like, 87 versions of this," DiPaola estimates. The challenge is to offer functionality that appeals to a broad spectrum of users—from those who want the app to work as a simple digital notepad, to "power users" who want the ability to keep track of very specific items (e.g., Golden Delicious vs. Fuji apples), make notes, create categories, and even break the list down into price per item for budgeting ease. The solution? The app opens

to a default Grocery List screen, with an Edit button that takes power users to their own page for additional functions.

Lesson learned: To make people devoted to your app, offer features no one else has—but make sure the design is flexible, customizable, and intuitive.

The most heated discussion revolves around the Save buttons on the Edit page. Some on the team argue that app users are aware that changes are saved automatically, so there's no need for buttons that take up precious screen space. Others think moms need to be reassured their changes are "safe." A compromise is reached: a large, central Save button stays, but a redundant button that had been in the upper-right corner is eliminated to cut down on screen clutter.

Next, one developer pulls out his iPhone to demonstrate a problem on the working List Bliss prototype. He shows that moving items on a list by dragging them around interferes with the Delete action. To fix this, the team decides that accessing the drag function will require an additional action—a tap or a hold—to distinguish between the two gestures.

Lesson learned: Sweat the small stuff. Every design element must be considered in terms of efficiency and functionality. Also, keep testing even the most minor functions, because as the app goes through its iterations, new problems can be created where none previously existed.

To celebrate the launch of List Bliss, DiPaola has commissioned a Mr. CheckPoints piñata. But even before the party is over, there will be troubleshooting (not to mention the scramble to create tablet and Android versions of the app). "It's inevitable there will be at least one bug, or a developer will get sick, so we try to prepare before the hurricane hits," he says.

It helps to have beta testers give perspective on simplifying user experience. "Sometimes you're just too close to the product," DiPaola says, noting that a great last-minute change made by his team involved consolidating two input fields into one. Bigger changes will be deployed in version 2.0.

Additionally, a few weeks before launch, inMarket built up a customer-support system. The team partnered with a company that establishes the infrastructure for a customer-support ticketing system and spent time bolstering the self-help section of the List Bliss landing page. That last item is one many developers don't realize they need until after launch, when they start to see the bad reviews from unhappy users.

Lesson learned: Don't be afraid to make last-minute tweaks or to let a trusted outsider test your product. Obvious solutions might not seem so obvious at the beginning of the process or to those deeply involved in the development. Try to anticipate potential usage problems and have customer-service options in place.

Although List Bliss has a big head start on user acquisition because of CheckPoints' existing user base, inMarket has planned a comprehensive marketing strategy for the new app: going after coverage in media and blogs; search-engine marketing; in-app advertisements; and Facebook data mining. And DiPaola is trying to keep things creative.

"For CheckPoints, we did a fun video showing Mr. and Mrs. CheckPoints shopping that was well-received," he says. "We're working on one for List Bliss, because it's good to have something entertaining that people can relate to, and will hopefully go viral and reach more users."

When it comes to reviews, it's important to hit the App Store "hard and high," DiPaola says. The more four- and five-star reviews you get at the beginning, the higher your app will rank on Apple's charts—and the easier it will be for people to discover your product.

Lesson learned: For the few apps that manage to go viral, great. But don't expect users to grow on trees. You need to get out there and woo them.

Critical Thinking

1. Use the article narrative to extrapolate the steps in the New Product Development Process for technology products.

2. As an app user, assess the validity of the 'lessons learned' of application development discussed in this article.

3. In your opinion, what are the advantages and disadvantages for businesses of doing in-house application developments as opposed to using self-service platforms.

Create Central

www.mhhe.com/createcentral

Internet References

Application Developers Alliance
    http://appdevelopersalliance.org/
Product Strategy
    http://www.productstrategy.net/

Jennifer Wang, "Lessons in App Building," *Entrepreneur,* August 2012. Copyright © 2012 by Entrepreneur Media, Inc. All rights reserved. Used with permission.

Article   Prepared by: Nisreen N. Bahnan, *Salem State University*

Brand Apathy Calls for New Methods

Turn Customer Preference from "No Brand" to "Some Brand"

DON E. SCHULTZ

Learning Outcomes

After reading this article, you will be able to:

- Differentiate between brand apathy, brand preference, and brand loyalty.

- Recognize how the competitive landscape has changed for businesses operating today.

- Identify a set of strategies that can successfully transform consumer apathy toward the brand into interest and potentially preference.

Brand managers are accustomed to seeing challenging numbers. Faltering economies around the world guarantee that. Yet management plows ahead—setting double-digit internal sales objectives, increasing market share and expanding retail shelf space—doing all the things that mollify shareholders and prop up stock prices.

There's increasing evidence that organic sales improvement, line extensions and acquisitions just don't do it today.

Some brands have tried more focused sales efforts on specific segments, expanded their online and interactive promotional tools, and adjusted prices through coupons and other promotions. Still, major national brands are challenged as never before.

Unfortunately, the news I have to deliver in this column isn't very encouraging. However, if brand managers understand the new competitive landscape and refocus their efforts on differentiated initiatives while adjusting their competitive mindset, all is not lost. A rainbow and pot of gold may not be just around the corner, but there may be an improved opportunity for national brands.

Brand managers historically have focused on the general marketplace (i.e., sales volume compared with a year ago, incremental distribution increases and the like). While paying attention to competitive brands, they've often been willing to give up short-term share points to generate sales volume. The result has been more market knowledge than competitive knowledge. Share has been important, just not that important, primarily because they've been incented to grow volume.

That game is changing. Following four quarters of profit declines, Procter & Gamble (P&G) has declared "no more market share losses." Moving from valuing sales volume (in the case of P&G, the base was organic sales growth) to market share doesn't sound like a big deal—but it is. Brand managers cut their teeth driving short-term, quarter-to-quarter sales increases.

Building share is a different ball game, requiring a new set of tools and techniques. Finely tuned brand strategies designed to shift ongoing consumer preference and purchase from competitive brands to yours on an ongoing basis are the orders of the day—long-term, not short-term, returns.

Not so difficult, one would think—only it is. Getting consumers to change brands and maintain that change through ongoing preference is much more difficult than simply getting short-term sales volume from in-and-out, deal-prone consumers.

Most fast-moving consumer goods markets consist of (a) a limited number of brand loyal buyers, (b) a large group of brand switchers, and (c) a growing bunch of unknowns or in-and-out buyers. That is, they only purchase when the price or promotion or communication is right. Promote to the switchers and sales often go up.

Observing this new emphasis on brand share growth, a Northwestern colleague and I decided to take a fresh look at brands, brand preferences, and brand shares. That's where we found the scary numbers.

A rainbow and pot of gold may not be just around the corner, but there may be an improved opportunity for national brands.

While one could argue that preference doesn't really reflect actual purchases, a person must be favorably inclined if a brand purchase is to be made. In addition, brand preference is forward-looking, while actual measured brand shares are historical. Thus, we believe preference is a relevant measure for most brands and their managers.

Using monthly online consumer reported preference information from the BIGresearch Consumer Intentions and Actions (CIA) panel, the consumer reported brand preferences were calculated for two product categories: breakfast products and salty snacks. (The data used was for August 2010 with a base of 8,000-plus U.S. respondents. See www.bigresearch.com for details.) Consumers also reported their retail grocery/mass merchandiser preferences. This dual retailer/brand combination is important. From previous research, we've found consumer retail store loyalty impacts national brand sales. If the preferred retailer doesn't stock the national brand, sales don't occur.

From the CIA data, a modified "Net Promoter" calculation, similar to the one Fredrick Reichheld of Boston-based Bain & Company developed, was calculated. Using a scale of 1 to 10 (1 being detractors or non-recommenders and 10 being promoters or people who favorably recommend), a Net Promoter Score was calculated first for the retail food store.

The store chain with the top Net Promoter Score was Publix, followed by Aldi and then HEB. Far down the list were some of the retailing giants, such as Wal-Mart and Safeway.

While these retail calculations were interesting, the brand results were even more so. For this, the brand preference rating in two product categories (using the same 1-to-10 system) was determined. That was then combined with the retail chain preference.

In the breakfast product category, when the chain and brand were indexed, the top brand was Cheerios, followed by Special K. The only brand with an index greater than 100 was Kashi. This simply means that Kashi brand preference is stronger than the retail store preference.

In the salty snack category, Frito-Lay (no specific product name) was the top indexing brand, followed by Tostitos. None of the national brands indexed more than 100, signifying to us that the retail chain store choice was stronger than the brand choice.

The really scary numbers in both categories, however, were the large numbers of "no preference" consumers. In the breakfast product category, 30 percent reported no preference. In salty snacks, 36.7 percent had no preference. Store brands (private label) registered a 4.1 share in breakfast products and a 6.8 share in salty snacks.

These scary figures seem to indicate that the share battle going forward isn't going to be getting consumers to prefer General Mills products over Kellogg's. The challenge is getting them to prefer "some brand" over "no brand." The national brand battle isn't between the leading national brands—or even the national brands against store brands or private label. It's against brand apathy.

Preference apathy is a tough task for a brand manager. If consumers don't care about the brand or don't perceive that it is even worth their time to learn about the category or the brand, most traditional marketing tools and concepts go right out the window.

When 30 percent or more of your product category consumers say their top choice is no preference, major rethinking needs to be done. Maybe P&G is right in shifting its performance evaluation to share-of-peer brand market, but how relevant is that when there is such a preponderance of customers who just don't care?

Critical Thinking

1. In your perspective, has the competitive landscape changed for businesses operating today? If yes, then discuss these changes.

2. With a small group of peers from your class, develop a list of DOs and DON'Ts to help businesses compete more effectively and enhance their market shares.

Create Central

www.mhhe.com/createcentral

Internet References

Branding Strategy Insider
   http://www.brandingstrategyinsider.com/brand-building
Loyalty 360
   http://loyalty360.org/

DON E. SCHULTZ is professor emeritus-in-service of integrated marketing communications at The Medill School, Northwestern University. He also is president of the Agora Inc. consulting firm in Evanston, Ill. He may be reached at dschultz@northwestern.edu.

Don E. Schultz, "Brand Apathy Calls for New Methods: Turn Customer Preference from "No Brand" to "Some Brand"," *Marketing Management,* Winter 2010, p. 8–9. Copyright © 2010 by American Marketing Association. All rights reserved. Used with permission.

Article Prepared by: Nisreen N. Bahnan, *Salem State University*

Branding's Big Guns

Dreaming of the day your business becomes a household name? Follow the examples of the 10 most trusted United States brands.

PAULA ANDRUSS

Learning Outcomes

After reading this article, you will be able to:

- Delineate the differences between cognitive and affective consumer responses to brands.

- Acknowledge the importance and effectiveness of brands building emotional relationships with customers.

- Identify common patterns that characterize brands that have successfully connected on an emotional level with their target markets.

There's no better way to dissect the how-tos of branding than to dig deep into the companies everybody knows and trusts. To accomplish this, *Entrepreneur* teamed with The Values Institute at DGWB, a Santa Ana, Calif-based think tank that focuses on brand relationships, on a consumer survey that explored the reasons some brands manage to stay on top.

What became clear: though they may not have the biggest sales or market share in their categories, today's most trustworthy brands have created relationships with consumers through experiences that trigger a visceral response.

"We're seeing more of an emphasis on brands building emotional relationships with consumers because it's powerful and it works," says branding consultant Jim Stengel, former global marketing officer of Procter & Gamble and author of *Grow: How Ideals Power Growth and Profit at the World's Greatest Companies.* "When you do it, you have a much stronger affinity, a much stronger business, much stronger growth and much stronger results."

"When we looked at brands [at P&G] that had a very, very strong emotional benefit vs. our competition," Stengel adds, "our shares were much, much higher. And the margin of growth vs. our competitor was much higher than those that had just a functional superiority."

Here, a look at the tactics used by America's most trustworthy brands to connect with consumers—and ways you can put them to work for your business.

1. Get Personal: Amazon

The online retailer of, well, just about everything, ran away with the list, posting the highest scores not just in overall brand trust but in every individual trust value.

That's no surprise to Brad VanAuken, chief brand strategist for The Blake Project consultancy. He says Amazon's exceptional product accessibility, functionality, and customer experience all converge to create a strong brand that consumers trust.

"With millions of products, 24/7 access, superior search and browse technology, user reviews and many other sources of in-depth product information, Amazon.com offers a superior purchase experience," VanAuken says.

He adds that the brand—with its low prices and free shipping on orders over a minimum total—is seen as offering value, while its one-click ordering and quick-shipping options help shoppers save time. Consumers also rely on Amazon to have all the products they're looking for, thanks to partnerships with other selling channels such as Partner Count merchandise.

While such a vast array of offerings could be perceived as impersonal, VanAuken says Amazon does an exemplary job of fostering relationships with consumers by helping them make decisions through recommendations of items based on past purchases, user reviews and ratings, and suggested complementary purchases. Consumers also have many options for forging a personal bond with the brand, including user profiles, reviews and ratings, wish lists, and Listmania lists for recommending favorite products.

2. Sell Happiness: Coca-Cola

Ice-cold Sunshine. The Pause That Refreshes. Life Tastes Good. Since its inception, the promise of the world's largest beverage-maker has been to delight consumers. "Everything they do is inspired by this idea of, How do we promote, develop and create happiness?" author Stengel says. Coca-Cola pushes this message across all points of customer contact, from Facebook to its custom vending machines, which allow consumers to concoct their favorite combinations of flavors. "They take the ideas of spontaneity and delight and infuse [them] into everything," Stengel says.

Putting aside the 1980s branding debacle that was New Coke, Stengel adds that the company backs up its focus on happiness with a consistently strong corporate identity based on longevity and heritage. "They have a deep and healthy respect for their past and for the people who have gone before them," he says. "They never forget why they started and where they came from, which means a lot to consumers."

> "[Coca-Cola has] a deep and healthy respect for their past and for the people who have gone before them. They never forget why they started and where they came from, which means a lot to consumers."
>
> —*Jim Stengel*, Branding Consultant

That trust is evident among respondents to our survey, who did not give Coca-Cola a single negative remark.

3. Live Up to Your Promise: Fedex

With a straightforward passion for the task at hand, FedEx has created a strong corporate identity. Not surprisingly, the company received its strongest ratings in ability, specifically for being able to achieve what it promises and for the efficiency of its operations.

In addition to providing what is seen as a reliable service, the brand has engendered trust through initiatives such as its "We Understand" campaign, says Kari Blanchard, senior director of strategy in the New York office of Future-Brand. "They've elevated the brand by recognizing that it's not just about the logistics of moving packages and boxes," Blanchard says. "They appreciate that it's people's treasures, livelihoods and futures, and that the contents of those packages mean a lot to people."

To further deliver that message, FedEx engages with consumers through its personalized rewards program and by interacting on social media channels. "When you've already nailed attributes like trustworthiness and reliability—things that are essential to the business but don't exactly make you fall in love with a brand—that's where thinking of your customer as a person and not just a number becomes crucial," Blanchard says.

4. Keep It Cool (And Fun): Apple

What other company has the public and the press waiting breathlessly for each new product release? The bottom line is whatever that new Apple product is, consumers trust that it will be smart and sleek and that it will improve the way they communicate, work or spend their leisure time. What's more, they'll enjoy the experience of making the purchase.

While Apple has always been about creativity and expression, the brand has kicked up the emotional quotient by creating retail stores that foster a sense of collaboration and transparency between customers and sales staff. "They hire empathetic people, and they don't measure their sales associates on sales," Stengel says. He calls Apple's approach to its stores "the best retail endeavor in history. They really want people to come in and be inspired, build confidence, and really feel better about themselves from the experience they had in the store."

Apple uses its retail outlets to show, not tell, consumers its brand philosophy, from the large tables, open spaces, and walls of windows to its well-trained associates (Apple's biggest brand advocates), who are armed with handheld checkout scanners that enable shoppers to make purchases without having to stand in line.

Apple uses its retail outlets to show, not tell, consumers its brand philosophy.

Some sour bits: the brand got lower than average scores for a sense of connection to Apple's corporate side, as well as for the perception that the company doesn't value customers' business or reward them for their loyalty. Those sentiments may simply be the result of Apple focusing on its core functions.

"Steve Jobs just thought about what was right for the brand and the consumer," Stengel says. "That focus is part of the reason they've done such a good job of creating new categories and products that continue to distance themselves from their competitors."

5. Design an Experience: Target

It's easy to forget that Target is a discount store. With its sleek, stylish ad campaigns and collaborations with high-end designers who create limited-edition merchandise that sends fashionistas into a frenzy, Target's public face often belies its mass-merchant status.

Further distinguishing it from its superstore brethren, Target consistently delivers an exceptional retail experience—from store design to merchandise selection to price and customer service.

"Target makes a real effort to provide an enjoyable shopper experience, but you still get quality merchandise at a good price," says branding consultant Rob Frankel. "As part of their brand persona, they make an effort to be warm and human, and that resonates with people and drives them to embrace it."

Thanks to easy-to-maneuver layouts and a consistent design, Target's retail outlets are easy and intuitive places to shop, giving customers confidence they will be able to find what they want, even on a vast selling floor. "It's not only more pleasant than their competitors; people actually enjoy being there," Frankel says.

Target customers also appreciate the brand's ability to design attractive yet affordable merchandise—most notably, an ever-changing array of trendy clothing and home accessories. "Target says [it's] going to give you a decent alternative that can hold up against more expensive fashion brands," Frankel says.

Customer service is friendly and consistent, as several survey respondents noted, from the way "cashiers look for people in line and direct them to a less crowded line," to the perceptions that "they, always have enough employees in the store at one time" and that "their customers are considered guests."

Frankel says businesses should recognize that providing a warm, human experience will foster the kind of trust that lets them command higher margins, drive traffic and enjoy better brand perception than their competitors. "No matter what you sell, if you don't give people a reason to go, they're not going to figure it out by themselves, because price alone just doesn't do it," he says.

6. Stay Consistent: Ford

In an era when the only thing that seems certain is change, Ford's consistent branding has established the company as a beacon of reliability.

The Blake Project's VanAuken points out that from its simple, one-syllable name to its iconic logo and emphasis on founding father Henry Ford, the company's brand identity stands the test of time.

"Everyone knows and admires the Ford story," he says. "Of the three Detroit-based automakers, Ford has the most consistent brand, product strategy and execution."

Ford also listens to and acts on its customers' needs, VanAuken adds, noting that CEO Alan Mulally is actively involved in interacting with customers through social media.

Those attributes forge a strong connection: the brand ranked high for stability and dependability, and respondents gave it the strongest average ratings for concern, specifically for behaving responsibly and caring about the well-being of employees and customers. Several respondents cited Ford's refusal to take government bailout money as evidence of the company's integrity.

> **"Once you have developed a unique and compelling value proposition for your brand, repeat it again and again."**
>
> —*Brad VanAuken*, The Blake Project

VanAuken emphasizes that consistency needs to reach all corners of any business. "Changing the logo, tag line and messaging on a frequent basis will ensure that nothing about your brand sticks in your intended customers' heads," he says. "Once you have developed a unique and compelling value proposition for your brand, repeat it again and again."

7. Can-Do Attitude: Nike

On its website, Nike declares its mission to "bring inspiration and innovation to every athlete in the world," adding, "If you have a body, you are an athlete."

It's that aspirational message and mainstream appeal that connects the athletic apparel company to consumers worldwide, according to branding consultant Kevin Lane Keller, professor of marketing at the Tuck School of Business at Dartmouth College. "Nike's always been extremely customer-focused, with a broad access point that makes the brand relevant to elite athletes as well as the everyday person," Keller says. "It's about self-empowerment and being your best, and the brand really does invite everyone to 'Just Do It.'"

Nike's constant product development, including introducing technologies such as Nike Air cushioning and Dri-Fit fabrics, is one of its biggest strengths, according to Keller, who says that consumers tend to equate innovation with expertise.

"When you're innovative, consumers are more trusting, because they think you really know what you're doing," he says. "Nike's first product was just the first step on this journey that's allowed them to completely transcend their roots as a quality running shoe to be everything athletic, all over the world, in all kinds of sports."

Keller says Nike gains trust points because celebrated co-founder Phil Knight is still involved with operations, a fact noted by one survey respondent who claimed to be "confident that [Knight's] company would always behave responsibly."

Notes Keller, "When the founder is still there, people respect the brand in a way that doesn't happen when the reins have been handed down over and over. Having his voice and persona still associated with the company keeps it closely connected to the consumer."

8. Forge Connections: Starbucks

After suffering a slump a few years back, the world's leading specialty coffee retailer has perked up its business and its brand by getting back to its original promise of bringing people together. "Starbucks has gotten much more in touch with the reason they're here, and that's to help create connections," author Stengel says.

From the free Wi-Fi to the in-store music to the large tables with room for groups and meetings, the company's stores are designed to help customers interact. "Go into any Starbucks, and business is happening and people are sharing, and the company understands that," Stengel says. "Everything in there is about connection, discovery inspiration and creation."

Startups would do well to note the company's innovative approach, which has enabled it to set the agenda in a category that has been around for centuries. "They carved out this dynamic niche with their brand and became very successful/ and there's still nobody else like them," Stengel says.

The key, he says, is to thoroughly understand category norms and competitors' strategies, and determine how to direct those toward your advantage. "If you're an entrepreneur entering a category, maybe you can't set the agenda, but if you can redirect that agenda, that's how you win," he says. "If you're going to enter a category and be a 'me too,' don't bother."

9. Serve up the Quirky: Southwest Airlines

This low-cost carrier has consistently set its own route in the airline industry creating a distinct personality through everything from open passenger seating to flight attendants who sing the safety demonstrations.

"Southwest has always been a very independent brand that's quick to break the norms of the airline industry" says Tim Calkins, clinical professor of marketing at Northwestern University's Kellogg School of Management. "From the seating assignments to the fact that it doesn't list in many of the big online reservation systems, it has always prided itself on being very different."

Calkins says much of Southwest's brand success comes from the fact that although its operations and corporate culture are idiosyncratic, those differences support the company's central function.

> **Although its operations and corporate culture are idiosyncratic, those differences support Southwest's central function.**

"Southwest has a fun, energetic corporate culture that's unique in the airline industry but at the core they are a very proficient operation that gets travelers from point to point in an efficient, affordable manner," he says.

While the airline received low ratings for not sharing information on decision-making, those protective measures may be among the reasons it continues to thrive. Several of the big carriers have tried to follow Southwest's model with low-cost subsidiaries (think Delta's Song and United's Ted), but none have been able to maintain them.

"You can see what [Southwest] does—they fly one kind of airplane, they don't charge for baggage and they have friendly employees—so you'd think someone could replicate that, but they can't," Calkins says. "The magic of Southwest is that even though the brand has many unique elements, all of the different pieces work together to serve its customers in a unique way."

10. Focus on the Customer: Nordstrom

When mythic stories circulate about your company's awesome customer service, you know you're doing something right. That's the hallmark of this upscale department store, which is rumored to have once graciously accepted the return of a set of tires, even though the store has never sold tires.

"Nordstrom is all about the power of delivering exceptional customer service that goes above and beyond a typical service experience," Northwestern's Calkins says.

Nordstrom scored strongly among respondents for concern for the customer, as well as for the quality of the products in its nearly 230 stores. Attentive service—which includes a liberal return policy, e-mailing digital photos of new items to regular customers, and sending thank-you notes after purchases—frees the Seattle-based retailer from having to focus on competitive pricing, which helps keeps profit margins higher.

"They don't pretend to have the lowest prices, but they don't have to," Calkins says. "When people go there they know they may pay a little more, but the service is so good that it makes it worthwhile."

Respondents criticized Nordstrom for not providing consumers with much information about its corporate decision-making policies, but Calkins contends that when building a brand identity, it's OK for your proposition to focus on one principal element, as long as you do it right.

"What makes this brand tick is the service experience, not the approach," he says. "Nordstrom has never focused on its company or its people; all of that positive energy is directed at the customer and the retail experience, and it's the secret to their success."

Cincinnati-based Paula Andruss has written for *Usa Today, Woman's Day*, and numerous marketing publications.

[**About the survey**] The Values Institute, which conducted the study, identified five values that influence trust in a brand: **ability** [company performance]; **concern** [care for consumers, employees, and community]; **connection** [sharing consumers' values]; **consistency** [dependability of products/services]; and **sincerity** [openness and honesty].

A total of 1,220 United States consumers were asked to rate each trust value on a five-point scale, from "very unimportant" to "very important." Additionally, five consumer perceptions were measured for each value; these included statements such as "They respond to feedback, about their products and services," and "They value my business and reward me for the loyalty." Each respondent rated two randomly selected brands; those who felt strongly were also asked to provide individual comments. The result is the "Trust Index," a composite score that indicates the level of trust respondents had with each individual brand in relation to the other studied brands.

Critical Thinking

1. By reading over the examples of successful companies presented in this article, what are some tactics a brand can use to build an 'emotional relationship' with its customers?

2. With a small group of peers in your class, develop your own list of three brands that have successfully connected with their target markets. Justify your choices.

Create Central

www.mhhe.com/createcentral

Internet References

Interbrand
   http://www.interbrand.com/en/
Marketing Research Association
   http://www.marketingresearch.org/brand-equity-models
The Values Institute
   http://www.thevaluesinstitute.org/

Paula Andruss, "Branding's Big Guns," *Entrepreneur*, April 2012, p. 50–55. Copyright © 2012 by Entrepreneur Media, Inc. All rights reserved. Used with permission.

Article   Prepared by: Nisreen N. Bahnan, *Salem State University*

Playing Well Together

CO-BRANDING among franchises appeared to have lost its luster in recent years. But new concepts are emerging to prove that strategic combinations of businesses can cut costs and broaden the customer base.

JASON DALEY

Learning Outcomes

After reading this article, you will be able to:

- Formulate a complete definition of co-branding strategy.

- Recognize the advantages of co-branding for organizations and their consumers.

If you flip through annual reports from Yum Brands, you'll notice an increasing frenzy starting in 1992 around "multibranding." A decade later, Yum—the holding company that owns and operates Taco Bell, KFC, Pizza Hut and, until last year, A&W, and Long John Silver's—hailed the concept as "potentially the biggest sales and profit driver for the restaurant industry since the advent of the drive-thru window."

Co-branding (also known as piggyback franchising and dual or combination franchising) is, at face value, a brilliant idea: take two franchise concepts, stick them in the same building and watch the revenue roll in. Not only does co-branding promise to save on operational costs like leasing, staff, kitchen equipment, building maintenance, and advertising, it can even out customer flow, especially if one concept appeals to the breakfast and lunch crowd and the other is destined for dinner. But franchise systems have touted co-branding's biggest advantage as providing a one-stop option for groups of people with different cravings. Tommy and Sally want chicken fingers but Mom and Dad want pizza? Come on in to our pizza parlor/chicken shack, and everyone will be happy.

In 2002, co-branded outlets accounted for $2 billion in sales for Yum. But just a decade later, Yum is quietly stripping down many of its co-branded locations, and in its 2010 annual report, hidden in the black-and-white financial section many pages beyond the color photos of smiling kids and well-groomed employees, the company admits it has suspended co-branding as a long-term strategy.

The last few years have been littered with corporate co-branding marriages that bit the dust. Wendy's asked Tim Hortons to the dance, but they broke up in 2006. Dunkin' Donuts tried to make it work with Togo's sandwiches, and Arby's fooled around with everyone on the block for almost a decade before deciding to stay single.

While co-branding does have some benefits, especially in airports and other specialized locations, the "something for everyone" model has not proved its worth. Yum found that adding A&W and Long John Silver's to other concepts did not add to unit revenue—co-branding those concepts just created headaches and increased costs. Co-branding can increase operational complexity, which can lead to substandard products and poor customer service. More important, the concepts need to mesh on the most basic level, drawing from the same customer base and making intuitive sense: franchises have found that skeptical consumers will pass up a baffling lobster-and-hot-wings merger for a single brand they understand—every time.

Many well-established brands have difficulty bending their strict operations rules to accommodate a partner, and they may run the risk of diluting their image if they sticker over their core concept with less-trusted brands. For example, Yum found that the limited menus at A&W and Long John Silver's were perceived as old-fashioned and boring, especially when paired with those at Taco Bell and KFC. Adding those smaller brands to an existing unit achieved little except to pull the focus from the more popular brand.

While the great co-branding experiment has more or less fizzled, the idea is not completely dead. Co-branding can be successful if it's done strategically between complementary brands, like salads and smoothies or pizza and another savory impulse snack. Many companies that have thought through their co-branding are finding the economies of scale the strategy produces are worth it.

"There are definitely some clear challenges in co-branding," says Steve Beagelman, president of SMB Franchise Advisors, who has worked with co-branded franchises over the last 25 years. "But if you can make it work, there are a lot of synergies and benefits, especially in making sure franchisees can make money. And that's ultimately what small business is about, especially in franchising. Let's say a franchisee has found a great location, but the costs are just too high. Co-branding gives you a real good opportunity to make that location work."

Selective Salons

Vas Maniatis built his Seva salon chain almost exclusively through co-branding, though his model is a bit different than putting two food concepts together. Instead, his small salons, which focus primarily on eyebrow threading, lash extensions and nails, are found exclusively in Walmart stores. While Seva is completely independent from Walmart, the salon chain's convenience, value pricing and speed make it appealing to the mass merchant's shoppers, according to Maniatis.

"Our customer is the Walmart customer, so co-branding to me has been huge," he says. "We're all about enhancing the one-stop shopping experience [that] Sam Walton built." Maniatis has opened 25 units in eight states since 2010 and hopes to double growth in 2012.

Seva didn't start out as a co-branded franchise. In fact, it didn't start out as "Seva" at all. For the first several years, the Chicago-based salon was called Simply Eyebrows and performed only eyebrow threading—a quick, less-painful alternative to waxing. Most threading takes place in malls at open-air kiosks; Maniatis hoped to improve the experience by offering a private session in a spa atmosphere. He was also focused on convenience and value, so a friend suggested he talk to Walmart about opening in a new development in Indianapolis.

A skeptical Walmart initially gave Maniatis the brushoff, but unbeknownst to him, a regional manager had been pushing for the concept, and when another tenant dropped out a year later, the space was offered for the salon. That first store was a hit, and in late 2009, two Walmart executives flew to Chicago to talk to Maniatis about a partnership.

"They basically said, 'Look, we love your concept,'" he recalls. But, he says, the execs thought it needed to be "bigger" and suggested adding other salon services and positioning the company as a Walmart exclusive.

Maniatis agreed, found a more appealing name and hasn't looked back. Co-branding with Walmart has not only given Seva huge traffic flow, it has freed up resources to develop other aspects of the business. "Our franchisees start with built-in traffic of 30,000 to 50,000 customers per week, with no marketing costs. That's given us an opportunity to do things that are state of the art in customer engagement," Maniatis says. "We've built an iPad-based paperless system . . . We have remote monitoring capabilities and can see our stores in real time and see what type of customer transactions work."

The only drawback to the co-branding relationship is that Seva can grow only as quickly as Walmart does, and the salon doesn't have a guaranteed spot in every development; it has to be chosen from a shortlist of approved tenants that include McDonald's, Subway and other elite franchises.

"It's been hard for us to open in as many spaces as we'd like," Maniatis admits. But, he adds, partnering with Walmart, takes the guesswork out of site selection. "The marketing's done by Walmart. The due diligence on where to locate is done by Walmart. We just need to focus on our core, which is our service, and engaging both the active and potential customer."

Sweet Spot

Sevas partnership is a dream scenario for co-branding. Other companies have more complex relationships, though they can be just as rewarding. Ted Milburn, vice president of franchise development for Nestle Tollhouse Cafe, which sells baked goods, coffee and frozen yogurt, has worked at other concepts that have co-branded—some successfully and others not. When he was approached with an opportunity to team Tollhouse with Haagen-Dazs, he thought the synergy would be perfect, evening out year-round customer flow and complementing both products. In 2011, the companies began opening co-branded locations across the country.

Not only do the co-branded stores smooth out the annual sales calendar, they appeal to the public with their synergistic offerings. "We eliminate the deal-breaker," Milburn says. "We cover the gamut, from cookies to frozen coffee beverages to smoothies to ice cream creations. Whatever people want, we can cover it. It would be different if we were co-branded with a pizza concept. People come in to a pizza place for pizza; we would be just an afterthought."

Dan Ogiba, director of development for Haagen-Dazs, agrees. "We're a complete dessert cafe," he says. "We looked at this as an opportunity to grow and for our franchisees to increase their revenues. We think serving larger groups outweighs any competition between our sweet products."

Focus Brands, which owns Schlotzsky's deli, Cinnabon and Carvel Ice Cream, thinks putting sweet treats together with sandwiches is a winning concept. Schlotzsky's and Cinnabon both bake their products daily; this appeals to franchisees, whose employees already have experience running ovens, according to Schlotzsky's president Kelly Roddy. Adding a Carvel element for a tri-branded store is a little more expensive, but Roddy thinks it complements the other offerings nicely.

"One of our concerns was that selling Cinnabon products would cannibalize purchases from our core Schlotzsky's menu," he says. "We found it didn't, and that it actually brought additional customers into stores and grew revenues with no additional labor costs, no rent, no managers or any of the things that come up with a separate unit."

Already, 165 Schlotzsky's have retrofitted Cinnabon ovens into their stores; Roddy projects that by year's end, more than 200 of the brand's 350 units will be selling cinnamon rolls. In 2011, 90 percent of new-store sales were tri-branded locations; in 2012, plans are to include Cinnabon and Carvel elements in all new Schlotzsky's units. So far, the co-branded stores are drawing in more customers in the 18 to 25 demographic, and more women.

"It has really worked out to be a home run for franchisees," Roddy says. He insists the co-branding isn't about shoe-horning Focus Brands concepts together willy-nilly, pointing out that significant testing and research indicated that the concepts would make a good partnership. "I haven't seen many co-branded concepts recently that work well and make sense as these do," he says.

Co-branding is not nearly as prevalent or hyped as it was a decade ago, but impressive numbers of franchises are giving it another shot. Hot dog chain Nathan's Famous is committed to growing almost exclusively through co-branding. Cold Stone Creamery has partnerships with Tim Hortons and the Rocky Mountain Chocolate Factory; Tasti D-Lite, which purchased Planet Smoothie, plans to give co-branding a test-drive.

While it's doubtful that co-branding will prove as revolutionary as the drivethru window, it may turn out to be a profitable strategy after all. "There is definitely a part of co-branding that really makes a lot of sense," SMB's Beagelman says. "It can help a franchisor grow quicker. It can help make sure franchisees make money. And for smaller franchisors, you can learn how more successful chains do things. It's not for every brand, but if you're flexible and are willing to listen, it can work."

Critical Thinking

1. In your opinion, what are the potential advantages of co-branding for organizations and their customers?
2. With a small group of peers in your class, develop your own list of successful franchise co-branding. Justify your choices.

Create Central

www.mhhe.com/createcentral

Internet References

Bloomberg Businessweek
http://images.businessweek.com/ss/09/07/0710_cobranded/1.htm
International Franchise Association
http://www.franchise.org/

Jason Daley, "Playing Well Together," *Entrepreneur*, April 2012, p. 87–92. Copyright © 2012 by Entrepreneur Media, Inc. All rights reserved. Used with permission.

Article   Prepared by: Nisreen N. Bahnan, *Salem State University*

The Devolution of Marketing

Is America's Marketing Model Fighting Hard Enough to Keep Up?

ANDREW R. THOMAS AND TIMOTHY J. WILKINSON

Learning Outcomes

After reading this article, you will be able to:

- Recognize that power has shifted from those who create innovative products and services to mega-distributors, who are increasingly in control of the global marketplace.

- Identify the pressures places on manufacturers from the mega-distributors.

The American marketing model is dysfunctional. Small and medium-sized companies, as well as large multinational firms, have been lured into a misconceived form of producing and selling. It goes like this:

- Invest blood, sweat, tears, and money to innovate a new product or service.
- Sell it through the largest distributor possible.
- Maximize the volume of sales through that distributor.
- Deal with the inevitable cost-cutting demands.
- Compromise brand integrity.
- Export capital, jobs, quality control and pollution to developing markets.
- Watch the innovation become a commodity.
- Lose money.
- Begin to develop new innovations.
- And then, start all over again . . .

A large portion of what drove us into the Great Recession is rooted in this dysfunctional pattern of distribution. Sell more and more through a mega-distributor—with much of the profit split by distributors and overseas manufacturers. Earnings obtained by the latter are reinvested into the United States, and then are lent to consumers so they can continue to spend beyond their means—thereby propping up the global economy.

Discussions are abundant about out-of-control lending, consumer spending, the impact of outsourcing, and the lack of sustainability. But little attention is paid to the harmful impact that the distribution strategies employed by mega-distributors have played—not only on innovators, but on the overall economy. As we talk to business leaders around the world, it is clear that many of them realize a fundamental shift has occurred: power has transferred from those who create innovative products and services to mega-distributors, who are increasingly in control of the global marketplace.

Mistakenly, many marketing departments see deals with mega-distributors as the way to boost sales and market share. In reality, the Megas live by high volume and low prices. They use their powerful leverage to demand price cuts and other concessions from suppliers. Companies end up with razor thin or nonexistent profit margins, even as their innovative products and services are treated like commodities by both the Megas and the buying public. Surprisingly, this transformation of the business landscape has occurred with little fanfare or real analysis.

The Blame Game

Let us be clear before you think that this is merely another attempt to blame Wal-Mart Stores, Inc., GE Capital, AutoNation, The Home Depot and others for the ills of the world: we do not blame the Megas for the distribution trap and what it has caused. As far as we know, no one has ever been forced to sell their products or services to someone else. Megas rarely, if ever, travel to visit potential suppliers. They wait for would-be vendors to show up. And boy, do they—in great numbers, each hoping to strike it rich!

Beginning in the early 1980s, innovative firms permitted, either consciously or subconsciously, outsiders into their companies. They allowed these outsiders to gain increasing control over sales and distribution activities. Innovative firms and the people who led them were responding to what management theorists were saying at that time. The "business gurus" talked about organizational transformation—emphasizing things like resources, capabilities, innovation, technology, and operational effectiveness. "Total quality management," "lean manufacturing," and "zero defects" were just a few of the solutions preached by business elites to companies of all sizes.

Drinking this elixir, thousands of companies that once had been in control of all aspects of their innovative development began to lose interest in sales and distribution, preferring instead that other companies take over this "business function." The concept of "core competencies" was provided as the justification for letting loose of control after the producing firm had exercised its unique set of value-adding activities. Why manage a string of dealers if your core competency—your basis of differentiation—is in research and development or manufacturing? Taking this advice, companies divested themselves of activities that were not perceived as value added. Sales and distribution were pushed aside.

One of the people who understood the ramifications of the new transformational thinking was Sam Walton. He and a raft of imitators stepped in to fill the power vacuum that the strategy gurus had helped create. The result was the evolution of massive distributors, which ultimately drove the sales and distribution of innovative products and services in the United States.

The Distribution Trap

Numerous manufacturers have seen their profit margins squeezed and their brands eroded because they decided to sell through the Megas. Rubbermaid, Levi Strauss, Goodyear, and many lesser-known companies have been literally trashed by the relentless pressure from the Megas to cut prices. Remember Jones Soda Co.? In 2006, this company showed profits of $39 million on $406 million in revenue. A distribution strategy initially based on selling through tattoo parlors and snowboarding shops morphed into one focused on Panera Bread, Barnes & Noble and Starbucks. But in 2007, Jones Soda began to sell to the Megas (including selling a limited selection to Wal-Mart), and ended up posting an $11.6 million loss for the year.

One website summed it up: "And just exactly what is Jones Soda doing for sale at Wal-Mart? Is Jones Soda now going to market itself as a value-priced soda, except with weird flavors?" (Source: www.bloggingstocks.com/2007/06/14/jones-soda-loses-its-fizz.) In September 2010, after suffering from years of quarterly losses, the company went all-out in marketing to the Bentonville, Ark., giant, agreeing to sell six packs of its most popular sodas to the Mega's 3,800 stores. This served to only further debase what had at one time been a popular, upstart brand.

The scope and magnitude of a Mega can quickly consume the brand equity of individual products and services. Private labels, discounting, lack of service and mass-market presentation have diluted the value of American brands. The distribution trap has squeezed margins by making products that were once viewed with respect easily substituted with either store brands or inexpensive knock-offs. In fact, the Megas can be viewed as instruments of brand dilution. The very act of discounting, which is the business model of the Megas, undermines the entire idea behind a manufacturer's brand.

In 1993, Rubbermaid, the long-time producer of high-quality storage products was named America's Most Admired Company by *Fortune* magazine. Rubbermaid offered 5,000 different items, producing nearly 400 new, innovative products each year. Most the company's history was defined by strong relationships with end-users through a network of independent distributors and dealers. However, beginning in the early 1990s, a new leadership team entered and committed to expanding sales through the Megas.

The CEO at the time, Wolfgang Schmitt, explained: "It's typically the bigger suppliers that can form the sort of close partnerships that retailing's behemoths are increasingly demanding. The goal is to boost sales and reduce costs for both sides by slashing inventories, shortening lead times and eliminating error: there is a healthy interdependence between us and people like Wal-Mart. We need them; they need us." Wal-Mart accounted for about 14 percent of Rubbermaid's business when, in 1994, disaster struck.

The key components of Rubbermaid products are polymer-based resins, which make up about one-third of the cost of any given product. The price of resins had been stable for years, but costs shot up in spring 1994 because of new global demand and a supply shortage resulting from problems at key refineries. Within 18 months, the price of resins nearly doubled—adding $200 million to Rubbermaid's costs. Focused as always on earnings growth, the company increased its prices. The price increases were met with derision by the Megas. The giant retailers objected to monthly price increases, and complained that Rubbermaid was unresponsive to the realities of the market. Wal-Mart, frustrated with the price increases, emptied shelves of Rubbermaid's "Little Tikes" line of toys, and turned the space over to Fisher-Price.

Left with no other real option, Rubbermaid felt compelled to change gears. In 1994, it began to compete aggressively on the basis of price, offering steep discounts to the Megas. Its margins quickly eroded, and cost-cutting measures were enacted, including the elimination of its dealer network, thousands of American jobs and the closure of nine plants. The company purged 6,000 color and size variations and cut the total number of products by 45 percent. These efforts produced only temporary relief. Rubbermaid was acquired by the Newell Corporation in 1998 for a mere $6 billion in stock.

The Outsourcing Compulsion

Another consequence of the distribution trap is outsourcing and offshoring. While the academic literature is replete with theories about foreign direct investment (FDI), the real motivator for much of the 23 percent FDI that is "contracted-out" has been entirely ignored. Producers are being literally forced to invest in overseas manufacturing by their mega-distribution partners. Outsourcing is a coping mechanism in response to relentless price pressures from the Megas. Companies locked into the distribution trap can substantially lower costs by shuttering domestic manufacturing operations.

Lakewood Engineering & Manufacturing Co. is a case in point. For years, this electric fan manufacturer sold its 20-inch box fan for $20. Responding to Wal-Mart's downward price pressure, the company opened a factory in Shenzhen, China in 2000, where labor costs averaged $0.25 per hour compared with $13 per hour in Chicago. By 2003, the fan was sold at the Mega for $10. In 2008, Lakewood employees, alongside local labor organizations, protested the company's decision to close its electric heater operations and move production to China. Wal-Mart buys 80 to 90 percent of the company's heaters.

Lakewood claimed that its hands were tied because it was heavily mortgaged to Wells Fargo Bank, which refused to lend it more money. The company's relationship with the Mega resulted in the layoff of 220 workers and the outsourcing of production. All too often, the compulsive embrace of offshoring by U.S. firms is not a function of internally generated goals and objectives, but is instead driven by the sheer demands of corporate survival.

One of the consequences of the outsourcing compulsion is environmental degradation in the developing countries where distributor-forced outsourcing takes place. In many emerging markets, environmental laws are lax or simply go un-enforced. These countries may be viewed favorably by multinationals, because they constitute "pollution havens"—with the cost of pollution absorbed by the people living in those countries, not by the multinational corporations or their customers. For example, China's industrial cities are so full of air pollution that their occupants rarely see the sun. The heavy reliance on coal

has polluted the air with suspended particles of liquid or solids that float in the air. These particulates—and China has lots of them floating around—are associated with respiratory problems and heart disease. In the U.S., the growth of municipal waste has grown in tandem with the contribution of retail trade to the gross domestic product. According to the Environmental Protection Agency, 55 to 65 percent of municipal waste is classified as "residential waste": it is the product of the buying habits of individuals and families. This has taken place because during the last 25 years, as consumer prices have dropped and as consumption has increased, people have purchased increasing amounts of cheap stuff from the Megas—which quickly wears out and is then discarded.

The rush to the cheapest possible price has not yet factored in these costs of environmental degradation. When that inevitably happens, prices will have to rise. In short, the offshoring of production, driven by the mega-distributors, is not sustainable. China and other emerging economies have traded extremely high economic growth for polluted air, water, and land. No country can pursue such a strategy indefinitely. In the coming decades, as emerging markets grow up, environmental concerns will outweigh the appetite for runaway growth, and the unreasonably low prices that Americans have come to expect as they make purchases from the Megas will end.

The Independent Solution

Falling into the distribution trap is not an inevitable outcome of American business practice. But companies like Red Ants Pants have prospered by avoiding the big-box stores and other mass-market retailers. Thirty-year-old company founder Sarah Calhoun became so frustrated with ill-fitting work pants, designed without the female figure in mind, that she started her own company. There are now 70 different sizes of the double-knee, double-seat work pants with their lower-rise front and higher-rise backs. By importing 12-ounce cotton canvas from India, and having it cut and sewn by a factory in Seattle, Calhoun is free to sell the premium priced pants ($119 a pair) to her target market: women who work for a living in the construction trades. A 1964 Airstream trailer decorated with red ants is the marketing vehicle of

Briefly

- Partnering with mega-distributors holds an irresistible lure for many companies.
- The Megas' business model depends on mass marketing, low price, and volume.
- Avoiding the Megas may mean less volume, but can have other advantages.

this small firm. Calhoun's Tour de Pants road trips allow her to make direct sales to groups of women at homes across the country. Personal contacts made through trade shows and conferences further extend her direct marketing approach.

Another example is STIHL Inc., a manufacturer of outdoor power equipment that has never sold its products through mass merchants. Instead, the company sells its innovative products through thousands of independently owned servicing dealers across America and throughout the world. An industry global leader in both market share and profitability, STIHL continues to embrace its founding principle of only selling the company's products through servicing dealers.

The Current Landscape

The rise of the Megas has created a groundswell of community-based efforts to help local independent businesses compete effectively and prevent chains and online giants from displacing local entrepreneurs. More than 100 such groups have organized in North America since 2000, including 70 affiliated with the American Independent Business Alliance (AMIBA), a non-profit dedicated to supporting these community efforts.

AMIBA facilitates group purchasing, cooperative promotions and advertising and other activities to help local businesses gain economies of scale. It also wages sophisticated "buy local" campaigns to promote the greater overall value local businesses often can provide to customers, as well as the vital economic, social, and cultural role they play in communities. Lastly, these alliances are advocates for the interests of local entrepreneurs in their local government and media. As their ranks grow, AMIBA aims to shift state and national policies that favor larger corporations at the expense of smaller community enterprise. Another effort to support local business is Independent We Stand, sponsored in part by STIHL. Independent We Stand focuses on the money spent at locally owned companies and how it re-circulates throughout the community. Whether it is the taxes that are paid, the payroll of the workers or the businesses' own spending, the impact of local-driven commerce makes a community a far better place to live.

The battle lines are being drawn for a new showdown between locally focused groups like AMIBA and Independent We Stand and Wal-Mart. The mega-retailer recently announced that it is targeting urban areas with the idea of introducing smaller stores like the ones it already operates across Latin America. In a recent *Wall Street Journal* article, Bill Simon, head of Wal-Mart's U.S. stores business, said that Wal-Mart hopes to open many of its "Neighborhood Markets" across the country. These stores will be like the smaller "bodegas" the company has set up across Latin America. According to Simon, Wal-Mart believes that the opportunity exists for "hundreds" of the smaller-sized outlets, which will offer customer staples and produce.

The Reality Check

For many companies, the lure of partnering with a mega-distributor is irresistible. These giants can put products in front of hundreds of millions of customers—and potentially bring in huge gains in sales and market share. But behind these high hopes may be a faulty premise that can lead to disaster. Whether out of naiveté, arrogance or greed, innovative companies expect that the Megas will care about the success of their products and services as much as they do.

What companies forget, or ignore, is that the Megas' business model depends on mass marketing, low price, and volume. Naturally, the Megas use their tremendous leverage to dictate tough terms to innovators. They insist on ever-greater price reductions and force companies to redesign products and services to better suit their needs. In the end, many producers discover that all the blood, sweat, tears, and money they have poured into their products and services has been wasted: their hard-won creations have been turned into commodities with razor-thin profit margins. From this perspective, the outcomes for the innovator are not surprising: the abandonment of brand integrity, the acceleration of the innovation into a commodity, and the inevitable cost cuts that result from offshoring and outsourcing.

Having created the process and product, and invested time and money, why would companies turn the final stage of the operation over to a third party? Business leaders do it all the time. It is their choice, and they must bear responsibility for what happens.

To avoid the negative outcomes described, companies must control their own distribution. This may mean selling directly to customers online or through company-owned retail stores. Or, it may mean striking strong deals with distributors and avoiding partners who will not agree to stringent terms. Of course, avoiding the Megas may mean less volume, but the advantages of doing so are likely to make up for it. Companies that keep a tight rein on distribution have a greater ability to control pricing, customer service and after-sales service. They can also build stronger, longer-lasting relationships with their customers. And isn't that what every company ultimately needs?

Critical Thinking

1. Explain the lure for manufacturers to partner with and sell their products through mega-distributors.

2. In your opinion, do small businesses that control their own distribution and avoid partnerships with mass-market retailers stand a chance at success?

Create Central

www.mhhe.com/createcentral

Internet References

Production and Operations Management Society
http://www.poms.org/

Supply Chain Musings
http://www.supplychainmusings.com/2010/11/supply-chain-sphere-of-influence.html

ANDREW R. THOMAS is assistant professor of international business at the University of Akron in Ohio, **TIMOTHY J. WILKINSON** is professor of marketing and Interim Dean of the College of Business at Montana State University Billings. They co-authored "The Distribution Trap: Keeping Your Innovations from Becoming Commodities" (Praeger, 2009), winner of the Berry-AMA Book Award for the best marketing book of 2010. They may be reached at art@uakron.edu and timothy.wilkinson@msubillings.edu, respectively.

Andrew R. Thomas; Timothy J. Wilkinson, "The Devolution of Marketing: Is America's Marketing Model Fighting Hard Enough to Keep Up?" *Marketing Management,* Spring 2011, p. 20–25. Copyright © 2011 by American Marketing Association. All rights reserved. Used with permission.

Article

Prepared by: Nisreen N. Bahnan, *Salem State University*

Made in America?

How to know which flag-waving products are true red, white, and blue.

Learning Outcomes

After reading this article, you will be able to:

- Comprehend the 'country-of-origin' concepts and its implications on consumer behavior.

- Identify and analyze various labeling strategies that companies use to infer country of origin.

Given a choice between a product made in the U.S. and an identical one made abroad, 78 percent of Americans would rather buy the American product, according to a new nationally representative survey by the Consumer Reports National Research Center.

More than 80 percent of those people cited retaining manufacturing jobs and keeping American manufacturing strong in the global economy as very important reasons for buying American. About 60 percent cited concern about the use of child workers or other cheap labor overseas, or stated that American-made goods were of higher quality.

And people would pay extra to buy American. More than 60 percent of all respondents indicated they'd buy American-made clothes and appliances even if those cost 10 percent more than imported versions; more than 25 percent said they'd pay at least an extra 20 percent. (Perhaps more surprising: according to a new survey of consumers in the U.S. and abroad by the Boston Consulting Group, more than 60 percent of *Chinese* respondents said they'd buy the American-made version over the Chinese even if it were to cost more.)

Clearly, most Americans want to know where products are made and want to buy those that will help create or keep jobs in the U.S.—an attempt applauded by economists like Jeff Faux, a distinguished fellow of the nonprofit, nonpartisan Economic Policy Institute, in Washington, D.C. "Consumers need to understand that all jobs and wages are interconnected," Faux told us. "When you buy foreign goods—and sometimes there's no choice—it means that fewer U.S. workers will have the money to buy the goods and services you sell."

But what does "made in the USA" even mean? And how can you identify what's made where?

In this special report, we'll decipher labeling laws and explain why a product that pictures an American flag might be made abroad, identify companies that still make products in the U.S., hear from economists about manufacturing trends, and provide our experts' assessment of the quality of some American-made apparel.

A Guessing Game

Few products except cars, textiles, furs, and woolens are required by law to reveal their American heritage. But when any manufacturer chooses to boast of an American connection, it must comply with federal rules designed to keep consumers from being misled.

Our evidence shows that if not misled, consumers are at least confused. Readers flood CONSUMER REPORTS with letters and e-mail seeking explanations as to why, for example, frozen blueberries from Oregon are identified as a product of Chile; why a company named Florida's Natural sells apple juice with concentrate from Brazil; why pants made in Vietnam are labeled "authentic, active, outdoor, American"; or why a T-shirt with the words "Made in the" above the U.S. flag comes from Mexico.

Though perplexing, such words and pictures don't usually violate regulations that are issued by the Federal Trade Commission, the agency responsible for protecting consumers from false or deceptive product claims. The key factors in determining whether a "Made in the USA" claim is deceptive, says FTC senior attorney Laura Koss, are the claim's context and whether it's likely to mislead a reasonable consumer. Ultimately, the line between legal and illegal is determined by the overall impression planted in consumers' minds.

But the line is blurry. Every case is different and subject to interpretation, Koss says. Most of the complaints the FTC receives are initiated by companies that are pointing a finger at competitors they claim are seeking an unfair advantage.

When a company definitely crosses the line, the FTC's priority is stopping the behavior, not punishment. If a company refuses, it faces civil penalties—in theory. In practice, the FTC has brought only one civil penalty case since the late 1990s, slapping toolmaker Stanley with a $205,000 fine in 2006 to settle charges involving the pedigree of its Zero Degree ratchets. (Stanley claimed that the ratchets were made in America, but the FTC noted that much of their content was foreign.)

The Types of Claims

"Made in the USA" claims can be "unqualified" or "qualified." Unqualified means that "all or virtually all" significant parts and processing are of U.S. origin. The product may contain a small amount of foreign ingredients if they're not significant—the knobs of a barbecue grill, for instance. Companies must be able to document any claim.

Qualified claims, the main cause of confusion, come in many forms, but each must tell the whole story. Take the new iPad Mini. The packaging says, "Designed by Apple in California, Assembled in China." That's an acceptable claim. By contrast, a company could land in trouble if it said "created in the U.S." without specifying the country of manufacture, since consumers are likely to interpret a vague, stand-alone term like "created" as all-inclusive. The FTC requires companies to post prominent, unambiguous statements (such as the actual country of origin) to leave an accurate impression.

Readers who have sent us complaints seem most irritated by foreign-made products whose makers have patriotic names (American Mills, Americana Olives, Great American Seafood, United States Sweaters, the U.S. Lock company) or whose packages have flag-waving slogans ("true American quality") or symbols (pictures of the flag, eagle, Statue of Liberty). But all of those products are likely to be legal as long as they leave a clear impression about where they're made.

Another type of labeling law, enforced by U.S. Customs and Border Protection with an assist from the Department of Agriculture, requires imported goods to bear a country-of-origin label when they enter the U.S. If an import combines materials or processing from more than one country, the agency considers the country of origin to be the last country in which a "substantial transformation" occurred—for example, the place where a computer was fabricated, not the country that supplied most parts.

The USDA's Agricultural Marketing Service is responsible for administering and enforcing country-of-origin labeling of certain foods. Large retailers must use signs, labels, or stickers to identify the birthplace of covered commodities (most meat, fish, fresh or frozen fruits, vegetables, and some nuts). That's why some brands of salmon are labeled both "wild-caught Alaskan" and "Product of Thailand." The fish was caught in U.S. waters but took a detour to Asia to be skinned and boned (to take advantage of cheaper labor) before making its return voyage. Under the law, that side trip must be noted.

Bottom Line

If you want to buy American products, these tips should help:

- Read labels carefully, using the info above.
- See the sidebar listing some of the companies still manufacturing in America.
- Consult websites that name companies making products in the U.S.: *americansworking.com, madeinamericaforever.com,* and *madeinusa.org.*
- Contact a manufacturer directly.

(Still) Made in the USA

According to the Bureau of Labor Statistics, American manufacturing lost almost six million jobs between 2000 and 2010. "Offshoring" became a buzzword with the implementation of the North American Free Trade Agreement in 1994. But the more recent hemorrhaging of jobs was due in large part to China's entry into the World Trade Organization in 2001, notes Ron Hira, associate professor of public policy at the Rochester Institute of Technology. A decade of BLS data reveals heavy job losses across more than a dozen manufacturing sectors, including apparel and textiles, electrical equipment, iron and steel production, computers, glass, leather tanning, and finishing.

Why are foreign nations so appealing to manufacturers? Simple economics, for starters. In 2010, compensation costs (wages and benefits) for manufacturing jobs in the U.S. were $34.74 per hour on average, according to the BLS. That's lower than in 13 northern and western European countries, but far higher than costs in China: $1.36 per hour (in 2008), based on BLS estimates. Another manufacturing powerhouse, India, has even lower hourly compensation costs than China.

But depending on the manufacturing sector, labor may account for only a small fraction of operating costs. So China may offer manufacturers "goodie packages" to relocate,

Car wars: Comparing pedigrees

Most vehicles are multinational, even those with iconic American nameplates, and many imports are surprisingly red, white, and blue. Case in point: the Chevrolet Spark (below left) and Toyota Sienna (below right). Only 10 percent of the Chevy's parts are American or Canadian; more than 75 percent (including the engine) are from Korea, where the vehicle is assembled, and the automatic transmission is made in Japan. By contrast, 75 percent of the Sienna (including its engine) is American. It's assembled in Indiana.

We know those facts because the American Automobile Labeling Act requires passenger vehicles, pickup trucks, SUVs, and vans to bear labels specifying the value of their U.S. and Canadian parts (as a percentage of the total value of all car parts), the country of assembly, and the country of origin of the engine and transmission. That information is typically on the vehicle's window sticker.

Woolrich vintage throw $129

On one side, this blanket (made in Woolrich, Pa.) is 84 percent wool and 16 percent nylon; on the other, it's nubby polyester and acrylic sherpa fleece. The fleece side is a stretchy double knit with a fuzzy texture to counterbalance the roughness of the wool on the flip side. It has an old-fashioned look, and the big, loopy chain stitch around the edge adds to the hand-sewn feeling, though it's made by machine, as is the rest of the blanket. If the edge were to wear out, the chain stitch would unravel, but it's purely decorative, so the blanket would stay intact. The sides are actually held together with a conventional serged seam that's concealed from view.

Bottom line. "It's a classic," our expert said. "Good fabric choices and construction details mean it's something you'll have for a very long time."

Orvis cropped cotton pants for women $54

They're made (in California) of a stretchy jersey knit, like T-shirt fabric but denser. The two pockets aren't pocket bags but are instead a single piece of fabric folded over itself—a cheaper design. The pants have an elastic waistband, a bar tack at each pocket to help prevent ripping, a T-shirt-style hem, and serged stitching that's reinforced at seams to prevent unraveling. Sewing at the crotch and hem is neat, but hanging threads as long as 4 inches could snag.

Bottom line. "The fabric is nice, but the pants seem pricey for what they are," our expert said.

including tax breaks, low-cost land rental, and reduced utility costs, according to Hal Sirkin, a senior partner with global-management consultants Boston Consulting Group. In exchange, U.S. companies might be required to take on local companies as business partners or cut other deals with area businesses or municipalities.

The appeal of foreign countries may wane, Sirkin says. "China gets more expensive every year. By 2015, Chinese wages will average $6.15 per hour, still well below the U.S. minimum wage, but American worker productivity is significantly higher. When you consider all the factors, the true cost to manufacture goods from China will be only about 10 percent cheaper than to make them domestically in another few years."

National security issues and an iffy supply chain are also concerns. "Natural disasters such as the 2011 tsunami in Japan can disrupt the product pipeline, leading to shortages of parts, products, and long shipping delays," says John Hoffecker, a managing director of global business consultants AlixPartners in New York. By 2015, the Boston Consulting Group predicts, cost advantages (in electricity, natural gas, and labor) over Japan and several European countries in a range of industries will give U.S. exports a big boost. As a result, the group says, the U.S. could add as many as 2.5 million to 5 million manufacturing jobs by the end of the decade.

Jeff Faux, a distinguished fellow of the Economic Policy Institute in Washington, D.C., is not sanguine about the nature of those jobs. "When you think it through," he says, "our default policy to compete in the global economy over the long run is to lower the wages and benefits of American workers, and no one at the top will admit that. There's no question a few jobs are coming back. However, they're jobs that once paid $22 per hour and are now paying $12. Globalization isn't the problem. The problem is that we started to accelerate the opening of U.S. markets to foreign goods, but without preparing our workers for the brutalization of competition. For 30 years leaders have said we need to train and upgrade the skills of American workers, but it needs to be done before signing these trade agreements, not after the fact."

Making it in America

Still, it's a stretch to say, as is commonly heard, that the U.S. doesn't make anything anymore. In fact, Sirkin says, the U.S. makes about three-quarters of all the manufactured goods (including components) it consumes. The chemical and plastics industries are thriving, thanks to declining natural gas prices, and foreign automakers including BMW, Hyundai, Kia,

Company manners matter

Although looking for U.S.-made products is important to most Americans, our national survey found that other corporate behavior matters at least as much.

All things being equal, would you be more likely, less likely, or neither to buy from a company that . . .	More likely	Less likely	Neither
gives back to the local community	92%	2%	6%
treats its workers well	90	4	7
expresses public support for causes you believe in	82	5	13
engages in environmentally friendly practices	79	7	14
is American, not foreign	78	6	17
has manufacturing plants in your home state	75	7	18

Mercedes, and Volkswagen have opened plants in the U.S. Master Lock returned ("onshored" or "insourced" in labor-speak) 100 union jobs to its Milwaukee lock factory. Among the companies that have dug in their heels and continued to manufacture domestically is Lenox, which says it's the only maker of fine bone china in the U.S.

Some companies are bucking the outsourcing trend even in industries that have largely fled the U.S.: large appliances, electronics, and apparel.

Appliances

In 2000, Michigan-based Whirlpool manufactured most of its front-loading washers in Germany. Now the company is in the midst of making a five-year, $1 billion investment in U.S.-based plants, facilities, and equipment. Of the products Whirlpool sells in the U.S., it makes 80 percent in U.S. plants. And it continues to ramp up production of front-loaders in Ohio, where it already makes dryers, dishwashers, freezers, and top-loaders.

"On the one hand, U.S. labor costs are often higher than in other countries," says Casey Tubman, Whirlpool's general manager of cleaning. "But when you look at the higher productivity for American workers and consider the fact that it's very expensive to ship something as big as a refrigerator or washer, we can quickly make up those costs."

Last year, KitchenAid returned the manufacture of hand mixers from China to the U.S., and GE opened two factories in Kentucky to make hot-water heaters and refrigerators. A spokesman for Sears told us that "through our manufacturing partner, Electrolux, more than 1,200 new American jobs will be created at a plant being built in Memphis."

There should be plenty of demand if the industry does come back. About a third of respondents to our survey said they'd tried to buy U.S.-made appliances during the past year. And more than half of respondents perceived such appliances as having much or somewhat better quality than those made abroad.

Electronics

A few TVs, cell phones, or digital cameras are made in America, but in December, Apple CEO Tim Cook said, "Next year, we will do one of our existing Mac lines in the United States." China-based Lenovo, the world's second-largest personal computer maker, announced last October that it would start making some PCs in North Carolina, bucking a trend "that has seen electronics manufacturing jobs migrate overseas for more than two decades," the company said. And Element Electronics, an American company, has been assembling LCD TVs in its Detroit factory since January 2012. The company says that opting for domestic production was "an emotional decision . . . maybe even a patriotic choice."

Apparel

The domestic industry has been scorched by job losses because of plentiful and cheap labor overseas. More than 90 percent of clothes and shoes sold in America are made elsewhere, according to Jack Plunkett of Houston-based Plunkett Research. Still, the industry is gaining traction in the U.S. There's growth among designers with output too small to attract the interest of international manufacturers, and among those who simply want to be part of a Made in America movement. And as you'll read in "American Made, But Well Made?" even some big names are offering at least a limited assortment of American-made garments and accessories.

To build on the momentum, President Obama, through the departments of Commerce and Labor, last fall launched the "Make It in America" challenge, offering $40 million in grants to applicants who come up with the best proposals to encourage "insourcing," spur foreign investment, and expand job opportunities through employee training programs.

Close to home (mostly)

Here's a sampling of companies that make or assemble at least some of their products in the U.S. Note that a company's entire output isn't necessarily American-made. And some primarily American companies may have manufacturing facilities in more than one country to meet demand overseas.

Housewares

All-Clad, Lodge, and Nordic Ware cookware; Bunn coffeemakers; Dacor; DCS, Viking, and Wolf ranges; Harden Furniture; Kirby and Oreck vacuum cleaners; Lasko (mostly fans); Pyrex glassware; Sub-Zero refrigerators.

Apparel and accessories

Allen Edmonds shoes, American Apparel, Chippewa boots, Filson apparel, Kepner Scott children's shoes, Pendleton woolens (the Portland Collection and wool blankets and throws), Stetson hats, True Religion and Texas jeans, and Wigwam socks.

Tools and home equipment

Briggs & Stratton mower and tractor engines, Channel-lock and Moody hand tools, Maglite flashlights, Purdy paintbrushes and rollers, Shop-Vac wet-and-dry vacuum cleaners, and Stihl gasoline-powered equipment.

Other products

Airstream trailers, Annin flags, Crayola crayons, Gibson and Martin guitars, Hillerich & Bradsby (Louisville Slugger wooden bats), Little Tikes and K'Nex toys, Sharpie markers, Steinway pianos, and Wilson sporting goods (NFL footballs).

Critical Thinking

1. Consumer ethnocentrism may be defined as one's belief that one's own system of tastes and preferences are better than that of another cultural group. Based on the article, what are some factors that may influence consumer ethnocentrism?

2. Look up the definition of "Country of Origin Effect." What impact can this concept have on consumer purchasing behavior?

3. With a small group of peers from your class, develop a list of DOs and DON'Ts to help businesses reduce the confusion consumers experience with relation to a product's country of origin.

Create Central

www.mhhe.com/createcentral

Internet References

U.S. Customs and Border Protection
http://www.cbp.gov/trade/nafta/country-origin-marking
Pew Research
http://www.pewglobal.org/topics/country-image/

"Made in America" Copyright 2013 Consumers Union of U.S., Inc. Yonkers, NY 10703–1057, a nonprofit organization. Reprinted with permission from the February 2013 issue of Consumer Reports® for educational purposes only. www.ConsumerReports.org.

Article   Prepared by: Nisreen N. Bahnan, *Salem State University*

The Rebirth of Retail

Innovator: Shopkick's Cyriac Roeding reinvents retail:
Meet Cyriac Roeding, the man reinventing shopping for the mobile era.

JASON ANKENY

Learning Outcomes

After reading this article, you will be able to:

- Understand the concept and importance of product innovation.

- Identify the traits of an innovator or visionary.

- Examine and assess theRoeding's 'shopkick' application, from the consumer's perspective.

The idea first came to Cyriac Roeding in 1994. The German-born business and engineering graduate student was studying Japanese management theory at Tokyo's Sophia University. "Everywhere I went, I saw people walking around with these clunky machines they called 'mobile phones,'" Roeding says. "I said, 'Wow, that's the next big thing.'"

The seed was planted, but the true form and scope of the idea remained elusive for more than a decade. In the meantime, Roeding pursued other successes. He founded a mobile marketing firm called 12snap. He served as executive vice president of CBS Mobile, where his interactive entertainment concepts were strong enough to win an Emmy Award nomination.

Still, the big kahuna—the eureka moment, the one that captured lightning in a bottle—refused to reveal itself.

"I have been looking for an idea that has the potential to become a really large company in mobile for 11 years," Roeding says. "When I started 12snap in 1999, it was during the dark ages of mobile, when text messaging was still a geeky thing even in Europe. For years I've been trying out different mobile-use cases, looking for the one with a chance to become huge."

Roeding left CBS Mobile in 2008 and traveled the world for nearly two months. Everywhere he went, from New Zealand to Nepal, he saw people on mobile phones. With each successive stop, the idea took shape.

"I wanted to develop a service where mobile meets the real world," Roeding says. "Your cell phone is the only interactive medium you carry with you in a noninteractive physical environment, and that changes everything. It makes the offline world an interactive experience."

The idea finally achieved critical mass in September 2008, when Roeding arrived at his new gig as entrepreneur-in-residence with Silicon Valley venture capital firm Kleiner Perkins Caufield & Byers. After poring over thousands of business plans submitted to KPCB's iFund (a $200 million investment initiative created to ignite software developer interest in Apple's then-fledgling iPhone) and finding nothing that crystallized his vision, he shifted his perspective from identifying a solution to pinpointing a problem.

"The number-one challenge facing every retailer in America is getting people through the door," Roeding says. "Conversion rates in the physical world are so much better than online—between 0.5 percent to 3 percent in the virtual world, and between 20 percent to 95 percent in the real world. So if foot traffic is so important, then why hasn't anyone rewarded people for visiting stores? The answer is simple: It's because nobody knows you came through the door."

So Roeding set to work on a smartphone-optimized rewards program offering customers discounts and promotions simply for entering retail stores—a model he describes as "the physical-world equivalent of an online click." Meetings with big-box retailer executives followed. "They all loved the idea," he recalls. "It was crazy. I still didn't have a company, the technology, a team or even any funding. I only had a PowerPoint presentation."

With kickbucks, retailers design their own rewards. The idea—or shopkick, as it's now formally known-launched last August, buoyed by $20 million in funding from KPCB, as well as venture firm Greylock Partners and Linked-In founder Reid Hoffman (also an investor in Facebook and Zynga). The startup's eponymous mobile application delivers "kickbucks" rewards to all registered iPhone and Android users who enter a participating retail location. Kickbucks can be collected and redeemed across any partner store and turned into gift cards, discounts, song downloads, movie tickets, Facebook Credits, or even charitable donations. As of late last year, shopkick spanned 1,100 individual United States retail outlets and 100 shopping centers with partners such as Best Buy, Macy's, Target, Sports Authority, Crate & Barrel and mall operator Simon Property Group.

"Shopkick transfers the online business model to the real world," says Roeding, CEO of the Palo Alto, Calif.-based company. "We're tackling a huge market with a big problem, and we're offering them a solution that works."

Roeding speaks about ideas in a deeply reverential, almost spiritual, tone. "I love building companies," he says. "I've always said that if the right people and the right idea pop up, I will drop everything to start a company. That's why I came to the United States I wanted to build something."

Roeding's entrepreneurial aspirations took a left turn when he landed in the entertainment industry, taking the helm of CBS Corp.'s fledgling mobile entertainment unit in 2005.

"At that time Disney had 270 people in its mobile department and CBS had zero," he recalls. "I met with [CBS executives] Nancy Tellem and Leslie Moonves and asked, 'Why are you talking to me? I'm an entrepreneur. I'm not a big-company person,'" he says. "And Les said, 'Because I want to turn this company into a company of entrepreneurs.'"

Roeding left CBS Mobile after three years at the top. Along the way, he pioneered a mobile video news-alert program, produced mobile games based on the network's prime-time hits and masterminded original made-for-mobile content across the three largest United States wireless carrier networks. Roeding also inked an early location-based mobile advertising partnership with Loopt, a still-growing mobile social networking startup that predates up-and-comers like Foursquare and Gowalla by several years.

At first glance, it may appear shopkick is yet another variation on the location-specific check-in paradigm championed by those firms, but Roeding cautions that the app is not a social networking tool.

"Our vision is to transform shopping into a personal, rewarding and fun experience for everyone," he says. "Shopkick is an app that is built around the act of going out and shopping. It's not about going out and letting your friends know where you are."

And unlike other location-enabled applications, shopkick doesn't rely on GPS triangulation. "If you want to reward someone for walking in your store, you cannot use GPS," Roeding says. "It's way too inaccurate. There's an error radius of about 500 yards, meaning I still don't know if you're inside the store, out in the parking lot, or across the street at a competitor."

Shopkick instead incorporates a patent-pending device located in each participating store. The box, which costs retailers less than $100 and is roughly the dimensions of a paperback novel, plugs into any power outlet, emitting an audio signal that's undetectable to the human ear but automatically picked up by a smartphone's internal microphone. Because the signal's range is limited to the perimeter of the store, users must physically enter the location to earn kickbucks. And as Roeding points out, because detection occurs via the mobile device, consumers retain control over the privacy of their presence information.

Retailers determine how many kickbucks a shopper receives for entering their business. Roeding says each walk-in can earn as many as 100 kickbucks, with 875 kickbucks earning a $25 restaurant gift certificate, for example. Retailers can leverage the shopkick app to deliver special offers, like a discount on specific merchandise.

The concept also extends beyond retail: in partnership with brands including Kraft Foods and Procter & Gamble, shopkick offers smaller rewards for scanning product barcodes, which extends the network to about 230,000 additional stores nationwide.

Shopkick receives a small commission fee for each kickbuck a customer earns. "It's essentially a cost-per-click equivalent, only we charge cost-per-visit," Roeding says. If a shopper makes a purchase after using the app, shopkick claims a percentage of that transaction as well.

Not only is the shopkick model different from services like Foursquare, its users are different.

"Eighty percent of Foursquare users are male and 70 percent are between the ages of 19 and 35," Roeding says. By contrast, he notes, "55 percent of our users are female. Forty-nine percent of all users are aged 25 to 39, and 13 percent are 40 or older. Only 6.5 percent are 13 to 17. It's the perfect shopper demographic."

Retailers credit shopkick with kicking their customer traffic into a different gear. Sporting goods chain Sports Authority has rolled it out to more than 100 of its United States locations. In late 2010 the chain doubled—and in some cases even tripled—kickbucks rewards to determine the potential effect on walk-ins. The promotion ultimately increased shopkick user walk-in growth 50 percent to 70 percent.

"You have to innovate in retail to be relevant," says Jeff Schumacher, Sports Authority's chief marketing officer. "We looked at other applications, but we felt shopkick's strategy was the best fit. Their focus is on driving frequency, and in retail, frequency is a powerful metric. Anything that incents the customer to come into the store more often is a win–win for us."

Schumacher declines to reveal how many Sports Authority customers actively use the shopkick application, but says the company is "quite pleased" with it. "We're trialing shopkick in our major markets, which is where we see the greatest density of smartphones," he says. "Our customers love it. Some of them are even asking for it in markets where we don't have it. Feedback has been very positive."

Shopkick's rapid growth corresponds with surging consumer interest in leveraging mobile technology to shop smarter. Shoppers relying on mobile solutions to search for price and product information, check merchandise availability, compare prices at nearby stores, browse product reviews and even purchase goods accounted for $127 billion in consumer spending during the 2010 holiday season—which represents 28 percent of the $447 billion the National Retail Federation forecasts United States consumers spent over the period—according to a survey conducted by research firm IDC.

"We're seeing a fundamental shift in how consumers are accessing information at the point of purchase," says Cathy Halligan, senior vice president of marketing and sales at PowerReviews, a company in San Francisco that provides social commerce solutions (including customer reviews) to retailers and brands. "Consumers now have access to product information while they're standing in the store. They've never had that before. It's a game-changer."

As of October, nearly 61 million United States consumers owned smartphones, up 14 percent from the preceding three-month period and translating to one out of every four American wireless subscribers in all, researcher comScore reports. And as smartphone penetration grows, the opportunity for startups like shopkick flourishes.

"We made the decision to focus only on smartphones—it makes the most sense," Roeding says. "There will be 150 million smartphone users across the United States by the end of [2011], and consumers who can afford to shop are overrepresented in that group."

His idea is growing, too. Shopkick is extending its platform into the small-business sector: at press time, the firm was planning to launch its SMB retail trials in the first quarter of 2011.

"We're very excited about moving into the small-business world," Roeding says. "You could never join a national program as a local player before. It just didn't work. But with kickbucks, the playing field is level."

He also plans to expand the core capabilities of the shopkick model. In conjunction with the annual Black Friday shopping frenzy, the company recently unveiled The 12 Days of Kickmas, a sweepstakes giving walk-in users a shot at winning one of a dozen daily prize packages, including a grand prize of 4.25 million kickbucks. Other initiatives are in the pipeline, and as shopkick grows and improves, retailer offers should become more sophisticated as well, with kickbucks awards and promotions eventually targeting consumers according to age, gender, geography, shopping frequency or purchase history.

"Shopkick is about shopping, and not anything else," Roeding says. "There are all kinds of things that shopping entails, and we want to improve all of them. It's about making the in-store experience amazing. It's not a tool. This is your world."

Critical Thinking

1. In your opinion, what are the traits of a true visionary?
2. Elaborate on the concept of Roeding's "shopkick."
3. As a consumer, how do you assess the "shopkick" app? Suggest some ways to improve it.

Create Central

www.mhhe.com/createcentral

Internet References

Product Development and Management Association
   http://www.pdma.org/p/cm/ld/fid=1
Visionary Marketing
   http://visionarymarketing.com/index.html

Jason Ankeny, "The Rebirth of Retail," *Entrepreneur*, February 22, 2011. Copyright © 2011 by Entrepreneur Media, Inc. All rights reserved. Used with permission.

Article   Prepared by: Nisreen N. Bahnan, *Salem State University*

Marketing Communication in a Digital Era

Marketers Should Focus Efforts on Emerging Social, Mobile and Local Trends

DONNA L. HOFFMAN AND THOMAS P. NOVAK

Learning Outcomes

After reading this article, you will be able to:

- Become familiar with the role of social media in today's world as more people spend more time interacting with others through social media applications.

- Gain a better understanding of technology and about what it allows people do.

- Examine five social media outlets that are poised to have a large impact on both marketing research and practice.

Today's web is all about social media. It is increasingly becoming less about technology and more about what technology lets people do. Through social media, Internet users can perform various actions online, from connecting with friends to sharing videos to buying products. But as social media applications proliferate and the dynamics of online social interaction continue to evolve, marketing managers are seeking a deeper understanding of how and why people use social media, so that consistent practices based on online consumer behavior can be developed. The need for such understanding is acute, especially as more people spend more time interacting with others through social media applications.

Trends and Implications

Before outlining a framework for how to understand consumer behavior in today's dynamically changing online environment, let's first examine five social media outlets that are poised to have a large impact on both marketing research and practice.

1. Portable Social Graphs

First coined by Facebook founder and CEO Mark Zuckerberg in 2007, a person's "social graph" is the set of data-based connections that indicate how people within a given social network are related to each other. Social graphs can be diagrammed with the people as "nodes" and "edges," or lines connecting the nodes indicating how people are connected to each other. Such diagrams are typically called sociograms and describe the connections among one's "friends" in a particular social network.

Since April 2010, Facebook has significantly broadened the reach of users' social graphs via "social plug-ins," or embedded features on external websites that keep people connected with friends from their Facebook social graph. Through these plug-ins, a person can, for example, broadcast that she "likes" a certain story on another site, without first having to log in to Facebook. Instead of being limited to just the Facebook interface, actions between Facebook friends can now happen around the web. Social plug-ins have made social graphs essentially portable.

With "like" buttons and other social plug-ins, marketers can now more easily integrate their web presence with consumers' social networking behavior. Social plug-ins can provide social proof or legitimacy to content and increase reach when used in the right situations (for example, if a customer were to like a particular movie on IMDb, Amazon could access those likes via Facebook and serve product recommendations to that user based on her IMDb likes). In addition, the use of social plug-ins

Briefly

- Track consumers' online behavior via their social graphs, "likes," "check-ins," and "information shadows."
- Analyze social media's evolution using the "4Cs" as a framework: connect, create, consume, and control.
- Focus your social media efforts using the LEAD model: listen, experiment, apply, and develop.

can drive traffic, promote word of mouth, increase interaction, and generate marketing insight into consumer behavior (through website traffic data and demographics accessible through the Facebook Insights Dashboard). Besides the "like" button, other examples of popular social plug-ins include the activity feed that shows users what their friends are doing on the marketer's site (through "likes" and comments) and the recommendations plug-in that provides a marketer's page recommendations personalized to users.

Currently, 250 million people use Facebook through other sites, instead of through direct visits to Facebook.com. But as the social graph becomes increasingly portable and users are able to take their friends with them as they travel around the web, we are left with the question of where this trend will lead. We have two predictions that we think will have important consumer behavior and marketing practice implications.

First, we believe that people will increasingly want to limit their social graph to their "real friends," ultimately ending the era of "promiscuous friending" and leading to more meaningful application of the social graph to marketing practice.

Second, because Facebook, not the marketer or the user, controls the information embedded in the social graph, we believe there will be a battle for control of the social graph, potentially leading to a backlash over ownership of social data and creating new regulatory challenges for businesses.

2. The Power of the "Like"

Social search, or human-driven search, incorporates one's social graph into any given search, giving more weight to content endorsed by users in one's social graph. A user can thus find content based on friends' shared bookmarks, tags, questions and answers, reviews, and ratings. This kind of search combines artificial intelligence with human intelligence, is evolving rapidly and takes on a variety of forms. Examples of social search include Aardvark and Quora (which match a user's question to someone in his network who may be able to provide an answer), Stumpedia (in which users index, organize and review search results based on their relevance to their

social graphs) and Scour (in which users vote and comment on the relevancy of search results).

At one extreme, social search results can be driven by the in-depth response of a single expert member of one's social graph, such as with Aardvark or Quora. At the other extreme, Facebook's social search, which is based upon likes, is driven by the collective behavior of a large group of people. It provides a much broader, but at the same time much shallower, dip into the social graph. When a user clicks the "like" button, it is tantamount to an endorsement of the content, which others in that user's social graph can then use as the basis for their own content searches. This "power of the 'like' vs. power of the link" phenomenon is changing the dynamics of organic search, essentially changing the way we search, from Googling to liking. More importantly, we are shifting from a reasonably objective search process controlled by a purportedly neutral third party like Google or Bing, to a mass frenzy of websites motivated to install "like" buttons out of fear that not doing so would make them invisible to Facebook's social search.

One critical problem this trend introduces is that it does not distinguish between different types of likes. There is, for example, a difference between people who like a product out of genuine preference for it and those who might be externally motivated to like a product as a result of simply seeing others perform the action. Another problem is that we don't know whether a like relates to purchase intent. Clicking "like" does not necessarily represent a commitment on the part of the consumer. A person might click "like" purely from a *wish* to buy a particular product, not because of any *plan* to buy it.

The concept of liking something is getting baked into social search. Two million sites and counting use social sign-in and all are using this social plug-in. This is a huge investment that will not be going away anytime soon, so marketers are stuck with "like" whether they like it or not. Looking ahead, marketers need to figure out how best to leverage all these connections.

3. The "Footstream"

The geolocation field is getting crowded. There are currently around 20,000 real-time location-based mobile apps through which users can "check in" and share their locations and activities. Of the 20,000, only a handful have an established following, with Foursquare currently leading the pack. Other examples include the Meebo MiniBar (a website that allows users to check in to any website and share content with friends) and Whrrl 3.0 (a social location-based game, in which users inspire each other to try new activities and experiences). Virtual check-in to a location, content or brand is analogous to a "like," and is another way the social graph is being redefined.

Not surprisingly, the check-in model is rapidly evolving and is serving as a focal point for the integration of online and offline retailing. Shopkick's mobile check-in application, for example, identifies the customer entering a participating store and gives Kickbucks points just for walking in. Check-in was, at first, largely about creating awareness and driving traffic, but it is moving in the direction of location-based points, rewards, coupons and incentive systems that draw from principles of game mechanics to encourage specific customer behaviors. For example, Foursquare has formalized seven types of marketing specials, such as the "Mayor Special" that identifies and rewards the most frequent visitor to a venue over a two-month period for loyalty. Shopkick can reward very specific consumer behaviors with Kickbucks, such as inspecting products being promoted in the store or even entering a dressing room. A merchant could also use check-in data to identify and push product specials to customers already at the store. Starbucks, for example, could use this data to push deals and coupons for a venti cappuccino.

This location data measures foot traffic, which advertisers can use to quantify return on investment. Some are calling this the "footstream," but as we've seen, the footstream goes well beyond merely counting the number of customers to measuring specific targeted customer behaviors. Many view the footstream as the solution to the "last 50 feet" problem, in that it allows marketers to engage and incent consumers when they are literally at the front door of the business. The footstream brings the social web into the store.

4. Social Data Mining

Through basic PC sensors (such as a mouse and keyboard) and more advanced smart-phone sensors (such as a touch screen, microphone, camera, motion sensor, proximity sensor, and location sensor), people are leaving what some have called "information shadows." These information shadows are a behavioral trail of one's visited websites, emails, instant messages, tweets, blog posts, photographs, videos, locations, and so on.

The advent of location-based sensors that use radio frequency identification (RFID)—which use radio waves and intelligent bar codes, like smart labels—near field communication (NFC) or short-range wireless and geotags—GPS data that indicate longitude and latitude of a tagged object (it's embedded in photos and videos with GPS-equipped smartphones and digital cameras)—will lead to an exponential increase in these information shadows.

Consider this: a single tweet has 40 fields of data associated with it. How many fields of data are associated with a person? Taking into account every upload from every location at every point in time, a single person has more fields of data than the total number of websites in the 1990s. This can be expanded if we incorporate internal sensors that monitor, for example, heart rate or other bodily functions. What we have, then, is a data mining problem that goes considerably beyond the footstream, to a veritable fire hose of data. A primary challenge for marketers in the coming decade is how to make sense of these information shadows and connect the dots for a deeper understanding of customer behavior.

> **Emerging technology trends suggest a convergence of augmented reality, real time, location and sensors that will make Facebook seem quaint.**

5. Smart Signs

There are two types of smart signs. The first is the digital sign, the simplest and most common form of which is a flat-screen television playing a loop of advertisements in a public place.

Digital signage can be seen in retail stores, doctor's offices, gas stations, restaurants, gyms, airports, train stations and taxis. The advertising medium has expanded into a multibillion-dollar business and has continued to grow relatively rapidly through the economic downturn of the past several years. Digital signage is now integrating identification technologies, such as tiny facial recognition cameras, in order to tailor advertisements to match audiences, as well as to record a consumer's response to ads.

As a consumer draws near to the screen, the camera-enabled smart sign can detect the consumer's age and gender, prompting the screen to run an ad that matches the consumer's profile. Facial recognition is the most common targeting method, but other digital signage systems employ RFID, Bluetooth and social networking. Most systems do not record individual identities at present, but there is little barrier to individual identification and profiling in the future. Although somewhat cliche in the digital signage industry, the famous advertising scenes from the movie "Minority Report," in which billboards can scan a face to determine one's gender and age and present ads accordingly, are the clearest dramatization of what this medium may ultimately be capable of doing. In fact, a Japanese company has already undertaken research in this direction of "gladvertising," using emotion recognition (EMR) software to serve ads according to one's mood.

The other type of smart sign is webcam-based augmented reality (AR), in which a camera either identifies a target or pattern on a physical-world object or uses motion capture to overlay digital information on top of a physical object captured via a webcam. Examples of augmented reality include the Ray Ban Virtual Mirror, which allows users to virtually try on different styles of Ray Ban sunglasses, and the United States Postal

Service Priority Virtual Box Simulator, which allows users to determine the correct box size for the item they want to ship.

Bloomingdale's Magic Mirror and Macy's Magic Fitting Room in-store AR installations allow customers to virtually try on clothing via a large-scale interactive mirror and receive remote feedback from their social network friends in the process.

Online marketers have been largely concerned about the relationship between online and offline retailing, but now they also have to worry about the convergence of online and offline with "social retailing." Digital signs (displays that recognize and target offers to individuals) and augmented reality (signs that overlay digital information on physical objects) will continue to converge in such a way that in the future, the sign will know it's you, suggest a dress just for you and digitally dress you—right there on the street. And clothing is just the beginning.

Managing What's Next

Based on a close examination of these five trends, we can expect considerable technology changes in the coming decade, driven by the fundamental laws of technology that suggest exponential increases in processing power, data storage, bandwidth, and number of Internet-enabled devices. As a result, we need to step back and use a framework to address these constant changes in social media and to help manage what is coming up next, and that framework must start with consumers in mind.

In our research, we argue that the fundamental interactivity of social media allows for four higher-order goals. These "4Cs" of connect, create, consume, and control not only are the fundamental defining characteristics of social media, but also define the goals that consumers pursue in connection with social media use. Thus, social media enable and facilitate interactions that "connect" people. These social media conversations occur through web- or mobile-based applications that people use to "create" (i.e., post, upload, blog) and "consume" (i.e., read, watch, listen to) content. Finally, social media applications give individuals a greater ability to manage their reputations and control content (e.g., page layout, tagging, rating) and online settings such as profile and privacy options.

All five of the trends we have discussed can be viewed through the lens of the 4Cs to understand why these trends have captured the attention of today's consumers. This understanding provides the starting point for developing digital strategy as social media continues to evolve. The chart on the next page summarizes the marketing implications of the five trends we examined in this article, in the context of our 4Cs.

Take the LEAD

Digital communications are increasingly becoming social, mobile and local. The web is moving far beyond its current state of connecting people and content, as billions of devices with embedded mobile functionality create an "Internet of things." Emerging technology trends suggest a convergence of augmented reality, real time, location, and sensors that will make Facebook seem quaint. The web is evolving rapidly, driven by exponential changes in technology and a thrilling abundance of innovation. Marketers have no choice but to keep up or fall far behind.

One way marketers can not only keep up, but also get ahead is to use our LEAD model. With the LEAD model, marketers listen, experiment, apply, and develop to help focus their companies' social media efforts against what sometimes feels like dizzying and dynamic change.

Listen

Marketers need to formally monitor and analyze what their customers are saying about them online, as well as what they are doing online. Ideally, marketers should put a formal process in place to monitor and analyze the conversations that customers are having about their brands, using the information as an early warning system, but ad hoc is better than nothing.

Experiment

Marketers can't just monitor. Start with simple pilot social media experiments, such as a Facebook brand page, YouTube videos or a Twitter stream. While ROI metrics for social media are still in the early stages, it's clear that these experiments pay off big-time in terms of increased customer awareness and brand engagement. Marketers can take first steps toward co-creation, and reach out to their customers through collaborative efforts to conceive new offerings and ad campaigns. Be aware that there really aren't any best practices or established business "models" yet, so marketers just need to get as much experience as they can as quickly as they can.

Apply

As experimentation proceeds, marketers are ready to gather the successes and start applying them systematically and on a larger scale. At this point, measuring impact is paramount, so it is important to track the results.

Develop

This involves developing integrated marketing programs that effectively integrate social media in marketing campaigns and go beyond simply viewing social media as just another channel for advertising.

By using a framework like the LEAD model, and remembering the 4Cs' fundamental aspects of how consumers behave online, marketers will be prepared as social media trends continue to evolve.

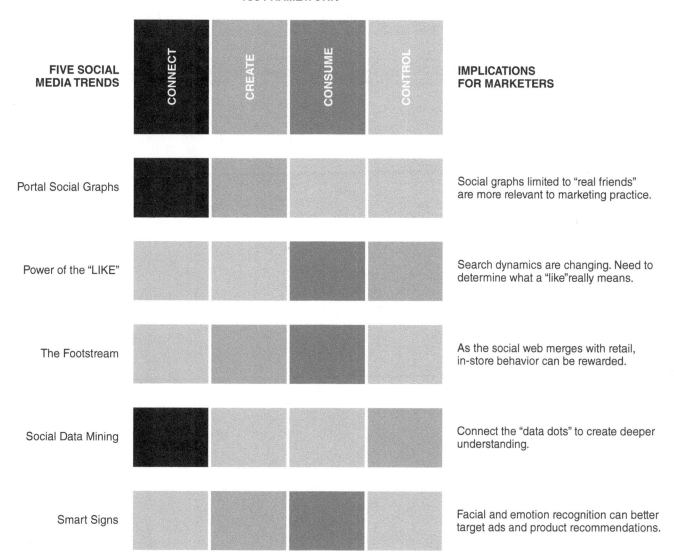

Marketing implications of five social media trends

Critical Thinking

1. Describe the five social media trends discussed in the article.
2. According to the authors, what are the four goals that consumers pursue in connection with social media use?
3. With a small group of peers in your class, evaluate the LEAD model. Do you agree or disagree with the implications?

Create Central

www.mhhe.com/createcentral

Internet References

Internet Marketing Association
   http://imanetwork.org/

Social Media Association
   http://socialmediaassoc.com/

Donna L. Hoffman is Chancellor's Chair, professor of marketing and co-director of the Sloan Center for Internet Retailing at the University of California in Riverside, Calif. **Tom Novak** is Albert O. Steffey professor of marketing and co-director of the Sloan Center, as well. They may be reached at Donna.Hoffman@ucr.edu and Tom .Novak@ucr.edu, respectively.

Donna L. Hoffman; Thomas P. Novak, "Marketing Communication in a Digital Era: Marketers Should Focus Efforts on Emerging Social, Mobile, and Local Trends," *Marketing Management*, Fall 2011, p. 37–43. Copyright © 2011 by American Marketing Association. All rights reserved. Used with permission.

Article   Prepared by: Nisreen N. Bahnan, *Salem State University*

Selling Green

Marketing a business as green requires a blend of transparency, practicality, and savvy. Here is *Entrepreneur's* five-step guide to how to do it right.

Matt Villano

Learning Outcomes

After reading this article, you will be able to:

- Define the concept "green marketing" and distinguish it from "green washing."

- Summarize and discuss the five steps to effective green marketing proposed in this article.

- Examine the possible negative impacts that "green washing" may have on a company's image and credibility.

In the world of marketing, green is the new black.

Have a recycling program? That's green. Use LED light bulbs? That's green, too. Heck, if you go so far as to encourage employees to carpool to work, you might as well be able to say your business is green.

And yet, green marketing—that is, *successful* green marketing—isn't nearly as easy as it seems.

It turns out there's more to eco-consciousness than simply being conscious of the environment. We asked a number of entrepreneurs and experts for insights on the components of green marketing that works. The gist: green only yields green when messaging blends transparency, practicality, and savvy.

1. See What Your Customers Want

Marketing your business as green is a great idea—provided your customers are into that sort of thing. Executives at Bardessono, a luxury hotel, and spa in Yountville, Calif., learned this the hard way.

Beware of "Greenwashing"

While marketing your company as green has undisputed benefits, misrepresenting one's greenness—a process known as "greenwashing"—can be disastrous to a company's credibility.

ConAgra, the food product company, is facing a class-action lawsuit for labeling its cooking oils as "natural," even though they're made with genetically modified ingredients.

Then there's Sigg. The Switzerland-based reusable-bottle manufacturer told its customers that its products were BPA-free, even though the bottles contained the chemical in their liners. When news of this hit the mainstream media, sales dropped precipitously.

Apparently, greenwashing is getting worse. According to the 2010 Greenwashing Report from the TerraChoice Group, an environmental marketing agency based in Ottawa, Ontario, more than 95 percent of all consumer products claiming to be green were found to commit at least one of the "Seven Sins of Greenwashing," which include not providing evidence, being vague or flat-out lying.

The best way to avoid these claims, according to Shel Horowitz, CEO of Greenandprofitable.com, is to keep messages consistent and support every claim with incontrovertible evidence.

"Transparency and honesty is the best approach," he says. "If you're accused of greenwashing and there's some stick to it at all, you're dead."

When the 62-room property opened in 2009, executives trumpeted the hotel's Platinum status from the Leadership in Energy and Environmental Design (LEED) program—the resort was one of only two such honored hotels in the United States. While the facility was a hit among environmentalists and green-obsessed journalists, it struggled with perhaps its most important group of constituents: customers.

The problem? Travelers accustomed to the luxury hotel experience perceived "green" to mean "sparse" and "uncomfortable" and booked elsewhere.

"Our messaging was great for occupancy but not so good for the average daily rate," says Jim Treadway, the hotel's general manager. "We had lost sight of the fact that our core customers value a luxury experience above all else."

Naturally, in 2010 Bardessono changed its tune, tweaking marketing messages to emphasize luxury first and green second. Almost overnight, bookings—at full price, mind you—soared.

The lesson: never assume everybody will love you just because you're green.

"It took us a while to realize the best message for our customers was, 'We're a world-class hotel and, oh yeah, we're green,'" Treadway says. "That might not be intuitive, but when you consider that your customers are the top priority, targeting your messages to their lifestyle certainly makes sense."

2. Define What Green Means to You

Describing something as "green" can be dicey, since the word often means different things to different people.

In one instance, it could summarize an off-the-grid production facility powered by solar energy. In other cases, it could signify the existence of a telecommuting program that helps reduce a carbon footprint.

Jenny Grayson, a Los Angeles-based consultant who helps companies go green, says it behooves companies to be totally honest and to define exactly what "green" means to them.

"Everyone right now, from Clorox to Huggies, is marketing themselves as 'natural,' but what does that really mean?" she asks. "Environmentally savvy consumers can become quickly disillusioned with a company when it doesn't live up to its eco-friendly claims," or when it doesn't explain how it's eco-friendly in the first place.

Personal explanations usually work best. Ava Anderson Non-Toxic, a personal-care-product manufacturer (and one of *Entrepreneur's* "Entrepreneur of 2011" award winners), explains on the company website how its founder, as a 14-year-old girl, became disillusioned with chemicals in beauty products due to their hazardous health effects.

Bill and Jane Monetti offer similarly personal insights on the website for their company, Eco-Command, which produces GoFlushless, a spray that neutralizes the odor of urine and reduces the need to flush a toilet. The Monettis detail how the product was born out of necessity when they purchased a home in the environmentally sensitive area of Maryland's Eastern Shore.

"Along with our new home, we acquired a well, septic tank, drainage field and an extreme awareness of every drop of water we use," they write. With this, it's easy to understand the company mission of "saving water, saving energy."

3. Connect the Dots

No matter how well a company defines green, being green alone is not enough—there has to be some substance behind the messaging to make it work.

Do Customers Care?

With businesses in just about every industry vying to market themselves as green, it's natural to ask: to what extent do customers care? The answer depends on where you look.

Some data indicates that increasing numbers of Americans are seeking out green products; according to the Organic Trade Association, organic food sales have grown about 20 percent per year over the last decade. What's more, Wal-Mart, that mass-market juggernaut, is now the world's largest buyer of organic cotton.

Still, when most companies gauge customers about what matters most to them, answers such as "greenness" or sustainability frequently come in behind key issues such as usefulness and price.

Saul Kliorys, environmental programs manager for Great Lakes Brewing Company in Cleveland, has taken surveys of this nature, and says green is always near the top but never finishes first. "On the whole," he says, "greenness doesn't sell products; products sell products."

Still, to be fair, certain demographics appear to be more concerned than others with whether products are, in fact, green.

Women, for instance, account for a majority of household spending, and many may be worrying about the chemicals in their kids' shampoo, or might be trying to avoid purchasing genetically modified food at the grocery store.

The bottom line: green likely isn't the sole factor determining customer behaviors in today's economy, but it undoubtedly is one of the few.

"Customers want good-performing products at prices they can afford that are healthy for their families and easy to get," says Park Howell, president of Park&Co, a sustainable marketing firm in Phoenix. "If a product has met all of those considerations and it's green, that's even better."

Green Allure

Jennifer Kaplan is a partner in green marketing firm Greenhance and the author of *Greening Your Small Business.* She is also an entrepreneur in her own right, having recently founded VineCrowd.com, a website designed to connect artisanal, independent wineries with consumers to buy, sell, discuss, compare, and share. Kaplan compiled this ranking of green marketing innovators from the past decade for the Green Marketing and Communications class she teaches at Golden Gate University in San Francisco.

1. Tide Coldwater Challenge

This landmark 2005 marketing campaign addressed the money saved by washing in cold water and the product's deep cleaning and whitening abilities, making green the ancillary benefit. The far-reaching campaign included national advertising, in-store programs, product sampling, a strong Internet presence, consumer promotions, and strategic alliances.

2. Jamie Oliver

The outspoken English chef and advocate of healthy food is a brand in and unto himself. He uses "disruptive media and public visibility" to communicate and motivate, creating a new kind of "infotainment."

3. Diesel Clothing: Global Warming Ready

In print ads promoting its 2007 spring/summer collection, the Italian clothing company depicted landscapes transformed by environmental disaster. The campaign proved that green marketing and tongue-in-cheek humor-when done well—resonate with young audiences.

4. GE Ecomagination

A massive 2008 multimedia campaign for Ecomagination established GE's green position in a competitive marketplace where credibility and believability are paramount to success. The resulting creative was simple, beautiful, and compelling and delivered the message in engaging ways.

5. HSBC: There's No Small Change

A highly successful 2008 print campaign elevated HSBC's environmental credentials and consolidated the bank's environmental leadership position—all without TV or radio.

6. TOMS Shoes: Project Holiday

For the month of December 2008, TOMS promoted its Project Holiday campaign to sell 30,000 pairs of shoes so it could give the same number of protective rubber shoes to kids in Ethiopia. The company exceeded its goal by 23 percent and raised unprecedented awareness for its cause—all without paid media.

7. Toyota Prius: Harmony

This 2009 multimedia campaign showed how the Prius delivers extra power, space, safety, advanced technology, and superior gas mileage.

8. Timberland: Earthkeepers

This 2009 global campaign showcased the Earthkeepers collection of eco-friendly apparel and included TV, print, and retail ads, as well as social media and a microsite that used 3D technology.

9. Method: Just Say No to Jugs

This cheeky 2010 campaign is typical of Method's marketing, mocking mainstream cleaning products as feeding a household's "jug" habit. The campaign relied only on print and online ads.

10. BMW Diesel: Ch-ch-changes

This 2011 campaign launched at Super Bowl XLV, communicated valuable information and a relevant message to the American audience about the environmental benefits of and changes in diesel technology.

Park Howell, president of Park&Co, a sustainable marketing firm in Phoenix, says that in the current economy, emphasizing how people can save *their* green by going green is the most effective approach.

"In these overwhelming efforts to come across as eco-friendly, most small businesses taking their products to market miss the most important differentiators: quality and price," he says. "Something that's good for the planet is nice, but in this day and age, the masses simply don't care about it as much."

Howell contends that the best green marketing campaigns address the "three Ps" of *profit, people,* and *planet,* effectively answering consumers' questions in the following order:

- Is it good for my budget?
- Is it good for my family?
- Is it good for the planet?

Howell adds that in most cases, green campaigns should avoid the word *green* and avoid incorporating green leaves into a logo. "Really, these tactics are just camouflaging a brand differentiator," he says. "Finding another way to tell your story will always end up delivering a targeted message to the people you want to reach."

4. Practice What You Preach

In an age when just about anyone can find out just about anything about the inner workings of a company online, transparency is key. For this reason, it's important for companies that market themselves as green to operate sustainably in many of their day-to-day operations.

At Green Apple Cleaners, a non-toxic dry cleaning business in New York City, this has meant no print advertisements whatsoever, steering away from the traditional approach within the industry. Instead, founder and CEO David Kistner has opted for virtual (and therefore paperless) services such as Groupon and Google Offers to bring in new customers.

"Could you imagine if one of our coupons came in the mail?" he says, assuming eco-conscious customers wouldn't remain patrons for long.

Other businesses have opted for different strategies. At Eco-Command, owners Bill and Jane Monetti have installed in their home water-efficient shower heads, aerators for sink fixtures and an Energy Star clothes washer. GreenChoice Bank, a green-themed bank in Chicago, issues debit cards with a 100 percent recycled plastic core and boasts electric car chargers in all of its bank parking lots.

Consultant Shel Horowitz, author of *Guerilla Marketing Goes Green,* says it doesn't matter how a company embraces eco-consciousness, so long as it does so on some quantifiable level.

"You need to walk the walk to some extent," he says. "The minute a customer calls credibility into question, that customer will start shopping somewhere else."

5. Reinvest in the Community

One of the most important attributes of sustainability is reinvesting dollars and energy into the surrounding community. It's a simple step—but it's also an initiative many green companies overlook.

Reinvesting in the community can take many forms. Green Choice Bank offers flexible loan terms to commercial clients who build sustainably. Ben & Jerry's, one of the first green companies, continues to donate significant money to nonprofits more than a decade after it was purchased by Unilever.

Great Lakes Brewing Company, a brewery in downtown Cleveland, has taken a different approach: it sources locally. All told, the brewery's restaurant uses local vegetables and herbs in dishes whenever seasonally available, as well as local eggs, milk, cream, butter and locally raised meats. Saul Kliorys, the company's environmental programs manager, says the brewery has gone so far as to manage and till part of the 16-acre Ohio City Farm in Cleveland, growing many of the herbs and vegetables itself.

"Why source from elsewhere when we can get what we need right here?" Kliorys says. "Being green isn't always about making the best choices for the planet at large; sometimes it's about making the best choices for the people in your own backyard, too."

Critical Thinking

1. What are the five steps to effective green marketing proposed in this article?
2. Define "green washing" and discuss the possible negative impact(s) it may have on a company's image and credibility.
3. With a small group of peers in your class, explain the following statement: "Green only yields green when messaging blends transparency, practicality and savvy". Do you agree with this statement?

Create Central

www.mhhe.com/createcentral

Internet References

Environmental Leader
    http://www.environmentalleader.com/category/green-marketing/
Green Marketing TV
    http://www.greenmarketing.tv/
Greenpeace Greenwashing
    http://www.stopgreenwash.org/
The Sins of Greenwashing
    http://sinsofgreenwashing.org/

Matt Villano is a Freelance Writer and Editor Based in Healdsburg, Calif.

Acknowledgements—Copyright of *Entrepreneur* is the property of Entrepreneur.com, Inc. and its content may not be copied or emailed to multiple sites or posted to a listserv without the copyright holder's express written permission. However, users may print, download, or email articles for individual use.

Matt Villano, "Selling Green," *Entrepreneur,* November 2011, p. 52-56. Copyright © 2011 by Entrepreneur Media, Inc. All rights reserved. Used with permission.

Article

Prepared by: Nisreen N. Bahnan, *Salem State University*

Social Gathering

Apparently you *can* teach an old dog new tricks: Just look to the social media efforts of stalwart frozen dessert franchise Tasti D-Lite. The Franklin, Tenn.-based company, in business since 1987, has become the poster child for online engagement in the franchise world.

KARA OHNGREN

Learning Outcomes

After reading this article, you will be able to:

- Recognize the role played by social media within a company's promotional mix.

- Analyze the social media campaign of Tasti D-Lite.

- Discuss the national vs. local engagement debate for franchises with regards to social media presence and management.

Along with operating an active blog and providing in-store iPads that serve as customer information kiosks and digital guestbooks, the company has instituted an innovative loyalty program. Patrons earn TastiRewards points by sharing their experiences with friends and followers online. Like with most rewards programs, customers earn points toward free treats each time a cashier swipes their TreatCard. But they can earn even more points if they link the loyalty card to online profiles. Then, when the card is swiped, a message—such as: "I just earned 5 TastiRewards points at Tasti D-Lite Columbus Circle, NYC!"—is automatically sent to the customer's Facebook and Twitter networks. The single swipe also checks the customer in on foursquare. Often, the automated posts include a link to a coupon, so a patron's loyalty generates a benefit to his or her entire network.

The company has found that one in five TastiRewards members are generating connections to at least one social network, and 18 percent of those are generating automatic checkins on foursquare.

"People are talking about our product online, and they're passionate about our brand, so we wanted to be part of the conversation," says BJ Emerson, vice president of technology and head of social media for Tasti D-Lite. "We've put some mechanisms in place where we're now rewarding our customers for their digital activity. People are responding very well to that."

Tasti D-Lite doesn't reveal sales figures. Last year, the company was unranked on the Franchise 500®; this year, it comes in at No. 331.

The 59-location franchise has found that its most engaging social media content isn't necessarily directly related to the business. For instance, when Emerson posted to the company's Facebook page a *Women's Health* article about the best songs for runners and asked fans, "What's on your playlist?" the responses rolled in. Tasti also offers value to its fans with promotions, like TreatCard giveaways during Tasti Trivia contests on Twitter.

Tasti D-Lite is smart for undertaking an active social media stance. According to a recent study by marketing agencies Ogilvy & Mather and ChatThreads, patrons of major fast-food franchises McDonald's, KFC, Taco Bell, Subway, and Wendy's were more likely to pull out their wallets after being exposed to social content on sites like Facebook and Twitter. Of people exposed to McDonald's social touchpoints, there was a 45 percent increase in the perception that the fast-food giant provided the "best value" for the money. And people who were exposed to social media for KFC were seven times more likely to spend more than they did before connecting with the brand online.

Still, franchises in general have been notoriously slow to adopt social media operations. "It's been years now, but we're still trying to educate franchisors and franchisees in why you

A New Slice of the Pie

Going social has paid off in a big way for the once-floundering Domino's Pizza franchise. Ramped-up social media efforts played a significant role in its nearly 10 percent year-end sales spike in 2010, according to Chris Brandon, a public relations manager for the company.

When Domino's introduced the "inspired new pizza" recipe in 2010, the company had about 500,000 Facebook fans and 10,000 Twitter followers. Now, it has more than four million fans and 100,000 followers—and a completely refreshed brand.

For Domino's Pizza, ramped-up social media efforts played a significant role in its nearly 10% SALES SPIKE at the end of 2010.

"A lot of people who had written us off or hadn't tried Domino's in a long time gave us a second chance after seeing the positive feedback on social media," Brandon says. "Through social media, we're able to find out how they came back, why they came back and if they're pleased they rediscovered us."

Domino's is still trying to figure out a way to push online engagement down to the local franchisee level, but for the time being, the executive team is sponsoring several interesting programs. For instance, the company has asked customers to share photos of their pizzas online, posted prominent signage of "Pizza Tracker" feedback in New York's Times Square and hosted a massive Facebook giveaway of its new Artisan Pizzas.

"We've learned that not only is social media great for keeping the consumer informed, but we're also able to get that real solid two-way interaction going," Brandon says. "It helps us to keep getting better, keep innovating and keep doing what we need to do to give people what they want." —K.O.

should be using online marketing tools," says Deb Evans, president of Computer Explorers, a tech education franchise, and co-organizer of FranCamp, a Nashville, Tenn., social media training event for franchises. "Yet there are a lot of companies that are jumping in now and testing the waters."

Evans says franchises need to be careful not to post earnings claims or other confidential information that could break federal disclosure laws. "It used to be all about what franchisors disclosed to prospects verbally, but now franchisors have to watch what they put out online, because that stuff never goes away," she says.

National vs. Local Engagement

There's a debate in the franchise world about the best way to manage social media outreach. Many franchisors try to keep their arms around social media from a branding perspective and tell their franchisees to stay out of it. Yet, with this method, it can be a huge challenge to effectively support all locations with relevant content on the local level.

Tasti D-Lite is at the other end of the spectrum: the company takes a position of leadership but walks beside franchisees to co-manage their social media efforts. "The franchisees are the ones who are local with their customers," Emerson says. "We need to steward the brand, but we want to empower our franchisees to use these tools—we don't want to control them."

Emerson says a franchise's multilayered business model makes adopting a sound social media strategy challenging. In designing digital Tasti D-Lite programs, the team had to consider how the initiatives would be implemented in the retail environment.

"I have to communicate to all of our franchisees, and they have to communicate to all of their employees, so that when someone comes in and shows their mobile device to get a deal, we don't look at them like they're crazy," Emerson says. "We might have a great online experience, which any franchisor can manage, but if the program fails at the line level, then we've failed."

Emerson still manages Tasti's parent Twitter and Facebook accounts, but in 2009, the company started encouraging franchisees to get involved on a local level, too. Tasti now has 35 individual Facebook accounts.

"We start to mention social media when potential franchisees come in for Discovery Days," Emerson says. "If they want to open a Tasti, we tell them we want to be a social-friendly brand, and we're looking for franchisees who are interested in engaging customers online. Then, during training, we'll spend a few hours on social media."

For Tasti franchisees who are new to the social media game and unsure what to share online, the company has created a content library of potential posts. From several years of trial and error, Tasti has a pretty good idea of what works and what doesn't online. Franchisees can simply pull content from the library and post it to their Facebook and Twitter profiles.

"We might have a Great Online Experience, which any Franchisor can Manage, but if the Program Fails at the Line Level, then we've Failed." —BJ Emerson, Tasti D-Lite

Massage and spa franchise Massage Envy also encourages franchisees to embrace social media. The Scottsdale, Ariz.-based company not only operates corporate Facebook and Twitter accounts and the Touch of Wellness health blog, but each month distributes to franchisees a social media calendar with suggested Facebook and Twitter posts that easily can be customized for individual locations. Additionally, at its annual convention last year, Massage Envy held several sessions on social media to help franchisees understand the benefits and prepare them with the tools they need to be successful, according to chief marketing officer Susan Boresow.

"Social media is a two-way street: We engage with our followers, and they in turn engage with us," she says. "We track the conversations taking place online and learn from them. We like to know when a customer had an amazing experience at one of our clinics and when they did not. This feedback helps us constantly improve our business and deliver our vision. Not to mention, our fans and followers appreciate being informed of new promotions and programs taking place at their local clinics."

Massage Envy uses targeted Facebook ads to attract new franchisees to buy into the 700-location system. Last year, the company implemented a 60-day advertising campaign targeting 12 million Facebook users in key expansion markets. The initiative generated more than 10 million impressions and nearly 2,500 click-throughs to the Massage Envy franchising website.

Tasti doesn't actively recruit potential franchisees via social media. However, new franchisees have said they chose Tasti over another franchise because of its position online and the loads of positive user-generated content.

"We went from complete social negligence about four years ago to social prominence, and it has become a competitive advantage for us," Emerson says. "This is who we are; it's part of our culture. And if you think this is for you, we'll train you to do it, too."

Critical Thinking

1. In your opinion, what is the role played by social media within a company's integrated marketing mix?
2. Discuss and analyze the social media campaign launched by Tasti D-Lite.
3. The article mentions the debate between national and local social media engagement for franchises. What side of the debate do you favor? Justify your response.

Create Central

www.mhhe.com/createcentral

Internet References

Social Media Today
  http://socialmediatoday.com/
Tasti D-Lite
  www.tastidlite.com/

Kara Ohngren, "Social Gathering," *Entrepreneur,* January 2012. Copyright © 2012 by Entrepreneur Media, Inc. All rights reserved. Used with permission.

Article   Prepared by: Nisreen N. Bahnan, *Salem State University*

Advertising's New Campaign

JENNIFER WANG

Learning Outcomes

After reading this article, you will be able to:

- Recognize the primary role played by women and mothers in household consumption decision-making.

- Comprehend the impact of interpersonal and word-of-mouth communication on persuasion.

- Assess the performance and success of various companies that have tapped into the powerful medium of conversation-building blogs.

others," as *Calvin and Hobbes* cartoonist Bill Watterson proclaimed, "are the necessity of invention." Look around online, and there's no doubt it's true: when it comes to innovation in digital commerce and media, moms rule. The current generation of moms is tech-savvy, highly educated, and controls a dominant 85 percent of household income. Moms are also the most social demographic—which means that when they see something they like (or dislike), everybody and, well, their mother, hears about it.

Many companies are attempting to tap into this base, but one has found a way to do so that goes beyond traditional advertising. BlogFrog, co-founded in April 2009 by Rustin Banks and Holly Hamann in the startup-friendly city of Boulder, Colo., provides free tools for mom bloggers to power their own online communities, live discussions and video broadcasts, then connects these platforms with brands like Coca-Cola that are willing to pay to be a visible part of those conversations.

"Brands have glommed on because we can get them out of the sidebar and into the main bar," says CEO Banks, referring to online advertisers' age-old struggle to get users to click on banner ads. Such ads are seen as a distraction, since successful ones force customers to click away from their original purpose; social media product placement, meanwhile, can seem pushy, while mass-pitching bloggers for reviews is seen as distasteful.

BlogFrog's "conversational marketing" products have disrupted business as usual, allowing advertisers to relate to customers via "brand communities" and "sponsored conversations."

BlogFrog's platform promotes a new type of social network, one that bases connections on what you're interested in, rather than on who you know. BlogFrog has 125,000 active members and 65,000 bloggers with a reach of 10 million parents per month, making it the largest mom-blogger network in the country. Tight communities have formed on the platform around topics such as food and fashion, as well as more serious issues related to military spouses, infertility, and special-needs kids. Some of these communities are even transcending the virtual world—in internet speak, BlogFrog members are meeting F2F (face-to-face) and ending up friends IRL (in real life).

"Moms are the most powerful consumer segment, and also the most underserved and misunderstood," says Hamann, who serves as vice president of marketing. "Before us, nobody was going there."

Many other services, such as Ning and Go Social, allow users to create niche social networks monetized by ad sales; the idea is that the aggregated blogs have increased power when it comes to traffic and search engine optimization, resulting in higher ad revenue. BlogFrog, however, goes the extra step and offers a way to monetize the content of the blogs themselves, through brand integration.

In a mere 18 months, BlogFrog has signed on major clients such as ABC News, the UN Foundation, Lego, Procter & Gamble and Intuit, as well as Coca-Cola. Annual revenue is on track to reach the multimillions (revenue doubled from the first to the second half of 2011); the staff has quadrupled from just five employees at the end of 2010; and the company is in its third office, a sprawling 9,500-square-foot space that's a far cry from the 600-square-foot room in which it launched. In March, BlogFrog closed on $3.2 million in funding, led by Washington D.C.-based Grotech Ventures.

Here's how it works. The network's brand communities are led by a team of bloggers, or "community leaders," carefully matched by topic interest and level of influence. (BlogFrog collects data based on metrics like quality of posts, blog traffic, and Facebook rankings.) Marketers pay a flat monthly fee depending on the number of bloggers, their reach and type of campaign. Sponsored conversations generally involve a larger blogger group that's asked to pose a question and call for reader contributions in the form of personal stories and comments, votes, or photos. Responses are aggregated and distributed to the brand's hub pages and to what BlogFrog calls "conversational ad units"— widgets that show campaign results in real time and serve to amplify the conversation and spread it across the web. Sponsored conversations, too, are cost-dependent on influencer reach and type of campaign; say, $20,000 for a four-week campaign with 40 bloggers with a combined readership of two million.

For example, organic dairy company Horizon signed on for a campaign around the question, "How do you sneak Omega-3s into your family's diet?" (No surprise: milk has a bunch.) Thirty bloggers were asked to talk about picky eating and get the community to share kid-friendly recipes. Not one word was company-supplied "advertorial." The campaign resulted in 2.1 million social media impressions on Twitter and Facebook and 3.7 million ad-unit impressions. Horizon has since sponsored three BlogFrog conversations and has signed an annual contract for 2012.

"Consumers want to be connected to relevant brands, yet so much of advertising today is irrelevant. BlogFrog is an attempt to bridge that gap and be genuinely helpful . . . and 2012 is about scaling and applying our products to categories beyond moms, and working with other kinds of influencers, like YouTube stars," Hamann says.

"Right," Banks agrees. "Elevated, authentic editorial brought to you by a brand is the future."

Banks started working as an engineer at Ball Aerospace in 2005. He'd moved to Boulder with his wife, Tara, and their 18-month-old, and they didn't know a soul. Stuck at home and stir-crazy, Tara began blogging and soon amassed a decent-size audience. Banks noticed that even though readers left plenty of encouraging comments, they couldn't communicate with one another directly. A simple fix occurred to him: a widget that would allow his wife to form her own online community.

Banks had coded his first Bulletin Board System (think an old-school online chat room and forum) and hosted it from his parents' closet at the age of 12, so after a few nights and weekends studying HTML, he managed to code a prototype and put it on his wife's blog. Fellow bloggers snatched up the technology like a new Baby Einstein product, and Banks realized he had a business opportunity on his hands.

Boulder's close-knit startup community steered him to Hamann, who 18 years earlier had packed up everything she owned in Maryland and driven west. She found herself in a startup utopia, where you could "have a good idea one day and be doing something about it the next."

When Banks approached her, Hamann (who has a 16-year-old) had already built teams and executed marketing for six startups, several with successful exits. Banks' idea to use technology to connect moms sounded like "nirvana" to her, and after several months of discussion, Hamann quit her job as vice president of marketing at a now-defunct music-event invitation service to work on the business plan full-time. A month later, in May 2009, Banks did the same.

"It was fun," Banks recalls, describing lengthy coffee-shop meetings and huddling on the front steps of the downtown branch of the library, leeching Wi-Fi. They hustled, attending mom-blogger conferences and talking to every brand agency they knew. By February 2010, they'd raised about $300,000— enough to hire a couple of staffers and secure proof of concept and a small office for their company, whose name riffed off the concept of "blog hopping."

As traction grew, BlogFrog got the attention of David Cohen, founder of the TechStars incubator, who led a second funding round of $600,000 in early 2011. At that point the team, which had been focused on the blogger community tools and brand communities, launched its first sponsored conversations.

Caitie Ramsburg, director of client services, says BlogFrog's strength is in its level of customization. "We dig deep for what brands want to get out of the campaign. We tie that into what women are already talking about and come up with an elevated topic or question," she says, noting that on average, the brainstorming sessions last a couple of days.

Then, with the help of a sophisticated algorithm that scores influence levels in a way that allows bloggers at all levels a shot at being picked, the team recruits the group that is most aligned with campaign goals. "A brand might want a health blogger in a particular income group with kids under the age of 10," Hamann says. "We have that information because we look at who they are and who they're connected to on several levels."

The advertising world is still feeling out social media's place in its future. "In advertising, you clinch the customer by being emotive," says veteran account manager Elaine Marino, and traditionally that has been done through TV and video. Now, she says, "we're going after the blog space."

Many agencies, eager to tap into the power of these social media influencers, have gotten behind the BlogFrog concept. "It's a better way for brands to approach marketing, because they make sure bloggers actually want to work with you," says James Clark, founder of Boulder-based boutique marketing agency Room 214, which brought Horizon to BlogFrog and has recommended similar campaigns for several other clients. Clark believes the conversational marketing method inspires more activity and loyalty than merely sending samples to random bloggers and hoping for a plug.

The process is also said to yield more honest feedback. Community members are more willing to respond and participate in discussions that are led by their peers, and the conversations give brands a chance to listen in, participate and attempt to boost their own likeability and perception as helpful. Horizon, for example, brought in expert nutritionists and food scientists to answer readers' questions. "We let community leaders run with it," Clark says. "We tell them the topics we like and if we're interested in getting opinions about something, but the communities are self-sustaining."

Other blog networks are partnering with BlogFrog, too. Chuck Moran—chief marketing officer of Burst Media, which represents indie websites across many verticals—is using the community-platform technology to syndicate content across his MomIQ parenting channel. "From a branding perspective, nothing is more powerful than having your target audience participating in a conversation, whether or not it's about a specific product," he says. Reader response to the sponsored conversations has been so great that Burst recently rolled out the platform for its Ella channel (targeting females 18 to 35 with relatively high disposable incomes) and plans to do the same for other communities.

BlogFrog's bloggers are also seeing benefits. The most successful blogs, which can have larger audiences than reality TV shows, can earn their domain owners six-figure incomes. In addition to obvious revenue streams like traffic-driven ad revenue, sponsored posts and product endorsements, popular bloggers can earn money from social media consulting gigs, e-book sales and sponsored conversations, and communities like those on BlogFrog.

Last year, BlogFrog paid out more than half a million dollars to its bloggers, who are sent monthly checks based on the communities and campaigns they lead, with the most influential and active making upward of $10,000 a year. Some bloggers who join the network see revenue increase an average of 50 percent, according to the company. BlogFrog's user metrics have also determined that bloggers on its platform see average time on their sites increase fivefold and page views per visit go up by 10.

Laurie Turk is behind TipJunkie.com, a blog that aggregates DIY and craft tutorials and gets about seven million page views per month. She notes that bloggers' income depends on skill set, influence, traffic, and contacts, but there's really no limit to how much they can make. "I don't need to use BlogFrog," she says, noting that when Banks first tried to recruit her, she refused until the platform had developed into a product that was relevant to her community. She also admits to being skeptical that the brand relationships would feel authentic. However, she says, "now I use BlogFrog for engagement, because they stay relevant."

What's most important to her is that the company provides mom bloggers the opportunity to wield their power and influence. "They're at the forefront of helping 'mom blogger' become a profession," Turk notes.

Shannon Shaffer, a former accountant and the voice behind the blog For the Mommas, agrees. As a BlogFrog community leader, she spearheads several brand campaigns per month—representing a small sliver of the income she generates from her site, which has approximately 500,000 unique visitors per month. "I only say yes to campaigns I think readers will enjoy," Shaffer says—like a recent one for Kraft Foods in which she shared easy recipes, some involving the brand's ingredients.

"BlogFrog does a really good job of matching, so it's a good relationship," she says. "It's not like in an ad network where you don't have the opportunity to say no. I'm a foodie, and I love saving money. BlogFrog has done a really good job of introducing brands to our readers without it being invasive. It's genuine information. If the brand is Kraft, it isn't that we're asking readers to buy Kraft products—it's recipes, easy weeknight recipes that we're coming up with and providing resources for. It's real, true content."

The bloggers themselves—and the amount of trust they are able to engender among their readers—are perhaps the biggest determining factor in BlogFrog's model. Although the company's method of increasing the distance between advertising message and consumer should result in greater trust, authenticity isn't guaranteed, notes Prashant Malaviya, associate professor of marketing at Georgetown University's McDonough School of Business. That depends on how transparent the blogger is in divulging her association with a brand, how loyal her readers are, how relevant the discussions are to readers' lives and even the ways in which readers find out about the community—via the brand itself or elsewhere on the internet. Blogs, Malaviya says, can lose influence if they're discovered to have "sold out," and those that discuss "deeper subjects are perceived to be more authentic."

On a crisp winter Friday afternoon, Banks and Hamann are showing off BlogFrog's new Boulder headquarters. A running trail abuts the back of the office building, just east of a hip downtown shopping area where healthy-looking denizens with shiny MacBook Airs are a common sight, even at the nicer restaurants.

Banks and Hamann seem an unlikely pair. Wearing a BlogFrog T-shirt, Banks looks the part of the classic startup guy, with laid-back energy and a genial, two-handed handshake. Hamann is trim, well-spoken, and professional in a sharp suit jacket.

The new office has a rooftop perfect for big summer gatherings, and plenty of room for growth. But at the moment, it's mostly empty. The team of 21 sits together (by choice) in a bullpen, and the conference rooms, named after famous frogs like Kermit and Jeremiah, are identified by taped-up sheets of paper. At least one animal-cracker box is being used to hold file folders. The walls are decorated with frog-theme paintings, the efforts of staff and friends from the last holiday party—most notably, a frogified version of Van Gogh's The Starry Night (by Hamann) and a surreal image of a frog peeking out of a blooming flower (courtesy of Banks' wife).

The office's makeshift, ephemeral decor is a fitting metaphor for the company's promising, if still nebulous, trajectory. "The landscape of the competition changes daily, and the demands are great," says vice president of engineering Doug Cotton.

On the consumer side, the platform needs to be scalable and intuitive to use on every device and browser; for enterprises to sign on, there must be proof, metrics-wise, that the system works. One never-ending task is to find ways to make Blog-Frog more viral—coming up with more campaigns, more brand products, and more tools. The latest, released in January, is Conversation Networks, which lets bloggers pool small niche communities into one larger one. Titus Stone, the company's lead front-end developer, likens it to a moving target.

"We take requests," he says, only half joking. "When the Live Discussion feature was launched, we started writing code and pushing it out while we were on the phone with bloggers asking us if it could do this or that."

While remaining based in Boulder, the BlogFrog team plans to open a New York office this summer to go after East Coast clients. Meanwhile, it is preparing to extend its network beyond moms to include blogs about food, fitness, fashion, entertainment, and tech. Up for grabs? A share of the rapidly growing social media advertising space—which Forrester Research expects to rise from $1.59 billion in 2011 to nearly $5 billion in 2016.

Critical Thinking

1. In what way is the current generation of moms different than previous generations?

2. With a small group of peers in your class, discuss the appeal of blogs in today's digital communication arena.

3. Elaborate on the following statement from the article: "From a branding perspective, nothing is more powerful than having your target audience participating in a conversation, whether or not it's about a specific product." Article 40. Advertising's New Campaign

Create Central

www.mhhe.com/createcentral

Internet References

Branded Content Marketing Association
http://www.thebcma.info/
Word of Mouth Marketing Association
http://www.womma.org/
Wommapedia
http://wommapedia.org/

Jennifer Wang, "Advertising's New Campaign," *Entrepreneur*, April 2012, p. 29–38. Copyright © 2012 by Entrepreneur Media, Inc. All rights reserved. Used with permission.

Unit 4

UNIT

Prepared by: Nisreen N. Bahnan, *Salem State University*

Global Marketing

"All too often, cultures are insufficiently studied or wrongly interpreted. It might seem that responsiveness to cultural differences should be second nature to marketers and therefore virtually reflexive. However, cultural differences continue to challenge marketers and can negatively affect the marketplace. Many times, disregarding local idiosyncrasies is like the introduction of a destructive virus on a culture."

— Michael Czinkota and Charles Skuba

According to the American Marketing Association, "Global Marketing is a marketing strategy that consciously addresses global customers, markets, and competition in formulating a business strategy . . . the multi-national process of planning and executing the conception, prices, promotion and distribution of ideal goods and services to create exchanges that satisfy the individual and organizational objectives," but the concept goes beyond this basic definition. It alludes to a firm's ability to establish the need for its products or services among consumers in different countries. The global firm must orchestrate its expertise, staff, skills and insights to deliver value to customers worldwide. The global firm comprehends the challenges in servicing customers locally while maintaining global standards, while successfully positioning its offerings against competitors. The firm is also cognizant of the need to develop global brands that are high in equity and loyalty.

Globalization across world economies is now a very much a reality, but one that is not fully understood. Generally, the concept of global markets "views the world as one market and is based on identifying and targeting cross-cultural similarities" (Ghauri and Cateora). Another perspective focuses on cultural differences, and dictates that each foreign market requires its own culturally adapted marketing strategies. Despite the varying positions, one certainty remains: marketing with a global perspective will continue to be a strategic element of U.S. business well into the next decades. Regardless of whether they wish to be, all marketers are now part of the international marketing system. For some, the end of the era of domestic markets may have come too soon, but that era is over. Today, it is necessary to recognize the strengths and weaknesses of our own marketing practices as compared to those abroad, and to acknowledge important economic, political, and social changes that have occurred that dramatically alter the landscape of global business. The articles in this unit were chosen to provide an overview of these changes, focusing primarily on the emergence of the Arab world and its thriving middle class that yearns for progress and modernity, yet has no interest in abandoning its religious traditions. Other selections call into question some of the key features of globalization, particularly those that affect the future of global brands, featuring companies which have traveled successfully across the globe with their brilliant marketing strategies.

Article Prepared by: Nisreen N. Bahnan, *Salem State University*

New World Order for Global Brands

J WALKER SMITH, ANDREW CURRY, AND STOKES JONES

Learning Outcomes

After reading this article, you will be able to:

- Differentiate between the concepts of globalization and global brand-building.

- Identify the four successive models that make up the history of global branding.

- Recognize shifting trends in global brand-building (fifth generation: co-creation model)

Although many beliefs about global brands feel more fragile than ever, there are many beliefs about branding and marketing that are increasingly sure.

In 2010, the Credit Suisse Research Institute published a report documenting the returns enjoyed by companies that focus on branding. Companies consistently spending at least 2% of sales revenue on brand marketing have substantially outperformed the S&P 500 since 1997, according to Credit Suisse's analysis, while the top one-fifth of these businesses outperformed the market by a huge 17% per year. While questions about globalization are rife, global brand-building continues to deliver unquestionable value.

However, the open question for marketers remains how to manage branding as part of globalization. Should global brand-building "push" or be "pulled" along? Should global brand-building be driven by a central strategy or by local markets? Developments in the global receptivity to brands demarcate a key pathway to the future.

Deconstructing "Global-Ness"

What does it mean to be a global brand? At root, of course, every brand is local. Yet so, too, is every brand potentially

global. For example, if a consumer discovers a Palestinian beer and brings six cases back to New York, where it becomes a minor rage in Tribeca, that brand has started to globalize. As this simple example illustrates, for the consumer a brand's global presence is, paradoxically, most tangible when a brand is most deeply embedded in a local situation. No brand has an exclusive monopoly on "global-ness," at least not in the traditional way in which global brands have been understood.

To understand where global brands are headed, it is useful to revisit the history of global branding. There have been four successive models of global branding.

First generation: export model

This could be considered the pre-history of global branding. This was the way of thinking by which branded consumer goods first found their way around the world. Developed market brands were basically unchanged from the manufacturing country as they moved to national colonies and beyond. The key business objective was to keep unit costs cheap enough to cover transportation.

Second generation: in-country model

In contrast to a branch office simply receiving goods, this approach involved the creation of a full-blown parallel company structure in expansion markets, including production facilities and, crucially, marketing departments to handle in-country marketing.

Third generation: standardization model

In reaction to the perceived costs of prior approaches, this model drew on convergence theories of development that saw global consumers becoming alike. Hence, consumers could be targeted with the same products and the same branding.

Fourth generation: "glocalization" model

This model was developed to balance the benefits of standardization with the need for local customization. This model works with an idea of brand elements that need to be held firm, such as name, logo or visual identity, versus those that can be modified as needed, such as positioning, target audience, and communications strategy. This is the prevailing model today.

The Coming Era of Co-Creation

A new model is now driving the future of global brands. It is practised already by many brands, though not yet recognized or spoken of as a true branding model. But it is coming on strong in a world hungry for new entry points into the global marketplace.

Fifth generation: co-creation model

This model extends the open-ended style of "glocalization" into explicit collaboration on equal terms between brand owners and host markets. It's not the top-down collaboration of customizing a global concept to a local situation but a deep, iterative collaboration in which the very concept of a brand arises bottom-up across several local situations at once.

This sort of fifth-generation brand model, operating through the progression of local market flows, can be seen today with several innovative global brands.

dENiZEN

dENiZEN was launched in 2010 in Shanghai—the first time Levi's has launched a brand from outside the US and the first Levi's brand to have its headquarters outside the US. The five-pocket jeans are aimed at 18-to-29-year-olds in China, Singapore, South Korea and, in the future, India. It is a target group Levi's referred to as "Asia rising."

In style and price, these jeans are all about this new global consumer and the local situations that give meaning and power to its global strategy. More importantly, these jeans represent a ground-up approach to building an international presence.

Shang Xia

Shang Xia is a Hermès luxury brand launched in 2008, opening its first retail store in 2010, targeting the Chinese market. Shang Xia pitches itself squarely into the tension over the ultimate source of a brand's identity.

Historically, Hermès expanded by buying existing brands, but Shang Xia is being launched from the ground up, using local knowhow and materials to build a global presence at a lower price point for this fast-growing market.

The brand is a stylistic hybrid of modern European design and Chinese craft, yet a Hermès representative has insisted that it is "a Chinese brand, developed in China with the Chinese team, based on Chinese craftsmanship and broadly made in China. We don't want any confusion."

This is the heart and soul of co-creation. The challenge for Hermès, as one scholar of the Chinese luxury market has noted, is that products specifically targeting the Chinese market are often "less welcomed than products that are totally foreign" in the first place. Hermès' co-creation model offers a resolution to this challenge.

Bonvi!

Launched in Ghana in 2009 by Amway, BonVi! was developed through a live prototyping project run in rural Ghana involving in-home interviewing and village charrettes with feedback on everything from product samples to the proposed color of the brand identity. BonVi! aims at a mass market using not only glocalization strategies to convert existing Amway products to fit local needs but also co-creation strategies to identify additional needs, learned from local collaborators, that can be met by new products within the global capabilities of Amway (such as water purification tablets).

From Processes to Meaning

As brands face forward, they will find that meaning more than processes will be a critical element of success. Co-creation puts meaning in the forefront of engagement. In the century ahead, global brands will find themselves having to straddle 150 years of past history and the legacies that has left for the future. Though the corporate focus on emerging markets is largely economic (following the shifts in global money), these very markets are more exposed over the near term to resource shortages, pollution and other threats to their viability. For example, Asia is highly vulnerable to water scarcity.

Future global brands will need to be mindful that one of the advantages of global brands in years past has been a tacit guarantee that products carrying their name would not kill or injure their consumers. In this sense, global brands of the future will need to be just as mindful of the functional bottom end of Maslow's hierarchy of needs as of its more aspirational top end.

Global supply chains make this harder to achieve. Consumers in affluent markets feel secure and distanced from risk when they read of vigilante consumers in China turning on a brewer alleged to have watered down beer, or when two people are tried and executed for their part in a powdered milk scandal. But these risks hit close to home when lead paint renders toys produced in China unsafe for the American market.

Brand risks are amplified by the co-creation model that, inevitably, creates brand divergence at the level of national or local markets. With consumers in different markets increasingly connected through digital networks and social media, inconsistencies will be identified quickly, then shared and publicized. Global brands will need to speak coherently across markets, even as they speak distinctively within them.

Global brands will be forced to shift much of the emphasis in their brand communications from rules to values and from processes to meaning, putting more pressure on the ways in which corporate culture is created, communicated, and internalized. This is a lesson Mattel learned from its toy recalls. Its first attempts focused on procedure, but this was not enough. Its subsequent efforts approached the problem by looking at the values of integrity and safety around its productions processes.

The Future of Global Brands

Looking across the trends that are shaping the global landscape in which transnational businesses operate, it is possible to pick out some clear implications for executives.

Emerging brands from emerging nations

Developing markets that weathered the global downturn better than other markets are showing their resilience through a flurry of M&A activity. As the BRIC countries continue to expand, with more affluent nations trapped in the debt overhang of the economic crisis, we will see BRIC-based businesses add brand assets to their existing portfolios of natural assets, production capacity and manpower. March 2011 data shows that 44% of privately held businesses in Brazil, Russia, India, and China are planning to grow by acquisition in 2011, up from 27% in 2010.

"Authentic" local brands from affluent nations

Many of the brand stories mentioned in the full report (see attribution, below) have been about how brands from the affluent world responded to the challenges of new markets. The historically strong brand skills of existing global brands will not vanish, even in this business environment.

However, global brands will need to be more responsive to their local circumstances, understanding more deeply why consumers in each particular market seek out their brands or disregard them. In the competitive context of these various marketplaces, the imperative of adaptation and indigenization will play out as a race against time and capital between established brand owners and new, acquisitive brand owners to co-create brands that will win the loyalty of emerging market consumers.

This is the race that will decide control of the "brand wealth of nations" in the years to come.

The Decline of the Iconic Brand

There will be too many brands chasing too few possibilities for iconic brands to dominate consumer relationships as they have in years past. No matter how good a strategy may be, it dunks a brand into the "red ocean of undifferentiation" if every brand adopts it. The ultimate challenge for brands has always been to overcome consumer indifference, and this challenge will grow in the global marketplace to come.

In response, brands will have to deliver ever greater value to consumers who favor them, even as brands fragment their identities through greater locally driven co-creation.

The End of Grand Strategy in Global Branding

An era of mixed strategies in global branding is emerging in which what happens at the center will be equally matched—if not overpowered—by what happens in local situations. The "glocalization" models of the fourth generation will be challenged increasingly by global brands that are co-created from the bottom up. Local customisation will give way to local co-creation as the underpinning of global success. A movement is under-way to shift toward toolkits to support a mix-and-match approach in which different elements can be woven together to respond to locally unique branding challenges.

The Contextual Brand Manager

In the marketplace ahead, successful global brand managers will be culturally and contextually adept, listening to markets in order to master and understand multiple cultures. Increasing numbers of global brand managers will move from emerging nations to work in all of a brand's markets, not just the home market. A key skill will be assessing local factors accurately and judging the correct elements to deploy. In today's global marketplace, what's required is an expedient, experimental mindset that is open to all possibilities. Brand judo, not brand brawn, will determine which brands win.

New Narratives

With many trades in ownership and the invention or reinvention of co-created brand propositions, national or local origin will no longer be a sufficient basis for brand authenticity. In an age of ever-smarter consumers, the battle of the brands will become a battle of narratives. Competing brands will attempt to tell more compelling stories about their values and purpose, from product to provenance to social and corporate commitment.

Conclusion

Notwithstanding the push of market forces to co-creation, there are counter-forces at work as well. Today's global brands got there first, giving them a huge order-of-entry advantage that new co-created brands will have to spend heavily to overcome. This challenge is intensified by the status enjoyed by many foreign brands among emerging market consumers. Indeed, as developing nations grow more prosperous, consumers there may spend even more on established brands.

The future of global brands of every sort will require a new approach to global brand building. The intersection of interests that defines global market opportunities now demands a fresh look at the marketplace. Uncertainty is bringing together a confluence of perspectives that is redefining global brands from the bottom up. The hierarchy of established global brands will be challenged by new, co-created global brands.

Established brand owners have the skill and experience to navigate these tricky marketing waters and should feel confident about their ability to create authentic new brands of their own, thereby appropriating some of the cultural authority that new brands might otherwise enjoy. Such adaptation can be a rich source of innovation and thus, even as a new marketplace unfolds, the dominion of Western brands is not likely to be wholly overturned by the future market forces of co-creation.

Critical Thinking

1. "While questions about globalization are rife, global brand-building continues to deliver unquestionable value." In your opinion, should global brand-building be driven by a central strategy (standardization) or by local markets (adaptation)?

2. List and briefly summarize the four successive models that make up the history of global branding. Discuss the latest fifth generation: co-creation model presented in the article.

3. In your opinion, what do the authors mean by the following statement: "for the consumer a brand's global presence is, paradoxically, most tangible when a brand is most deeply embedded in a local situation?" Do you agree?

Create Central

www.mhhe.com/createcentral

Internet References

Global Policy Forum
http://www.globalpolicy.org/globalization.html

Global Strategy
http://www.global-strategy.net/

Globalization 101
http://www.globalization101.org/

The Center on Global Brand Leadership at Columbia Business School
http://www8.gsb.columbia.edu/globalbrands/

The Global Brand
http://www.theglobalbrandonline.com/

J. Walker Smith; Andrew Curry; Stokes Jones, "New World Order for Global Brands," *Market Leader*, Quarter 1 2013. Copyright © 2013 by Warc. All rights reserved. Used with permission.

Article

Prepared by: Nisreen N. Bahnan, *Salem State University*

Understanding the Arab Consumer

Vijay Mahajan

Learning Outcomes

After reading this article, you will be able to:

- Understand the important cultural and environmental factors that characterize consumers in the Arab world.

- Recognize the dynamic changes occurring across economies in the Arab region.

- Appreciate the inter-connectedness between religion and lifestyle and consumption for Arab consumers.

Critical Thinking

1. According to this article, what is the reality of the consumer market in the Arab world, and how is this reality different from the stereotyped notion adopted by the rest of the world?

2. With a group of peers in your class, discuss how "Islam molds the region's economy, touching every consumer and company."

3. In your role as a consultant, come up with a list of five recommendation for a U.S. company marketing a new product in the Arab world.

Create Central

www.mhhe.com/createcentral

Internet References

Global Islamic Marketing Conference
http://www.globalimc.org/
Pan Arab Research Center
http://arabresearch.iniquus.com/

Vijay Mahajan, "Understanding the Arab Consumer," *Harvard Business Review,* May 2013. Copyright © 2013 by Harvard Business School Publishing. All rights reserved. Used with permission.

Understanding the Arab Consumer

HBR.ORG

Harvard Business Review

MAY 2013
REPRINT R1305L

THE GLOBE

Understanding the Arab Consumer

A growing middle class that yearns for progress and modernity has no interest in abandoning its religious traditions. *by Vijay Mahajan*

The Globe

Understanding the Arab Consumer

A growing middle class that yearns for progress and modernity has no interest in abandoning its religious traditions. *by Vijay Mahajan*

The low-profile Arla Foods, Scandinavia's largest manufacturer of dairy products, had become a major player in the Arab world by 2005. The Dano-Swedish cooperative's brands, such as Lurpak, Puck, and the eponymous Arla, dominated the Middle East's markets for butter, cheese, and cream, and its sales in the region reached a record $550 million that year. Then the cartoons appeared.

On September 30, 2005, a Danish newspaper, *Jyllands-Posten*, published an article titled "The Face of Muhammad" along with a dozen cartoons that depicted Islam's prophet unflatteringly. Muslims the world over were incensed, and in January 2006 Saudi Arabian clerics called for a boycott of Danish goods. Within days, most retailers in the Arab world had pulled Arla's products off their shelves. The company mounted a massive communications cam-

PHOTOGRAPHY: REUTERS/KHALED AL-HARIRI

COPYRIGHT © 2013 HARVARD BUSINESS SCHOOL PUBLISHING CORPORATION. ALL RIGHTS RESERVED.

FOR ARTICLE REPRINTS CALL 800-988-0886 OR 617-783-7500, OR VISIT **HBR.ORG**

paign to distance itself from the cartoons, pointing out that it had been doing business in the region for 40 years. But even though the clerics lifted the ban in April, the company's sales for 2006 were only half the preboycott levels.

In 2008, just when Arla's sales had nearly recovered, 17 Danish newspapers republished one of the controversial cartoons. Sales plummeted again, costing the company around $274 million. Arla fought back, but its revenues didn't rebound until 2010—an indication of how powerfully Islam affects Arab markets. In fact, its influence is much stronger in the Arab world than it is in nations with large Muslim populations such as Indonesia, India, and Bangladesh.

In the post-9/11 world, Islam's resurgence has made multinationals jittery about investing in the 22 countries that constitute the Arab League. The Arab world, runs the stereotyped assumption, is a closed society of mullahs and militants, fatwas and jihad, whose leaders hate foreigners and whose young men and women are taught to despise Western products and culture. Add the political turmoil and armed conflicts of the Arab Spring revolutions—which ousted rulers in Egypt, Libya, Tunisia, and Yemen—and it's easy to conclude that the region is unstable, chaotic, and closed for business.

Like many other notions about the Arab world, this one is a figment of the imagination. From 2008 to 2010 I traveled through 18 Arab League countries, visiting many markets and companies and speaking with more than 600 people—from CEOs and entrepreneurs in skyscrapers to shoppers in souks and bazaars. Everything I saw and everyone I met suggested that the Arab market is *not* divorced from the rest of the world. Consumers there have the same demands as people everywhere, and despite the turmoil the region's markets are growing, globally interlinked, and intensely competitive.

If the Arab League were a single country, its 2011 GDP would have been more than $2.3 trillion, making it the world's eighth-largest economy—bigger than India or Russia. Its per capita income would have been around $6,700—higher than that of China and India. (See the exhibit "Per Capita GDP in the Arab World.") More than half the population is under 25 years of age, making it one of the world's most youthful markets.

The region's draw is no longer solely the top of the economic pyramid. A growing middle class of more than 150 million people (the total population is over 350 million) is busy earning and spending. (See the exhibit "The Arab Middle Class.") Household consumption accounted for as much as 44% of the region's economy, higher than China's 35% but less than India's 56%. No wonder Middle East expert Vali Nasr wrote in his 2011 book, *Forces of Fortune,* "All across the region, a whole new economy is rising, mixing local values with surging consumption and building ever richer ties to the global economy, and this trend is not only every bit as powerful and important as the threat of fundamentalism, it is more so."

The Arab nations are in many ways no different from Brazil, India, and China two decades ago: They're big, complex—and easily ignored. But what makes the Arab market more complicated, even threatening, is that Islam and Arab culture are intertwined. The religion is central to society *and* business, governing most facets of the marketplace. Its influence isn't fading; the same Arab consumers who yearn for progress, modernity, and inclusion don't wish to abandon their religious and cultural traditions. Thus, Arabs like and respect Western brands—but only as long as those brands don't conflict with their values. Companies that gloss over the interplay between culture and religion, believ-ing them to be mutually exclusive, ignore a critical factor for success in the region.

Respecting the Five Pillars of Islam

Not all consumers in the Arab world are Muslims, but Islam molds the region's economy, touching every consumer and company through its five pillars.

Shahada. In the Koran, Islam's sacred book, the belief in monotheism and the acceptance of Muhammad as Allah's prophet is encapsulated by the rhythmic Arabic phrase, *lā 'ilāha 'illā l-Lāh, Muhammadun rasūlu l-Lāh* ("There is no god but God, and Muhammad is the messenger of God"). This declaration of faith is the first pillar of Islam. The *shahada,* as it's called, has several layers of implications and interpretations.

Companies that gloss over the interplay between culture and religion ignore a critical factor for success in the region.

Figuring them all out, especially for business purposes, isn't always easy. Islamic jurisprudence depends on sayings or acts of approval or disapproval ascribed to the prophet Muhammad, called *hadith,* as tools for interpreting the Koran. These can be subjective. Moreover, Sunnis (the majority in Saudi Arabia), Shias (Bahrain's dominant community), and Ibadis (Oman's most common denomination) rely on different sets of hadith, so companies operating in the Arab world must understand the nuances of each.

Breaches of the shahada's letter or spirit have a major impact on corporate fortunes and reputations, as Arla unwittingly found. "We took 40 years to build a business in the Middle East, and we've seen it come to a complete stop in five days," a company spokesperson told BBC News in 2006. Western businesspeople in particular need

THE GLOBE

If the 22 nations that constitute the Arab League were a single country, it would be the world's eighth-largest economy.

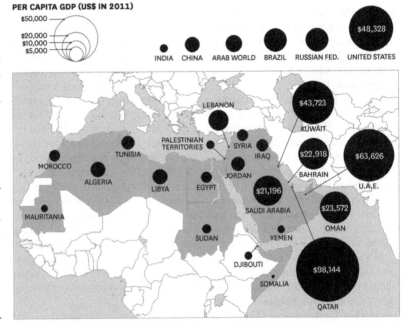

PER CAPITA GDP (US$ IN 2011)

SOURCES IMF'S WORLD ECONOMIC OUTLOOK DATABASE, WORLD BANK'S WORLD DEVELOPMENT INDICATORS DATABASE, AND CIA'S THE WORLD FACTBOOK (ACCESSED JANUARY 2013). DATA FOR SUDAN DO NOT INCLUDE SOUTH SUDAN. DATA FOR THE PALESTINIAN TERRITORIES AND SOMALIA ARE ESTIMATES BASED ON 2010 DATA. COMOROS IS NOT DEPICTED ON THIS MAP.

to understand that Islam's rules are perceived to have derived from divine command, as Frank Vogel and Samuel Hayes point out in their book *Islamic Law and Finance: Religion, Risk, and Return.* However, Arab consumers are quick to forgive: After Arla appealed to the Islamic values of tolerance, justice, and forgiveness, it became the first Danish company to be exempted from the boycott.

Foreign companies should distance themselves from anything that could be construed as offensive to Islam. For example, Islam forbids the depiction of Allah's image, including the writing of his name. Many companies have had to change logos and packaging to fit in. In the late 1990s, for instance, when Unilever Arabia executives saw the new corporate logo days before its global launch, some felt that from a certain angle it resembled the word *Allah* written in Arabic. In another market, the executives would have ignored the risk, but they knew better than to do so in Saudi Arabia. Despite the costs, Unilever Arabia worked with global headquarters to develop a new logo before its launch.

Although Islam is the bedrock of their culture, Arabs often prefer businesses to draw a line between religion and commerce. Advertising with overtly religious tones hardly ever works. When Procter & Gamble launched Tide liquid in Arab markets in the 1990s, it decided to use a series of ads showing how easily women could use the product to wash their veils. The company was careful to present the act as an everyday chore without religious overtones, making it clear that it understood the dynamics between business and culture in the Arab market.

Salah. Formal worship, or *salah,* consists of the repetition of a unit of actions and words five times a day. Be it the muezzin's calls to prayer or the arrows in hotel rooms pointing toward Mecca, the holy city Muslims face during prayer, there's no getting away from salah in the Arab world.

Prayer sets a routine to which foreign companies must adapt. In countries such as Saudi Arabia, companies must shut

briefly three times a day; it's against the law to prevent employees from praying. Factories and offices stop work, meetings break up, and stores close. Once prayers are over, people go back to business as usual.

The dedication to daily prayers can vary from one Arab country to another, but regardless of the local custom, prayer times set the rhythm for the day. That has not been lost on some companies. For instance, Titan Industries, the Indian watchmaker, has developed a clock for the Arab market that displays the time for each daily prayer. Apps such as alQibla, which displays precise prayer times and indicates the direction of Mecca through GPS and mapping software, are available in the iTunes store.

Zakat. Islam requires that Muslims donate 2.5% of their wealth every year. Because it is one of Islam's pillars, *zakat,* as Muslims call the donation, generates a guaranteed annual pool of philanthropic dollars.

Calculating the amount of zakat generated in Arab countries is next to impossible. Most Arabs make their donations privately

and informally, so there are no records. Moreover, the donation is a percentage of personal wealth in excess of a certain amount—not a percentage of income—which makes it even more difficult to estimate. While my extremely conservative calculations suggest that the annual collection could be around $3.3 billion, local experts claim that it easily tops $25 billion a year, or about 1.3% of the region's economy in 2010. By comparison, individuals, companies, and foundations in the United States together donate around 2% of GDP every year to charity.

Through zakat, Arabs have created one of the world's largest philanthropic annuities. Unfortunately, its use is almost entirely unorganized, which creates an opportunity for the global social sector. In the past, governments or ruling families oversaw the collection and distribution of the funds. However, fewer Muslims give their money to state-owned organizations nowadays; they don't trust the power brokers to put the money to the best philanthropic use. Moreover, the fragmented nature of the do-

FOR ARTICLE REPRINTS CALL 800-988-0886 OR 617-783-7500, OR VISIT **HBR.ORG**

The Arab Middle Class

COUNTRY Population	TOP OF PYRAMID	MIDDLE CLASS	BOTTOM OF PYRAMID
ALGERIA 36 million	17%	55%	28%
BAHRAIN 1.1 million	7%	60%	33%
EGYPT 80.4 million	13%	34%	53%
JORDAN 6.3 million	20%	41%	39%
KUWAIT 3.7 million	22%	57%	21%
LEBANON 4 million	10%	60%	30%
LIBYA 6.5 million	15%	35%	50%
MAURITANIA 3.5 million	3%	30%	67%
MOROCCO 32.2 million	13%	32%	55%
OMAN 3.1 million	6%	63%	31%
QATAR 1.8 million	8%	70%	22%
SAUDI ARABIA 28.2 million	13%	65%	22%
SUDAN 32.7 million	8%	46%	46%
SYRIA 20.8 million	3%	57%	40%
TUNISIA 10.7 million	22%	52%	26%
UAE 5.4 million	11%	60%	29%
YEMEN 25.1 million	4%	60%	36%

SOURCES POPULATION DATA ARE FROM IMF'S WORLD ECONOMIC OUTLOOK DATABASE AND WORLD BANK'S WORLD DEVELOPMENT INDICATORS DATABASE (ACCESSED JANUARY 2013). DATA FOR SUDAN DO NOT INCLUDE SOUTH SUDAN. POPULATION DISTRIBUTIONS ARE THE AUTHOR'S ESTIMATES BASED ON SOCIOECONOMIC DATA FROM SEVERAL COMPANIES IN THE REGION. NO DATA WERE AVAILABLE FOR COMOROS, DJIBOUTI, IRAQ, SOMALIA, AND THE PALESTINIAN TERRITORIES.

nations in most Arab countries makes them far less effective than they could be.

If Arab countries, collectively or individually, pooled the zakat collections and managed them professionally, they could achieve amazing things. Take, for example, Sudan's Zakat Chamber, which attracts much of the country's zakat collections. It took in roughly $250 million in 2010 and disbursed much of it to programs that promote development and self-sufficiency, especially among women. The organization distributes seeds for agriculture and flour for baking, which women use to grow or make products they can sell.

Governments do not necessarily need to oversee zakat funds; financial experts from Islamic banks could manage the money, and Islamic scholars and philanthropy experts could create a system for disbursing the funds in an efficient manner. According to several experts, the money could provide microfinance loans as well as health and welfare services for needy citizens. The hurdle is that Arab governments strongly believe that caring for people is their job and worry that others who do so are just trying to score political points.

A few pioneers have developed innovative ways to enhance the value of zakat giving. For instance, Abdul Latif Jameel Company in Jeddah, Saudi Arabia, funds a program—to which employees can make zakat contributions—that trains blue-collar workers, supports budding entrepreneurs, and incubates small businesses. The Jameel family decided that such a program would be more helpful to the community than their employees' monetary donations. Although expensive, the program has trained hundreds of workers for better-paying jobs and has helped launch dozens of small businesses since 2002. Indeed, it might be the forerunner of a zakat-based model of corporate social responsibility in the Arab private sector.

Sawm. During the month of Ramadan, which marks the revelation of the first verses of the Koran to the prophet Muhammad, Muslims practice *sawm*, or fasting during daylight hours. (Non-Muslim

foreigners in the Arab world are exempt, although as a courtesy they shouldn't eat or drink in public during the fasting hours.)

The period of Ramadan is both spiritual and celebratory, with the emphasis varying among Arab countries. Governments in the region mandate a two-hour reduction in office hours, which poses a challenge and an opportunity: Consumers have more time for leisure (and for spending), but it can be tough to keep businesses open because employees often can't work long hours. Most organizations turn the clock upside down, realizing that people will stay awake from dusk to dawn and sleep late or leave early.

Foreign and local companies have made the month of Ramadan as important for sales as the period between Thanksgiving and Christmas is in the West. Most Arab

retailers sell as much during this month as they do the rest of the year. Television advertising rates go up during Ramadan as networks launch new shows, and mobile phone usage shoots up as people connect with friends and family. Arabs go shopping into the wee hours of the morning, so malls and stores stay open, and companies offer huge promotions.

Paradoxically, food and beverage companies in the Middle East see sales rise dramatically during this period of fasting. That's because Arabs get together with family members and friends to break their fasts with special meals, and restaurants offer buffets for postsunset and predawn meals. Sales get a final boost leading up to *Eid al-Fitr* (the Festival of Breaking the Fast), the day that marks Ramadan's end, when Muslims pray, feast, and exchange gifts.

Ramadan isn't good for all business, though. Because the Islamic calendar is based on the lunar cycle, it doesn't synchronize with the seasons. From 2008 to 2018, Ramadan occurs in the summer, which results in changes in consumption trends. For instance, soft drink and perfume sales generally rise during the summer months and during Ramadan. When they overlap, companies in those industries enjoy only a single sales spurt. Smart players plan campaigns at other times of the year to boost sales.

Interestingly, a backlash is brewing against Ramadan's commercialization and the conspicuous consumption that sometimes characterizes it. Sensing the winds of change, some multinational companies are focusing on family togetherness, generosity, and spirituality in their advertising. In 2009, for instance, P&G announced that for every pack of Tide White Musk customers in Egypt purchased during Ramadan, it would donate one garment to a needy family. It built credibility by working with Resala, a well-respected NGO, secured an endorsement from a government minister, and signed up Hakim, a popular singer in Egypt, as the campaign's ambassador. By the end of Ramadan, P&G and its customers had combined to provide 640,000

During the hajj, companies in Mecca, Medina, and Jeddah capitalize on the surge in demand for everything from souvenirs to headache cures.

garments to needy children, and Tide's volume share of the Egyptian detergent market had risen by 3 points.

Hajj. The hajj to Mecca—a duty that able-bodied Muslims must carry out once in their lifetimes if they have the means—is one of the world's largest pilgrimages. The annual influx of over 1.5 million Muslims into Saudi Arabia creates numerous business opportunities. Although official figures are scarce, reports estimate the hajj's impact on the Saudi Arabian economy at $42 billion in 2011—almost 7% of GDP.

Several hotel chains, Arab and foreign, have capitalized on the need to house millions of people during the annual pilgrimage, which lasts just under a week. The InterContinental Hotel in Mecca stands meters away from the Kaaba, Islam's most sacred site, and the chain has several properties in Medina, another holy city for Muslims. Even though they triple their fees during the hajj, hotels in Mecca enjoy full occupancy every night of the pilgrimage (compared with a 65% occupancy rate the rest of the year). In 2011, the Saudi Arabian government licensed the construction of 500 new hotels in Mecca, which has become a perennial boomtown in the region.

The hajj is a religious experience, but consumption is often part of the pilgrimage. Hundreds of local and multinational companies in Mecca, Medina, and Jeddah capitalize on the surge in demand for everything from souvenirs to headache cures. P&G promotes just about all its products during the hajj, but those that people can take home as gifts sell best. Perfume sales peak, and small appliances, such as electric razors, fare well, especially those that are unavailable in the visitors' home markets. For consumer electronics companies such as Sony and Samsung, the sales boost dur-

ing the hajj is equal to a month of revenues. Samsung moves much of its staff from the rest of the country to Mecca and Medina during the hajj, and its point-of-sale displays feature headlines in four or five languages to cater to foreign visitors.

The hajj has become so alluring an opportunity that some Arab companies are using it as a launchpad for global expansion. Because the pilgrimage draws a large group of first-time visitors to Saudi Arabia, companies can test their brands on a new group of international consumers each year. They build brand recognition among the pilgrims through intense marketing and sales activities in Mecca and Medina and then establish retail footholds in their home countries. Arabian Oud, which creates perfumes using oud (agarwood), has 52 stores in Mecca and Medina, which account for roughly 11% of the company's global sales during the hajj, and has built a network of 550 stores in 28 countries by following Muslim pilgrims home.

YALLA! **"LET'S GO!"** You hear it everywhere in the Arab world, and despite the region's political and social challenges, it encapsulates the vibrancy of the marketplace. The only other Arabic word you hear more often is *yanni,* "that is" or "that means." It's a throwaway word, but it underscores the Arab people's deep yearning to be understood. Only companies in the Arab world that are able to cope with the energy of its yalla future while coming to grips with its yanni past are likely to flourish in the region. ▽   **HBR Reprint** R1305L

Vijay Mahajan is the John P. Harbin Centennial Professor of Business at McCombs School of Business at the University of Texas at Austin. He is the author of *The Arab World Unbound* (Jossey-Bass, 2012).

Business Not As Usual

Harvard Business Review

HBR.ORG
The Revival of Smart

Credits